The Irish District Court

A Social Portrait

The Irish District Court

A SOCIAL PORTRAIT

Caroline O'Nolan

CORK **cup** UNIVERSITY PRESS

First published in 2013 by
Cork University Press
Youngline Industrial Estate
Pouladuff Road, Togher
Cork, Ireland

British Library Cataloguing in Publication Data
A CIP catalogue record for this book is available from the British Library.

ISBN 978-1-78205-048-3

Typeset by Tower Books, Ballincollig, County Cork
Printed by Gutenberg Press, Malta

www.corkuniversitypress.com

In Memory of Malcolm Vincent

Contents

Glossary

RESEARCH LOCATIONS

CCC	City Centre Court
SDC	Suburban Dublin Court
NEC	North Eastern Court
RC	Remand Court

ORGANISATIONS

AA	Alcoholics Anonymous
An Garda Síochána	The Irish Police Force
CS	Courts Service
CSO	Central Statistics Office
DJELR	Department of Justice, Equality and Law Reform
FÁS	Foras Áiseanna Saothair – Irish National Training and Employment Authority
GNIB	Garda National Immigration Bureau
HSE	Health Service Executive
IPRT	Irish Penal Reform Trust
IPS	Irish Prison Service
ITIA	Irish Translators' and Interpreters' Association
JAAB	Judicial Appointments Advisory Board
LRC	Law Reform Commission
ODPP	Office of the Director of Public Prosecutions
ORAC	Office of the Refugee Applications Commissioner

LEGAL TERMS

Audi alterem partem	Literal meaning is to hear the other side. This principle requires both sides to be heard before a matter can be adjudicated upon.
Barring Order	An order made under the Domestic Violence Act, 1996 which requires a violent person to leave the family home and prohibits the person from further violence or threats of violence, and from watching or being near the family home
Bridewell	Court complex in Dublin city centre
CSO	Community Service Order

Gary Doyle Order	An order that the defence be supplied with prosecution witness statements
ISIS	Irish Sentencing Information System
TR	Temporary Release

OTHER

DAR	Digital Audio Recording
DPP	Director of Public Prosecutions
ECHR	European Convention on Human Rights
EEA	European Economic Area. The EEA currently includes thirty countries; Iceland, Liechtenstein, Norway, and the twenty-seven EU member states.
EU-12	The group of twelve countries that joined the EU in 2004 and 2007
EU-13	The countries other than Ireland and the UK that were EU member states prior to 1 May 2004
EU-15	This is the group of fifteen countries that were members of the EU prior to expansion in 2004.
IFSC	International Financial Services Centre
LEP	Limited English Proficiency
NET	North Eastern Town
PPS	Personal Public Service. A PPS number is a unique numeric identifier used in transactions with state bodies.
RTO	Road Traffic Offence

Prologue

It was late in the afternoon when Bridget Murphy[1] was brought into court from the custody cells. The late hour seemed to have taken a toll on Judge Murray. He is normally genial and courteous but in the previous hour he had lobbed several terse comments at a number of solicitors whom he considered were wasting the court's time and had sparred once or twice with the court presenter[2] whose applications he normally accepted without demur. He seemed tired and a little tense and had consulted his watch a number of times.

Bridget Murphy is an elderly woman, diminutive in stature with a waif-like physique; several solicitors shared quizzical glances and raised eyebrows when she was produced from the custody cells. Judge Murray asked why Ms Murphy was in custody and was informed by the court presenter that there was an objection to bail. The court presenter said that bail was being opposed because Ms Murphy had a history of bench warrants and faced numerous section 4 theft charges. The court presenter seemed to gird himself in anticipation of an attack. It wasn't long in coming.

Judge Murray looked through the wad of charge sheets in front of him and said in an irritated tone: 'She's not exactly a criminal mastermind, look at this . . . goods valued at €4.72 . . . and another one for €10.36 . . . what is it you expect me to do, Guard? This is an awful waste of the court's time . . . do you really want me to send her to the Dóchas?[3] It was evident that Judge Murray found the prospect of Ms Murphy's detention repugnant and was essentially making it clear that he wanted the objection to bail to be dropped.

The court presenter talked to the arresting Guard. I couldn't hear their conversation but the body language of the Guard suggested that he was unhappy at this turn of events. Meanwhile, the defence solicitor briefly consulted with Ms Murphy. The consultation seemed to be a one-way conversation; I did not see Ms

1

Murphy speak, but the solicitor seemed to take an absence of dissent as agreement. The solicitor then rose and announced that his client wished to enter a plea on all charges.

This application meant that the prosecution did not have to withdraw their objection to bail as the issue of bail had effectively been bypassed. While this saved face for the prosecution, it was a strategic move on the part of the defence, who correctly gauged that Judge Murray's attitude suggested that he would deal leniently with the charges. Judge Murray looked at the court presenter as if he was challenging him to disagree with the plea; the court presenter said that the prosecution was happy to proceed. The facts were presented in a very perfunctory manner by the court presenter and Judge Murray immediately announced: 'Section 1(1) Probation Act.'

The Irish District Court: An Introduction

This is a book about a powerful Irish institution which plays a pivotal role in regulating Irish society – the Irish District Court. The Irish District Court is the initial point of contact with the court system for all persons accused of criminal offences. It disposes of more than 90% of criminal cases in the state, and is responsible for the majority of committals to Irish prisons. It is a vital part of the court and wider criminal justice system. The book draws on extensive observations of proceedings in a number of District Court venues presided over by various District Court judges. The brief vignette set out above is an introductory account of proceedings observed in the Irish District Court and is just the first of a collection of such accounts presented in this book, which will provide readers with an appreciation of what it means to be 'in court'.

This initial short sketch highlights how criminal court outcomes can be influenced by an array of factors that are not always captured in official statistics; it also reveals that certain criminal justice processes may in effect be reserved for a limited cohort of society. In practice, the punishment meted out to those who commit minor criminal offences such as those disposed of by the Irish District Court is not simply dependent on the gravity of the offence, or even on the criminal history or personal circumstances of the offender. It may depend on the character and humour of the presiding judge, the appearance and demeanour of the defendant or on previous interactions between the defendant and other criminal court actors.

Offenders who have troubled the court on previous occasions may be treated with impatience and intolerance.

> JUDGE O'HIGGINS: . . . he has a record with not just one but a number of suspended sentences . . . maybe some of those sentences should not have been suspended . . . Shane Brennan is a blackguard . . .
>
> SOLICITOR: The offences are minor, Judge.
>
> JUDGE O'HIGGINS: That doesn't change the fact that he's a blackguard . . . he's a blackguard . . . four months or community service of 150 hours . . . let's get you back doing some good for the community you seem determined to disrupt . . . probation report on [deleted] . . . if you so much as raise your voice I'll lock you up for as long as I can. (FN75)[4]

The uncertainty regarding criminal court outcomes is especially evident in the Irish District Court as the sentencing discretion allowed to Irish District Court judges is relatively generous. The degree of sentencing discretion enjoyed by Irish District Court judges results in a great deal of disparity in the punishments applied by the court. An understanding of how sentencing discretion is applied in practice can only be gleaned from observing and reflecting on court proceedings. This book uses courtroom observations to provide a unique and illuminating account of how decisions are reached in criminal courts.

The Irish District Court deals with a very large volume of offences every year. If we consider that each year over half a million offences are disposed of by the District Court and the offences dealt with include a wide array of charges that cover road traffic offences, public order offences, criminal damage, animal cruelty, evasion of excise duties and other taxes, as well as more serious offences such as burglary and assault, it is not unreasonable to conclude that many Irish adults will at some stage in their life find themselves 'in court'. A court appearance in respect of an unpaid speeding fine or failure to display an National Car Test certificate (NCT) may be a source of irritation rather than worry. But for those charged with more serious offences, and for those with a history of previous criminal convictions, being in court is much more than an inconvenience, and as this book highlights, for a significant proportion of such defendants it may result in a period of incarceration.

Given the large numbers of people who at some stage in their life find themselves in court, it is perhaps surprising that there has not been greater public scrutiny of the work of the District Court to date. However, the insights provided by this book suggest that the explanation for why there has been no sustained demand for greater transparency and accountability in the work of the court is that those that are most affected by the decisions of the District Court are those that are the least powerful in Irish society. The book allows the reader to assess the structure and organisation of the Irish District Court and invites him/her to consider whether those who are accused and convicted of minor offences are appropriately treated and punished.

Press reporting of District Court proceedings often focuses on the comedic and farcical elements of court workings. It can sometimes be amusing to hear the accounts of the drunken escapades which are routinely presented in court or to listen to stories of a bungled attempt to steal 'three pairs of socks' or goods of a similar value. With the notable exception of Nell McCafferty's account of the District Court, journalistic reports on the District Court often afford little attention to the pathos that can attach to some court proceedings. From time to time the comments of and sentences imposed by District Court judges have caused a flurry of controversy, but for the most part their decisions are not publicly questioned, and the continued absence of a comprehensive analysis of sentencing decisions, or even a record of all court proceedings, has not excited anything more than an occasional ripple of disapproval. Similarly, the extent to which District Court decisions shape the Irish prison population is not widely recognised, discussed or questioned.

The Irish District Court is presided over by a small number of men and women who are largely protected from censure and whose body of work is subject to little in the way of review or scrutiny. While individual decisions by District Court judges may be reported and commented on in the press, information is not provided regarding the mass of sentencing decisions reached by individual judges. It could be argued that this lack of accountability, coupled with the broad sentencing discretion afforded to Irish judges, relies unduly on the bestowal of benevolence by judges and presumes that judges will be invested with exceptionally high levels of wisdom. This book suggests that this may be unwise and highlights the rather extraordinary level of trust that is placed in the men and women appointed as judges of the Irish District Court.

The extent of the sentencing discretion afforded to Irish District Court judges means that outcomes are greatly and perhaps overly dependent on the presiding judge. Differentiating between 'good' and 'bad' judges is not at all straightforward, as can be seen by the different comments of two Gardaí regarding the same judge.

> GARDA 1: This judge is really nice.
> GARDA 2: Too fuckin' nice. (FN 18)

Similarly, another judge characterised by one solicitor as 'a tough hoor' was described by a second solicitor as someone who 'gets the job done'. While some are loquacious and verbose, others are brusque and concise.

> SOLICITOR: He would be suitable for community service if you were mindful of that.
> JUDGE GILLIGAN: I'm not. (FN20)

The many extracts from courtroom proceedings presented in this book clearly show that the disparate sentencing philosophies and orientations of District Court judges result in a lack of coherence in sentencing which ultimately undermines the work of the court and may also weaken public confidence in criminal justice processes.

Irish District Court defendants are now global in origin but the court continues to deal with local offences, and for the most part relies on practices and procedures which are long-standing. This book largely presents accounts of non-Irish/non-UK nationals, referred to as foreign nationals, who have appeared as District Court defendants. In this way, the book considers the offences and procedures common to all defendants, as well as the offences and procedures particular to foreign defendants. The book also provides an assessment of the scale of the presence of foreign nationals before the court, describes the types of charges they face, and considers differences in the observed offending pattern of Irish and foreign nationals. It allows us to form a picture of the foreign nationals who appear before the Irish courts, their residency status in Ireland, their country or area of origin, and their gender, age, employment status and socio-economic class. It also enables us to assess the procedures adopted by the court to ensure their fair treatment.

The book also presents an assessment of the sentencing practices of the District Court, and in particular sentencing decisions in respect of foreign defendants. Sentencing decisions in respect of both Irish and foreign defendants are considered so that differential or discriminatory sentencing practices can be identified. To begin, we will examine the emergence of the greatly increased diversity in the origins of District Court defendants by considering how migration has affected the Irish criminal justice system in recent years.

Migration and the Irish Criminal Justice System

The Celtic Tiger era of high economic growth, which began in the 1990s, prompted sustained and diverse inward migration which resulted in substantial changes in the Irish population and a reshaping of the Irish social and cultural landscape. From the late 1990s, for the first time in Ireland's history, inward migration became a force which wrought significant changes in the ethnic and racial profile of the Irish population. Whereas in the past Ireland's migrant population constituted a small and for the most part not readily distinguishable section of the population, the accent, language and appearance of many new migrants ensure that they are very visible in Irish society. It has become clear over time that the changes to the Irish population are permanent and on such a scale that they warrant a re-evaluation of policies and institutional practices in many, if not all, areas.

Changes in the profile of those processed by the Irish criminal justice system were not unexpected given the wave of inward migration and the proliferation of migrants in the key age cohorts associated with criminal activity. However, as very limited or no information is recorded by the various arms of the Irish criminal justice system regarding the nationality/race/ethnicity of the people it processes, we cannot trace how non-Irish nationals progress through the Irish criminal justice system or evaluate the scale of their presence at various stages. We do not know, for example, if non-Irish nationals are disproportionately represented among persons arrested/tried by indictment/convicted/placed on probation.

We do, however, have information regarding the presence of non-Irish nationals in Irish prisons. Statistics published by the Irish Prison Service (IPS) chart a very marked and rapid increase in the proportion of non-Irish persons committed to Irish prisons from 2001 onwards.[5] During the period from 2001 to 2010, while the overall pattern is of a marked increase in the committal of non-Irish nationals to Irish prisons, when we look at the committal pattern for different national groups we see that this increase was not uniform. Between 2001 and 2010 a very large increase in the numbers of EU nationals committed to Irish prisons was recorded. EU enlargement in 2004 and 2007 partially explains this increase and similarly explains a decline in the committal of 'other Europeans' from 2004. Committals of persons of Asian origin increased rapidly between 2001 and 2007, declined in 2008 and 2009 but then increased marginally in 2010. The committal of persons of African origin also fluctuated during this period but the overall trend was upwards. However, there was no significant increase in the committal of UK, American or Australasian nationals to Irish prisons between 2001 and 2010 (see IPS 2003a–2011). In 2006 UK nationals accounted for more than a quarter of the recorded non-Irish resident population (see http://cso.ie./ statistics/nationalityagegroup.htm). In 2001, UK nationals accounted for 2.4% of persons committed to Irish prisons. This proportion remained more or less stable but with a slight downward trend during the period 2001–10. The growth in the flow of non-Irish persons committed to prison was therefore accounted for by a growth in the numbers of 'new' migrants within the Irish prison system. Given this and the difficulty of distinguishing UK nationals from Irish nationals, courtroom observations of non-Irish nationals concentrated on non-Irish, non-UK nationals who are referred to throughout this book as foreign nationals.

Overall the proportion of non-Irish nationals committed to Irish prisons peaked at just under one-third in 2007, having increased from just over 16% in 2001. The pattern of committals to Irish prisons changed significantly from 2008. In 2008, committals to prison for non-payment of a court-ordered fine jumped from 1,335 to 2,520 or 18.6% of total committals.[6] In 2009, and again in 2010, there were further dramatic increases in the numbers committed to prison for non-payment of a court-ordered fine with committals in this category numbering 4,806 in 2009 and 6,683 in 2010 and accounting for over 31% of total committals in 2009 and almost half (48.5%) of all committals in 2010. Alongside the increase in committals for non-payment of a fine, there has been a fall in the proportion of non-Irish nationals committed to Irish prisons to 22.2% in 2010 (24.2% in 2009 and 29.4% in 2008). It is not clear if the change in the pattern of committals has affected the share of total committals accounted for by non-Irish nationals.

Since 2003 the IPS has also disclosed the numbers of non-Irish nationals committed to prison for breaches of immigration legislation. Non-Irish nationals committed to Irish prisons for breaches of immigration legislation account for between 73% (2003) and 16% (2010) of committals of non-Irish nationals to Irish prisons during the years from 2003 to 2010 (see IPS 2004–2011). As is explained fully in Chapter 4, persons committed to Irish prisons for such breaches include persons who are held in administrative detention and are not charged with a criminal offence. It is not possible to identify such persons from the published details, but as Chapter 4 shows, it is thought that they may account for a significant proportion of those committed to prison in respect of immigration breaches. The statistics published by the IPS therefore suggest that non-Irish nationals have a greater involvement in the criminal justice system than is in fact the case.

The increased presence of non-Irish nationals in Irish prisons raises questions regarding the treatment of non-Irish persons by the Irish criminal justice system from arrest to sentencing. These questions prompted the research which this book draws upon.

Migrants in the District Court

Criminal justice outcomes are impacted by decisions made at a succession of key junctures. The discretion exercised by criminal justice actors may greatly influence how criminal behaviour is sanctioned or indeed whether behaviour is labelled as criminal and subject to sanction. As criminal justice outcomes are a product of a cumulative process, they should ideally be assessed by tracing cases from inception to punishment and analysing the decisions by all criminal justice actors along the way as well as by examining institutional and legislative frameworks. In the absence of the resources required to adopt such an approach, locating research in the criminal courts provides a means of observing and assessing the work and attitudes of the various arms of the criminal justice system as well as examining the sentencing decisions of the court.

Population diversity has placed additional demands on the Irish criminal courts and in particular the Irish District Court, which deals with a very large volume of offences and offenders and which relies on procedural efficiency in order to get through its substantial daily list. This book presents an account of the Irish District Court at a time when diversity among defendants had become routine rather than exceptional but was still often viewed as problematic. Courtroom procedures to deal with foreign defendants have evolved with little evidence of planning and still vary between court locations depending largely on the attitude of the presiding judge. The speed of change in the Irish population, which has resulted from substantial and sustained inward migration, has meant that within a relatively short space of time the origins of those who appear before the Irish District Court are no longer local or even national but global in character. The brief snippets set out below give a little insight into the many challenges faced by courtroom actors who were perhaps more used to dealing with a less eclectic group of defendants in the past.

> SOLICITOR: Can you certify for an Urdu interpreter, Judge?
> JUDGE: Is that a dialect? (FN19)
>
> SOLICITOR: Is there an Austrian interpreter in court? (FN1)
>
> JUDGE: Is there an objection to bail?
> PROSECUTOR: Yes, Judge, the defendant is the subject of a deportation order.
> SOLICITOR: My client is the subject of a deportation order, Judge, but the deportation order cannot be executed as it has not been possible to secure the necessary travel documents and he is seeking to be declared stateless.
> JUDGE: Well . . . that won't be decided today or tomorrow . . . what do we do in the meantime? (FN41)

Despite these changes, the court has been expected to continue to dispense with the daily caseload with little in the way of additional resources. The Irish District Court remains a local court with limited jurisdiction but it has had to adapt to take account of the greatly increased diversity of the persons who now appear before it on foot of criminal charges. As this book reveals, there is a tension between ensuring fair procedures are afforded to all defendants . . . and perhaps especially those with limited English proficiency . . . and getting through the court's allotted workload.

This book explores the scale, presence and treatment of foreign defendants in the Irish District Court and considers how the District

Court has dealt with the additional demands which have stemmed from dealing with increased diversity. While the presence and treatment of foreign defendants before the District Court is the central focus of the book, readers are also presented with a description and an assessment of the wider work of the court and of courtroom actors. The Irish District Court deals with minor and mundane criminal matters and consequently it is very easy to overlook the very important influence it has on the Irish criminal justice system and on wider Irish society; this study details the significance of the role played by the District Court and allows public scrutiny of the decisions of the court, which the absence of court transcripts has largely prevented to date.

The book points out that the narrow focus of the bulk of law enforcement efforts means that the immigrants who are criminalised will largely mirror those within the native population who are criminalised. Therefore, the study contends that the particular structural disadvantages faced by immigrants are only likely to result in the hyper-criminalisation of a limited section of the immigrant population. The majority of the defendants in the Irish District Court, and in particular persistent offenders, are unemployed or work in low-paid unskilled or semi-skilled jobs rather than being from the professional and managerial classes; this is the case for defendants of all nationalities. Therefore, it is the Irish bricklayer, the Polish agricultural labourer or the unemployed Nigerian chef, rather than the American architect, the Irish IT specialist or the Indonesian doctor, who are most likely to appear before the Irish District Court.

It should also be recognised that while the disproportionate presence of lower socio-economic class defendants is driven by different behaviour patterns and by the allocation of law enforcement resources, interactions with criminal justice actors and institutions are influenced and mediated by education and social class. Law enforcement officers may hesitate before arresting the articulate and urbane, regardless of their nationality.

A Brief Overview of this Book

As no transcripts are available of Irish District Court proceedings, and given the limited research previously carried out (which does not provide a detailed picture of how District Court proceedings are conducted), it was considered that the work and organisation of the

District Court are not widely known or understood. This is addressed in Chapter 1, which sets out a 'thick' ethnographic account of the court. This account provides the reader with an understanding of the roles of the various key courtroom actors and an appreciation of the manner in which matters are processed and the environment in which decisions are reached.

Chapter 2 presents a picture of both Irish and non-Irish District Court defendants. The range of offences dealt with by the Irish District Court ensures that the court deals with a broad cross-section of Irish society. However, the modal defendant is a young male from a lower socio-economic background. This is the case for both Irish and non-Irish defendants. The non-Irish defendants observed are described and compared with the resident non-Irish population.

Chapter 3 deals with the core work of the Irish District Court – sentencing. It points out that Irish judges impose criminal sanctions without the assistance of an over-arching sentencing philosophy and without sentencing guidelines – a system that ensures sentencing inconsistency. This chapter draws on courtroom observations to explore the factors which influence sentencing decisions and considers if and how nationality/residency status impacts sentencing decisions.

Chapter 4 describes and critiques the legislative provisions which gave rise to foreign defendants facing immigration charges in the District Court. The chapter describes how these charges may be faced by persons gaining entry to the state and persons already resident in the state, and it draws attention to the possible adverse consequences of the legislative provisions in place at the time that fieldwork was conducted and in particular the potential impact of such legislation on policing practices. In addition, recent changes in immigration legislation which arose as a result of a judicial review instigated by a District Court defendant are set out and discussed.

Chapter 5 addresses the procedures adopted in the District Court to ensure defendants with limited English proficiency (LEP) receive a fair trial. The chapter notes concerns regarding the standard of the interpretation services provided and the frequent failure of the court to adjust the pace of its work to accommodate the interpretation process.

The Conclusion outlines the key findings of the research that underlies this book. It situates these findings in relation to current debates about the criminalisation and incarceration of foreigners in European criminal justice systems and argues that for the most part only immigrants of lower socio-economic class will contribute to penal expansionism.

The Appendix sets out the research methodology adopted, including details of the research sites which are referred to throughout the book as DSC (Dublin Suburban Court), CCC (City Centre Court), RC (Remand Court) and NEC (North East Court).

Chapter 1

Anatomy of a Workhorse
The Irish District Court

The Role of Lower-Tier Courts

Courts are organised in a hierarchical structure with jurisdiction determining the tier or rank of a court. Lower-tier courts are courts of limited and local jurisdiction. The decisions of lower-tier courts can be appealed to superior courts. In short, lower-tier criminal courts dispose of minor offences, are constrained in the penalties they can impose, and in certain circumstances their decisions, both verdicts and sentences, may be appealed to higher courts. But as we will see when we look at the Irish District Court, lower-tier courts can exert a critical influence on the criminal justice system, an influence that could easily be overlooked because of the limitations placed on their powers.

Superior courts in all jurisdictions dispose of serious crimes. The criminal character of the offences brought before such courts is normally indubitable. This is not necessarily the case in lower-tier courts. We can expect unanimity within society regarding the criminal nature of rape, murder and armed robbery, but such unanimity is unlikely in the case of at least some minor criminal offences. Is it clearly 'criminal' to be drunk and disorderly in a public place? Is it irrefutably 'criminal' to fail to pay a speeding fine? This ambiguity about the criminal nature of certain minor criminal offences can be seen clearly if we look at the offence of drink-driving. Whether or not a driver's blood alcohol level is sufficiently high to render her guilty of drink-driving is both temporally and spatially dependent. With the same level of alcohol in my bloodstream I may be guilty or not guilty of drink-driving depending on where and when I drive. The offences dealt with by lower-tier courts are therefore more influenced by societal and cultural norms than those dealt with by superior courts. The offences dealt with by lower-tier courts also reflect policing priorities and practices and the level of police resources required to secure convictions. Public order offences are more easily detectable and prosecuted than minor fraud offences, and convictions are also more certain. Crimes such as public order offences and possession of illicit substances yield high detection rates because recorded crime largely equates to crime detected by the police. It could be argued therefore that such crimes present a positive, and perhaps unduly positive, impression of police activity which may encourage their prosecution.

The Importance of the Irish District Court

The District Court is the lowest tier of the Irish court hierarchy. It has been described as the 'workhorse' of the Irish judicial system (Rottman, 1984), a designation that reflects the large volume of cases dealt with by the court, and the generally commonplace and petty nature of the matters it deals with. The minor and routine character of the matters dealt with ensures that court outcomes attract little public scrutiny. The continuing lack of court transcripts or audio recordings of court sittings means that there is an opaque quality to District Court proceedings, which places limits on accountability and makes academic research more difficult. The lack of public and academic attention belies the importance of the court and the key role it plays in the Irish criminal justice system. The District Court is the initial point of contact with the court system for all those charged with a criminal offence and disposes of more than 90% of criminal matters. District Court judges enjoy the 'broad' (O'Malley, 2000; McCullagh, 1992) sentencing discretion afforded to all Irish judges but have only local and limited jurisdiction.[1] The court is responsible for the majority of committals to Irish prisons and therefore has a pivotal influence on the flow of people into Irish prisons.

Review of Literature

The most important source of information on Irish courts is the Courts Service of Ireland (CS). The CS was incorporated following the enactment of the Courts Service Act, 1998, pursuant to the recommendations of the First Report of the Working Group on a Courts Commission (1996). One of the functions of the CS is to provide information on the courts system to the public, which it does through its website, press announcements and publications. It is certainly easier now than in the past (Rottman, 1984) to get an overview of the workings of the courts, but when we try to get information on the 'micro' operations of these institutions, and in particular the District Court, we still find extraordinary data deficits.

To date little research has focused specifically on the work of the Irish District Court or the sentencing practices of District Court judges. Statistical information regarding District Court sentencing patterns is limited (Law Reform Commission, 2003) and does not provide sufficient information to review sentencing practices of individual judges.[2] Concern has been expressed regarding inconsistency in such practices, and the information that is available seems to support this concern as Courts Service (CS) statistics reveal significant variation between court offices in the type of penalty imposed for the main offence categories.[3] If we look at public order/assault charges we see that in 2007, 12.1% (CS, 2008a:76–7) of all defendants convicted of public order/assault charges received custodial sentences. However, the incarceration rate imposed by individual court offices varied between 2% and 26.5 % (CS, 2008a:76–7). The statistics for 2006 reveal a similar total incarceration rate of 11.6%, and an even wider variation in the incarceration rate for individual court offices, which ranged from 3.3% to 30% (CS, 2007:165). It is regrettable that the Courts Service annual reports for 2008, 2009 and 2010 do not include an analysis of District Court dispositions by office (CS, 2009, 2010, 2011).

The inadequacy of statistical information about Irish criminal court outcomes has been decried by many commentators (Rottman, 1984; LRC, 1996; O'Malley, 2000; Bacik, 2002; Seymour, 2006). Hamilton (2005) has suggested that the phrase 'here be dragons', coined by cartographers in the past to depict uncharted areas and used by Brewer et al. (1997) to describe the data deficit on crime rates in Ireland, accurately describes the almost complete absence of statistical data on sentencing practices in Ireland. Sentencing databases are routinely maintained in other jurisdictions. They provide a means of evaluating judicial decision making, and as such are an important means of providing a check on the powers of the judiciary. They facilitate research that can confirm consistency or detect patterns of disparity and discrimination in sentencing. As Bacik notes: 'The routine collection and publication of data on sentencing, . . . would be hugely beneficial in terms both of enabling greater public awareness as to actual sentencing practice, and also of facilitating the judiciary by providing guidance as to sentencing consistency' (Bacik, 2002:369).

Bacik (2002) describes the provision of training for new District Court judges through various initiatives including an induction course, a handbook and a period of 'shadowing' an experienced District Court judge, combined with the scheduling of two meetings of District Court judges and an annual residential conference, as the bones of a sentencing information system. Sentencing information is now also provided by the Irish Sentencing Information System (ISIS), which refers to a steering committee set up to plan for and provide information on sentencing. ISIS has undertaken a number of pilot projects in various tiers of the criminal courts, and the information compiled can be accessed at www.isis.ie. A limited database has been compiled in relation to matters sentenced in the Dublin and Cork Circuit Courts (see Conroy and Gunning, 2009). A pilot project was also undertaken in Dublin District Courts in 2009 and a database compiled in relation to 121 cases. The database provides information about the offender, including details of nationality.[4] Although the database is modest in size, it is a welcome initiative.

A number of studies have provided an analysis of sentencing practices in specific District Courts (Needham, 1983; Boyle, 1984; Rottman and Tormey, 1985; Lyons and Hunt, 1988; Bacik et al., 1998; Hamilton, 2005). However, research has been limited and has not been sufficient to present a comprehensive review of sentencing patterns (Bacik et al., 1998; Walsh and Sexton, 1999; Hamilton, 2005).

Several largely descriptive studies provide us with snapshots of the sentencing practices of the District Court. Boyle (1984) selected a sample of 899 cases which represented 5% of the total offences disposed of in the Galway District Court in the three-year period 1978–81. The sample was weighted to include one indictable offence for every two non-indictable offences. This is likely to have biased the sample towards more serious offences as current caseloads indicate that indictable offences only account for around 12–14% of total cases disposed of in the District Court (CS, 2007, 2008a, 2009, 2010, 2011) and this proportion is higher than was previously reported (McCullagh, 1996:179). Boyle contends that the proportion of people charged with indictable crimes who opt to be tried in the District Court is very high (90% in the Galway sample) because of the limited term of imprisonment that can be imposed by the District Court. He claims that this constitutes 'a form of statutory plea bargaining' and concludes that there is a need for restrictions on the District Court's jurisdiction to dispose of indictable offences.

The results presented by these studies indicate substantial variations in sentencing practices. In Boyle's sample, only forty-one offenders were sentenced to immediate imprisonment (4.6%). Boyle attributes the low rate of imprisonment to the minor offences dealt with by the court in Galway. Needham's study (1983), which was also based on a sample of cases from the Galway District Court for the same period, indicated that prison sentences were imposed on 11.2% of those convicted of indictable offences. Rottman and Tormey's survey (1985) of criminal cases disposed of during a four-week period in 1984 revealed that over 15% (20% of those who pleaded guilty) of all cases disposed of by the District Court in this period (2,783) resulted in imprisonment. The variations in the rates of imprisonment reported suggest a lack of consistency in sentencing practices but may also reflect considerable variation in the case mix dealt with by different courts.

A study of larceny convictions in the Dublin Metropolitan Area of the District Court suggests that women offenders are treated more leniently than their male counterparts (Lyons and Hunt, 1988). Larceny was chosen as it is a crime commonly committed by both males and females. The sample size in this study was very small: 108 females and 120 males. The sample size was limited by the numbers of females convicted of larceny in the period, all of whom were included in the study. The presence and treatment of women and children in the court is also explored in McCafferty's journalistic account of the District Court (1981).

In order to assess the severity of punishments, Lyons and Hunt devised a penal ladder by ranking the punishment options available to judges. They ranked probation as the lowest level of punishment, below fines or suspended sentences. This ranking system is potentially problematic and indeed the authors note that the ranking system they adopt is not consistent with that adopted in a number of studies which ranked probation as a punishment equivalent to a small fine (Farrington and Morris, 1983; Kapardis and Farrington,

1981). The study controlled for previous convictions and for the severity of offences, which were categorised according to the monetary value of the goods stolen.

Lyons and Hunt's results indicate that seven out of ten women offenders were sentenced more leniently than male offenders, but many differences were not statistically significant. The authors note that the model adopted proved a better fit in predicting sentences for male offenders than female offenders, and they suggest that this indicates that other variables not included in the model impact on the sentencing of women. Earlier research conducted by Farrington and Morris (1983) in the UK also suggested that gender-specific sets of variables impact sentencing. Farrington and Morris (1983) identified marital status, family background and parenthood as more important factors in the sentencing of females than males. Lyons and Hunt's conclusion that their results 'suggest quite strongly that males and females are treated quite differently before the courts' (1988:137), and their assertion that patriarchal notions of women's role in society are influential in the sentencing of women (1988:138), may overstate the significance of the sentencing differences found in this study, and ignores the possible impact of the small sample size.

Bacik et al. (1998) set out to examine the association between the levels of deprivation in the community of the individual offender, and District Court appearance and sentence severity. The District Court was chosen because of the lack of previous academic research and because it was considered that the low level of public scrutiny of District Court proceedings may contribute to inconsistency in sentencing patterns.

The study used data from the records of the Bridewell District Courts in Dublin city. A sample of 2,000 cases was selected from the court records for 1988 and 1994. This was reduced to 1,603 by only including the most serious offence when an individual defendant was charged with multiple offences. Offence seriousness was categorised and severity of punishment measured in accordance with the scale used by Farrington and Morris (1983). The relative and combined effects of sex, age and community deprivation on the risk of court appearance were measured. The study developed a 'standardised court appearance ratio' (SCAR) which took account of the different age profiles of communities and allowed a comparison between the expected court appearances and the actual court appearances of offenders from areas with different levels of community deprivation. The median SCAR value in the most deprived communities was found to be almost twelve times that in the least deprived communities.

When sentencing was reviewed, the sample of cases dropped to 1,283 due to inadequacies in the records. Details of prior previous convictions were not available in the District Court records, but two proxy measures were included to take account of previous convictions. These were the presence/absence of bench warrants and other outstanding offences. These variables, along with being male, were found to significantly increase the likelihood of a custodial sentence. Defendants from deprived areas were found to be 49% more likely to be imprisoned than other defendants when other variables were controlled. Bacik et al. conclude that their findings pose 'serious questions about the impartiality of the sentencing process' (1998:26). However, the study's failure to control for prior criminal convictions means that this conclusion must be interpreted with some caution.

Hamilton (2005) reported on the study conducted in 2003 by two Irish Penal Reform Trust (IPRT) researchers in the Dublin Metropolitan District Court. Details and outcomes were recorded in respect of 356 individual defendants. This study was essentially descriptive in character but was supplemented with qualitative research in the form of interviews with solicitors.

Hamilton presents anecdotal evidence of inconsistency in judicial decision making. She reports one interviewee referring to a practice of 'judge-shopping' in an effort to present cases to judges known for their leniency. She contends that, rather than District Court judges seeking to operate in unison, judges are free to make decisions in accordance with their personal moral dictates. This inconsistency in sentencing was also highlighted by Walsh and Sexton in their report on Community Service Orders (CSOs) (1999). They pointed out that there was a wide variance in the relationship between the length of a CSO and the default term of imprisonment, and recommended that this relationship should be more specifically correlated. It is also evident from their study that while some judges use CSOs routinely, other judges may rarely or perhaps never impose CSOs.

In their study of child pornography and the punishment thereof, O'Donnell and Milner (2007) interviewed seven District Court judges and five Circuit Court judges, all of whom had been directly involved in cases taken under the Child Pornography Act, 1998. In determining sentence, all judges assessed the gravity of the offence. A number of judges also considered the age and circumstances of offenders, their willingness to participate in treatment and their likelihood to re-offend. Two of the District Court judges referred to using the Sentencing Advisory Panel guidelines for the judiciary in England and Wales to assist them in deciding whether to accept or reject jurisdiction (2007:136–7). O'Donnell and Milner's research provides some insight into the sentencing practices of Irish District Court judges but it should be remembered that their focus was on very specific offences which are likely to come before the court infrequently.

Riordan's study also focused on a particular category of offenders, drug-abusing offenders who were suitable for diversion for treatment. His study of drug-related cases in the Dublin Metropolitan Area included a focus group in which eight District Court judges participated and discussed the issue of drugs in the criminal justice arena, the manner of identifying offenders suitable for diversion to treatment and judges' expectations of outcomes following treatment. Riordan acknowledges that his position as a District Court judge facilitated the convening of the focus group, which was held 'on the fringes of a Judges' Conference' (2000:33). The inadequacy of treatment services for drug-abusing offenders was unanimously agreed by all focus group participants and identified as a factor which resulted in judges imposing punitive sanctions rather than seeking therapeutic interventions.

District Court judges have no duty to explain why they have imposed a custodial sentence. The Working Group on the Jurisdiction of the Courts rejected the Law Reform Commission's recommendation[5] that District Court judges should give written reasons for imposing custodial sentences on the basis that the recommendation was impractical given the workload of the District Court and the absence of recording facilities (Working Group on the Jurisdiction of the Courts, 2003). In the IPRT study, Hamilton notes that reasons were given for only 42% of the custodial sentences imposed and that those reasons rarely gave any insight into the rationale for imprisonment. Rationales that were referred to indicated the absence of any coherent policy (2005:2). Immediate terms of imprisonment were imposed on 12% of the study group. This proportion was lower than that recorded in most previous research

(Rottman and Tormey, 1985; Bacik et al., 1998; O'Mahony, 1996) but considerably higher than the proportion in Boyle's study (1984). The study indicated that 63% of the custodial sentences imposed were for six months or less, and 38% of sentences were for periods of less than three months. These findings are consistent with the observations of other commentators (O'Donnell, 2001). The routine use of short prison terms is criticised strongly by Hamilton, who claims that they are 'a particularly pointless form of imprisonment, placing a huge strain on penal resources yet with minimal deterrent or rehabilitative effect on the offender' (2005:3). However, Vaughan's research (2001) points to only limited support among District Court judges for restricting the use of short terms of imprisonment.[6]

It should be noted that in 2010 Scotland introduced legislative restrictions on the use of short prison sentences (see Criminal Justice and Licensing Act (Scotland), 2010), and long-standing restrictions on the use of short prison sentences are in place in countries such as Germany, Austria and Portugal (Kuhn, 1997) and in Western Australia (Eley et al., 2005).[7] Finland and Sweden have also introduced measures to reduce the imposition of short custodial sentences (Eley et al., 2005). In the Irish context recent developments promote a change in use of short term prison sentences. In 2010 the Inspector of Prisons suggested that it may be appropriate to automatically suspend short-term sentences (Reilly, 2010:96). This sentiment is reflected in the provisions of the Criminal Justice (Community Service Amendment) Act, 2011 which requires judges to consider a CSO as an alternative to the imposition of a period of imprisonment up to twelve months. The Act also stipulates that judges may consider a CSO for periods of imprisonment in excess of twelve months.

Courts Service publications and research findings (Redmond, 2002; Hamilton, 2005) highlight that fines are the most common form of punishment imposed by the District Court. Redmond suggests that 'enquiries in the court process about offenders' means and capacity to pay fines would appear to be non-existent or at best cursory' (2002:53). This view is echoed by Hamilton (2005), who further suggests that setting inappropriately high fines may result in the indirect imposition of custodial sentences.[8]

Lysaght (2004) describes the operation of the Court Poor Box, which is almost unknown outside the realms of the District Court,[9] as an example of judicial innovation which he notes may derive from a desire to avoid injustice but which may also promote sentencing inconsistency and be interpreted as an inappropriate encroachment on the role of the legislature. The LRC recommended that the operation of the Court Poor Box be put on a statutory basis and further recommended that contributions to the Court Poor Box should only be sought on admission of guilt, and not when charges are struck out, or after conviction, in place of, or in addition to, a fine (LRC, 2005). These recommendations have not yet been implemented.

Evidence regarding the penal philosophy of District Court judges is limited. Questionnaire responses by them indicate that judges expect custody to produce beneficial effects mainly through deterrence and incapacitation, but Vaughan (2001) contends that research shows that judges are overly optimistic in this regard. Maguire (2008) used sentencing vignettes and interviews to explore the sentencing rationale of District and Circuit Court judges. More than a quarter of all sitting District Court judges participated in her research.[10] She describes a practice of 'cumulative sentencing' whereby repeat offending results in the gradual application of more severe penal tariffs. Healy and O'Donnell's study of accounts of court proceedings in local papers principally examines reported details of District Court proceedings (2010). Their study suggests that judges as a group understand offending behaviour to be largely within the power of the individual to control, and not to be primarily associated with external social conditions. Judges also demonstrate a strong belief in the capacity of individuals to redeem themselves, which is reflected in their sentencing practices. This means that although previous convictions will result in harsher punishment, judges may seek to afford defendants an opportunity to display willingness to reform by suspending prison sentences or adjourning cases.

Setting the Scene: Life in Court

A sense of the atmosphere in which District Court sittings are conducted and an understanding of the way the business of the District Court is actually transacted is largely absent from the current body of literature. It is hoped that the remaining sections of this chapter will largely bridge that gap and provide an authentic picture of the work of the court.

To understand life in the Irish District Court we need to appreciate that the sheer volume and mundane nature of the court's work results in a fundamentally different atmosphere from the hushed, solemn and almost sacred atmosphere one might expect in a higher-tier courtroom. The physical courtroom is the same; indeed some courtrooms are used interchangeably for District, Circuit and High Court proceedings, but no jury is present in the District Court. Matters are tried summarily, which means that judges decide whether the guilt of accused persons has been proven, and also decide on the appropriate sentence.[11] The judge therefore is the key figure in the District Court and he/she will dictate the pace of courtroom proceedings and control the behaviour of those assembled in court. Although a lot of behind-the-scenes work takes place outside the court, this should not give one the impression that District Court judges simply rubber stamp matters decided on between the defence and prosecution. All sentencing decisions are reached by judges without consultation and usually without a period of consideration. Sentencing decisions are considered in Chapter 3.

District Court proceedings often take place with a background hum of noise which at times can reach such a volume that the intervention of the presiding judge is required to restore it to a tolerable level. The seating arrangements adopted could be described as tribal in nature and contribute to the ever-present buzz of noise. A small troop of Gardaí is usually assembled in the court,[12] normally sitting and conversing together at the front. Solicitors and barristers are also grouped together at the front of the court and they talk among themselves and to their clients, who approach them at intervals. Defendants and those who accompany them tend to congregate at the back of the court; perhaps the presence of a sizable group of Gardaí at the front of the court is off-putting for some.

Some defendants are carefully dressed in formal clothes, but most wear casual clothes such as tracksuits or jeans. Not all those in court are sober; this can lead to noisy outbursts which at times can give rise to collective mirth. Among those present in court, one often finds people with the slurred speech, clumsy movements and unpredictable behaviour consistent with drug use. During the proceedings observed, people have shouted out, sung, threatened witnesses and Gardaí, and thrown bottles and mobile phones; this behaviour sometimes resulted in people being removed from the court and a short spell in a cell for some of those removed. At times the antics of a defendant or a member of the public can move court proceedings close to farce, and can certainly provide entertainment to many of those assembled.

The Court registrar, an employee of the Courts Service, sits directly below the presiding judge. She decides on the order in which cases will be heard, calls out the names of defendants in court, and passes files to the judge. She also carries out a myriad of other duties including preparing bail bonds, preparing bench warrants and custody warrants, recording details of sentences imposed and signing attendance sheets for interpreters. She can be an invaluable reference point for judges when a question arises regarding a procedural issue.

The probation officer is usually a somewhat isolated figure who has no direct colleagues to confer with, and when called on to consult with a convicted person generally does so outside the court.[13] Interpreters, when present, normally sit as close to the front of the court as they can. Prison officers accompany defendants who are serving a sentence into court. Such defendants arrive into court handcuffed to a prison officer. The handcuffs are normally removed once the defendant is in the body of the court and applied again before the prisoner leaves the court. At times the late arrival of defendants in custody can mean that matters have to be put back to 'second calling'. In RC, which is attached by an underground tunnel to a remand prison, almost all defendants are in custody prior to their court appearance and are produced from custody by prison officers. A prison officer also sits in this court throughout all court proceedings.

People come and go throughout the day but by afternoon the numbers in the courtroom are usually considerably fewer than in the morning and it is easier to maintain decorum. More serious and contested matters are usually dealt with later in the day when the courtroom is quieter. An air of solemnity often descends on the court, if only for a brief time, with the imposition of a custodial sentence.

The matters considered by the District Court are generally unexciting and commonplace in character, and hence tend not to engage the attention of all those present. Most people in the courtroom, including many solicitors and barristers, display little interest in the majority of cases that come before the court, and it is not unusual to see people passing the time in court by reading books and newspapers, consulting Argos catalogues, doing crosswords and sudoku puzzles, texting and even making mobile phone calls.

The limited public interest in court proceedings means that in Dublin, court reporters tend to descend on the court only when a person accused of a high-profile crime is due to appear. In NEC however, despite the very minor nature of most of the matters before the court, several reporters for local newspapers attended all court proceedings observed.

Before considering the role of the key actors in the District Court, it is helpful to briefly consider conviction rates and procedures in this court.

Convictions and 'Strike Outs'

Conviction rates in the District Court are high. In 2010, conviction rates ranged from 73% to 84% for those facing public order, assault, drugs, theft or sexual charges (CS, 2011:62). The conviction rates in 2009 ranged from 74% to 90% and in 2008 from 75% to 82% (CS, 2010:56, 2009:64). A considerably lower conviction rate of 58% was achieved in 2010 (2009:60%; 2008:60%) in respect of those charged with road traffic offences (RTOs). For all offence categories, the principal reason why convictions are not secured is because charges are struck out; the particularly high proportion of 'strike outs' for RTOs (39/37/36%) explains the lower conviction rates achieved for this offence category (CS, 2011:62, 2010:56, 2009:64).

Charges may be struck out on the application of the prosecution or the defence. When the prosecution applies for a 'strike out' they do not have to explain their application to the court. In such instances one can infer that the charges are struck out because the prosecution is flawed in some way, and is not expected to be successful. This could be because there is an error on the charge sheet or summons, or because a key witness has retracted their statement, or some other difficulty has arisen in relation to the prosecution of the charge, or because documents have been produced in respect of RTOs. However, when 'strike outs' are requested by the defence, a reason why the case should not proceed must be put before the court. Applications for 'strike outs' by defence lawyers are often made when the prosecution fails to expedite matters with reasonable promptness. So, when instructions from the DPP are still outstanding after a number of adjournments, or disclosure orders have not been complied with by the prosecution, or witnesses fail to appear in court and further adjournments are sought, the defence is likely to apply for a 'strike out'. In some circumstances a judge may direct that the 'strike out' be recorded as a state application even though the impetus for the 'strike out' came from the defence. This is what happened in the case outlined below:

> Jamal and Hussan J are co-accused and I assume that they are brothers or cousins. Their barrister tells the court that the state has not complied with a disclosure order which should have been met by a date more than two months previous. Judge Gilligan states clearly and forcefully: 'If the disclosure order has not been complied with the matter will be going out.' He stresses the last word 'out'. The barrister, sensing victory, says: 'Judge, one of my clients has travelled from the UK.' The court presenter asks that the matter be put back to a second calling, although you sense that he is ready to admit defeat. It is some time before the case is again recalled. The defence barrister reasserts that the 'Gary Doyle'[14] order has not been complied with. The judge looks at the court presenter as if daring him to argue that the state can justify its failure to comply with the disclosure order. The court presenter asks that the matter be struck out. The judge declares: 'Strike out on application of the state.' (FN20)

If the prosecution suggests that further charges are expected, or the case is complex in nature, or has international dimensions, it is likely that a judge will be reluctant to direct that the charges be struck out. In some circumstances a 'strike out' may be a product of skilled and ardent representations on the part of the defence lawyer, and in similar circumstances charges against an unrepresented defendant may proceed. It should be noted, however, that a 'strike out' does not prejudice future charges and it is possible in most cases for the DPP to bring the defendant before the court again on the same charges.

Pleas, Contested Charges and Adjournments

When charges do proceed, defence advocates use a variety of somewhat obscure terms to indicate that a defendant is pleading guilty or not guilty. One frequently hears that 'the facts are admitted', or 'there is a plea in that matter'; it seems almost as if the term 'guilty' is too indelicate and unequivocal to be used. Only a small proportion of defendants ultimately contest the charges brought against them. A 'not guilty' plea is also normally couched in somewhat coded language and is usually indicated by phrases such as: 'that matter is going ahead', or 'that matter is proceeding', or 'that is a contested matter'.

CS statistics do not identify the proportion of acquittals in the District Court. It seems that acquittals may be included as 'dismissals' in the CS statistics although this term strictly speaking refers to a judicial decision to terminate court proceedings prior to a verdict being reached. We can infer that the proportion of successful 'not guilty' pleas is not large as very few charges are dismissed by the court. In 2010 dismissal rates for defendants ranged from 2.2% for defendants charged with drug offences to 3.3% for defendants charged with public order/assault (CS, 2011:62). In 2009 dismissal rates for defendants ranged from 1.6% for those charged with sexual offences to 3.8% for those charged with public order/assault (CS, 2010:56). Similarly, in 2008 dismissal rates for defendants ranged from 1.6% for those charged with drug offences to 4.2% for those charged with RTOs (CS, 2009:64).

Why does the District Court find such a small proportion of defendants 'not guilty'? Most defendants do not contest the charges against them. Some may seek a hearing date as a delaying tactic even though they ultimately intend to plead 'guilty'. If defendants plead guilty at a hearing date, this may mean, as in the example below, that even for a first offence they will not be given the benefit of the Probation Act.[15]

> ... the solicitor told the court that his client had a sum of money in court of €200 and was prepared to make a donation to charity if he could leave the court with no conviction.[16] Judge Power was not receptive to this proposal and said: 'Well, it's a hearing date, he's had opportunities to plea before this.' The solicitor suggested that acceptance of guilt is a 'process of osmosis'.[17] The defendant was convicted and fined €100. (FN30).

During interview, Ms O'Brien, a solicitor, noted that in her experience the clients most likely to instruct her to plead 'not guilty' as a means of postponing sentencing are Irish clients who have experience of the criminal justice system. She stated:

> Typically our Irish clients would say, 'get it put back today', which means if it's the second or third remand pleading 'not

guilty' . . . when ultimately a few weeks or a month or two away they're going to be pleading guilty, they just want to postpone the evil day . . . and I would have thought that non-nationals who are less familiar with the system are perhaps a bit less likely to do that.

In many instances judges do not challenge defence requests for further adjournments and accede to them on what can only be considered fairly flimsy grounds. However, in some instances, as the examples set out below show, judges do challenge efforts by the defence to secure further adjournments and express their impatience at defence lawyers' failure to deal with matters expeditiously.

At the beginning of the morning session Judge Williams let off a warning shot to a solicitor who requested another court date to allow him to take instructions from his client. Judge Williams said: 'Don't be wasting court time on section 6 and section 4 matters[18] unless there is something different or complicated about the offences.' He then instructed the solicitor to discuss the matter with his client and directed: 'Let the matter stand.' Later when another defence solicitor requested a remand to get instructions from her client he commented with some irritation: 'It's not a murder trial . . . the man is alleged to have taken one box of beer.' This matter was also 'let stand'. (FN40)

In both of the above cases, when the matter was recalled, 'not guilty' pleas were entered by the defence and a hearing date was set. The entreaties by Judge Williams did not therefore succeed in expediting matters. Similarly:

Judge Nolan berated one solicitor who told the court that his client was in RC by way of explaining his absence. Judge Nolan reacted with impatience and irritation and wanted to know how this had happened and whether the solicitor was going to be paid for his appearance in court today when his client was in Remand Court (RC). The solicitor did not provide an answer regarding whether he would receive payment. On another occasion when a solicitor said: 'I'm seeking disclosure today,' Judge Nolan said: 'Why not next week or next year? Weren't you in the court on the last day . . . why didn't you seek it then? Bit of a waste of time this morning.' (FN43)

This extract highlights Judge Nolan's impatience with what he interprets as prevaricating tactics on the part of the defence. His comments also suggest that he suspects that sometimes the failure to progress matters may be motivated by solicitors' desire to maximise their fees rather than because they are simply following their clients' instructions.

This sketch of proceedings in the District Court gives the reader a preliminary sense of how the business of the Irish District Court is conducted. In the remainder of this chapter, colour and depth will be added to this initial sketch so that a more detailed picture of the everyday life of the court emerges. The role played by the prosecution and defence lawyers in the District Court is described and analysed. It is noted that much of the interplay between the prosecution and the defence takes place outside the court proceedings; this ensures the work of the court is minimised as both parties are generally aware in advance what applications will be made to the court and whether or not they will be contested. The distinction between the role of solicitors and barristers is described and the relationship between defence solicitors and barristers is also considered. The chapter points out that proceedings in the District Court rarely result in adversarial battles between the prosecution and the defence, whose primary role is often to present a credible case for mitigation to the court rather than to contest the charges faced by his client. Noting that many defendants in the District Court do not have legal representation, the chapter details how, and to whom, legal aid is granted. The chapter also draws attention to specific challenges which may arise in defending foreign nationals. Before turning to the roles played by the prosecution and defence, this chapter first describes the most powerful actors in the court, the judges.

District Court Judges

The Irish District Court is presided over by District Court judges, who sit alone. Currently the maximum permitted number of District Court judges is sixty-four. District Court judges are appointed by the president based on binding recommendations of the cabinet. Persons who wish to be appointed to judicial office are required to so inform the Judicial Appointments Advisory Board (JAAB). The JAAB was established by the Courts and Court Officers Act, 1995 in response to claims that judicial appointments were unduly affected by political allegiances and patronage (Ward, 2007). The JAAB identifies and informs the government of suitable persons for appointment to judicial office. The name and details of seven suitable applicants are normally put forward by the JAAB. The JAAB makes its selection on the basis of the criteria laid down in section 16(7) of the Courts and Court Officers Act, 1995, which essentially identifies reasons why applicants should not be put forward by the board rather than transparently meritocratic criteria (see Bacik et al., 2003; Ward, 2007). The JAAB is not empowered to recommend candidates in order of merit (Ward, 2007:51). Critics of the current system claim that it has not succeeded in eliminating political patronage from judicial appointments (see Carroll, 2005; Ward, 2007:52).

Persons appointed as District Court judges must be qualified solicitors or barristers with a minimum of ten years' experience of professional practice. In recent years the vast majority of applicants for appointment as District Court judges have been solicitors (JAAB, 2011, 2010, 2009). The office of District Court judge is a full-time appointment, attracts a generous salary and pension rights and provides an almost total guarantee of job security.[19] It is also noteworthy that until recently the Irish Constitution expressly prohibited any diminution of judges' remuneration during the term of their office; this provision attracted a great deal of media attention and public debate in the current era of cost cuts and a constitutional amendment regarding judges' remuneration was passed in 2011.[20]

In countries with common law traditions such as England and Wales, Canada, Australia and New Zealand, lower-tier criminal courts are presided over by magistrates, who often sit as part of a group. Magistrates may include lay magistrates who have no legal training or experience. Magisterial appointments may be part time, and may be remunerated by the payment of an allowance rather than a salary. Hence, Irish District Court judges differ from lower-tier judges in other jurisdictions by virtue of their legal experience and training, their security of office and their isolation on the bench. The judges of the Irish District Court therefore comprise a small, elite and privileged group whose day-to-day decisions greatly impact the Irish criminal justice system and the wider Irish society.

Prosecuting Minor Offences

Although the same presumption of innocence applies to defendants in the District Court as it does to defendants in higher courts, it has been suggested that the standard of proof that the prosecution is required to meet in the District Court is lower (see Devins, 2009). A book of evidence must be prepared by the prosecution for all cases tried by indictment. This is not required for cases tried summarily. Simply put, the prosecution has to do less work to secure convictions in the District Court than in higher courts, and convictions will usually be secured more rapidly in the District Court (LRC, 2003).

The level of proof typically presented in the District Court can be illustrated by reference to one of the most common charges dealt with by the court, a charge under section 4 of the Public Order Act, 1994. Section 4 stipulates that it is an offence for a person 'to be present in any public place while intoxicated to such an extent as would give rise to a reasonable apprehension that he might endanger himself or any other person in his vicinity'. Normally the charge is not contested and the arresting Garda presents the facts to the court in a formulaic fashion. The Garda will note in his evidence that the defendant was arrested in a public place and will refer to how he formed the impression that the defendant was intoxicated. From the evidence presented in court it seems that 'a strong smell of an intoxicating liquor' emanating from a defendant is generally key to this impression being formed. It is also necessary for the Garda to cover the legislative requirement that the defendant must present a danger to himself or to others in his vicinity in his evidence. If a Garda fails to refer to these matters in his evidence, the charges may be dismissed. To satisfy the court regarding the defendant's inebriation at the time of his arrest, and the danger he presented to himself or others, it is common for Gardaí to note in the course of their evidence that the defendant was 'unsteady on his feet', or 'had difficulty standing upright', or was 'swaying onto the road and into the path of traffic', and consequently had to be 'arrested for his own safety'.

The observations conducted suggest that when defendants try to defend a section 4 charge by offering any one of a myriad of defences (such as claiming that they were not drinking on the night in question; that they only had two drinks prior to their arrest; that they could not have been drunk because the hotel they were in had run out of beer; that they were mistakenly taken as being drunk because they had an eye infection which caused their eyes to look red and bloodshot), they are simply not believed.

Although such defences are very unlikely to succeed, they can usually be used to secure adjournments, and hence postpone sentencing. In NEC when a solicitor acting for an Irish defendant who was clearly well known to the court indicated that he was seeking a hearing date in relation to a section 4 public order charge, Judge O'Higgins looked exasperated. Noting this, the solicitor went on to explain his client's intention to contest the charges, adding that his client claimed that he had fallen down because he had a weakness in his legs which was being treated by medication. Judge O'Higgins turned to the defendant somewhat wearily and said: 'I know you have weak legs, and they go beneath you, and you're on medication . . . but you are fond of a few drinks Mr Murphy . . . more than a few.' The hearing date was granted. (FN80)

Who Acts as Prosecutor?

In the substantial majority of cases decided in the District Court, matters are not referred to the Office of the Director of Public Prosecutions (ODPP) (Devins, 2009), and hence the roles of investigating and prosecuting an offence are not clearly delineated. In such cases the role of the prosecutor is assumed by a court presenter, who is a Garda of the rank of sergeant or higher.[21] Court presenters of higher rank receive greater deference from other courtroom actors.

For more serious offences, An Garda Síochána prepares and submits files to the Solicitors' Division of the ODPP for Dublin cases and to the local state solicitor for cases outside Dublin. Solicitors from these offices conduct certain summary prosecutions in the District Court (ODPP, 2009:55). Such prosecutions will normally relate to more serious charges, but may also include charges brought against individuals considered to be serious offenders. Investigative files are submitted to the Directing Division of the ODPP for directions. The Directing Division directs initiation or continuance of a prosecution and provides ongoing instruction and legal advice to An Garda Síochána, the Solicitors' Division and local state solicitors.

When dealing with minor indictable offences, the prosecution normally has no incentive to refer the charges to the Circuit Court for trial by indictment. In such instances the court presenter will inform the court that the DPP directs summary disposition and the judge must then consider whether he will accept jurisdiction. Jurisdiction is not automatically accepted; judicial discretion may therefore override the directions of the DPP. The defendant may also be given the opportunity to opt for trial by indictment.[22] For less minor indictable offences the prosecution may direct that the offence may only be tried summarily on a plea of guilty.[23] This practice could be viewed as a form of plea bargaining whereby the prosecution trades the certainty of a conviction against the limited sentencing powers of the District Court.

When indictable offences are considered serious, the prosecution will usually be referred to the Circuit Court or, for charges of murder or rape, to the Central Criminal Court. When the DPP directs trial by indictment, solicitors from the Solicitors' Division and local state solicitors usually attend preliminary hearings in the District Court for indictment cases and are responsible for the preparation of the book of evidence.

Evidence

Much of the prosecution evidence presented in the District Court is witness testimony and in many instances the chief prosecution witness is the arresting Garda. In situations when the evidence of a defendant is not consistent with the evidence of a Garda, it is likely to be difficult to persuade the judge that the defendant's version of events is closest to the truth. Some judges may be particularly disinclined to question the veracity or accuracy of a Garda's evidence. As one solicitor put it: '. . . this judge now[24] . . . he will almost always believe the Guards . . . no matter what' (FN4). This attitude is also evident in the comments made by Judge Williams while passing sentence on a man who pleaded 'not guilty' to charges under section 4 of the Public Order Act, 1994. Judge Williams said that he was satisfied that the defendant 'was polluted with alcohol' at the time of his arrest, and that 'his judgement was significantly impaired'. Judge Williams indicated that he thought it probable that 'the defendant's recollection of events was likely to have suffered as a result' (FN47). This categorical statement regarding the defendant's condition at the time of his arrest was based essentially on the arresting Garda's description of him as being 'extremely intoxicated', and the defendant's admission that he had been drinking. The judge's comments also show how he has reconciled the competing versions of events presented by the defendant and the arresting Garda by concluding that alcohol had clouded the defendant's recollection of events.

Other forms of evidence presented by the prosecution in the District Court include CCTV footage, results of alcohol breath tests in drink-driving cases, and drug analysis certificates. Less routinely, Gardaí from the Documents Section may be called upon to present evidence regarding contested charges of false instruments. While there are frequent requests by the defence for CCTV footage, no CCTV footage was shown during the courtroom proceedings observed.[25] It seems that in most instances the CCTV footage is incriminating and does not aid the case of the defence. In such circumstances, even though the CCTV footage has been requested by the defence, it will not be shown in court if ultimately a guilty plea is lodged. In many instances, therefore, requesting CCTV footage may be motivated by a desire to defer conviction and sentencing rather than an expectation that it will establish the innocence of the defendant.

In the case of drink-driving charges, evidence is given in court of readings taken by an 'Intoxilyzer', which indicate the level of alcohol in a defendant's body. Even if the charge is not contested, the readings are relevant in that the period of disqualification from driving is determined by the level of the reading. If drink-driving charges are contested, Gardaí will be required to present evidence in court regarding the time of arrest and the time the breath test was conducted, the required observation period prior to conducting the test, the competence of the Garda who conducted the test, the temperature and humidity in the room where the test was conducted, and in some instances efforts to contact doctors to take blood samples. For drug charges to succeed, a certificate of analysis in relation to drug samples seized must be presented in court.[26] Delays in obtaining certificates of analysis are common.[27]

No District Court proceedings were observed during which other forms of forensic evidence such as fingerprint evidence or DNA evidence were presented. It is clear that there are limited resources available for forensic testing, and testing associated with more serious offences is prioritised (Kopp, 2008).

Defence Counsel and Legal Aid

The Role of the Defence Advocate

A good defence advocate is a wordsmith who can craft his client's life history into something heroic at best, or at worst present the court with the possibility, however slim, that the defendant is still redeemable and capable of reformation. This involves weaving together selected facts from the defendant's past to present the defendant in the best possible light. Many defendants have histories which are more distinguished by failures than achievements, and it is often simply not credible for the defence lawyer to suggest that the offence before the court was an aberration and the defendant is a solid upstanding citizen who is unlikely to trouble the court again. In such instances the defence seeks to devise a storyline which does not misrepresent the facts, but which does not necessarily seek to present the truth.[28] Every effort is made to create an impression of a defendant who is capable of seeking redemption and reform. Not surprisingly perhaps, judges do not accept such storylines without a certain amount of cynicism, and at times a lawyer's efforts to present their client in a favourable light can be derailed by a few apposite questions from the judge. This is clearly shown in the following field note extract:

> Paul Sheehan pleaded guilty to a collection of serious driving offences; in all, ten charges for driving without insurance and a similar number of charges for driving without a licence. We were told by his solicitor that he is forty years of age and his first wife has sadly passed away. We also learned that his second wife has very serious health problems and was recently diagnosed as having a brain tumour. As the couple have four young children, the defence solicitor noted that a custodial sentence would be particularly difficult for her client at this time when he was needed to assist with the care of the children. Judge Healy listened impassively to this account and after considering matters briefly he noted that a number of the convictions against Mr Sheehan were in respect of domestic violence and Mr Sheehan's wife had in fact taken a barring order out against him which he understood to be still in place. This information put a rather different complexion on this man's situation (FN56).

However, on many other occasions advocates were able to accentuate the elements of their clients stories that they knew would be viewed favourably by the court. In the extract set out below, the solicitor stresses that her client is a responsible member of society by pointing out her family responsibilities. She also highlights her efforts to improve her employment prospects by training as a nurse, and indeed the choice of profession underscores the basic storyline of a caring, responsible individual. She emphasises that the theft occurred when her client was under stress and hence does not reflect her underlying character. She mentions her client's immigration status because she is able to point out to the court that her client, a foreign national, is legally resident in the state.

> Vida D was called at 2.45 p.m. She is an African woman who is represented by Ms O'Shea, who indicated that her client is pleading guilty. The prosecuting sergeant told the court that the matter is a s.4 theft charge, and that cosmetics valued at €71 were taken by the defendant from Boots in Jervis Street. She has no previous convictions. Ms O'Shea told the court that her client is a 27-year-old Ghanaian national and mother of two children. She has a Stamp 4 status as the mother of two Irish-born children.[29] She came to Ireland in 2003 and is now studying nursing. Ms O'Shea told the court that her client is at a loss to account for her actions and can only say that she was under some considerable stress at the time which may have resulted in this behaviour which is completely out of character. Ms O'Shea then concluded by repeating that the defendant is the mother of two young children. Judge Moore said: 'The nature of the items does not indicate necessity.' Ms O'Shea replied that her client was experiencing some difficulties at the time of the offence. Judge Moore applied the Probation Act (FN50).

It is not always so easy for the defence advocate to find redeeming features in their client's history, as the following extract shows.

> Stefan D is in custody prior to his court appearance. His solicitor tells the court, 'Judge, we're anxious to complete matters,' and indicates that her client is pleading guilty on all charges. This man has amassed a number of fairly minor charges including several public order charges, a theft charge, and a s.13 'failure to appear' charge. His solicitor, Ms Burke, tells the court that the defendant previously had terrible drink difficulties but that he has now 'turned his life around'. The man still has 'an occasional drink' but it is no longer on the disastrous scale it was in the past. Ms Burke asks for leniency. She also notes that her client has no income at present as he is not working and is not in receipt of social welfare. Judge Williams then asks about previous convictions and the prosecuting Guard indicates that the defendant has 'quite a few', which date back to 2007. 'Quite a few' is never firmed up. Judge Williams imposes three terms of imprisonment of two, three and four months to run concurrently (FN47).

In this case the defendant has a criminal history and is before the court in respect of further multiple incidents of offending. Although the offences are minor, the persistent offending makes it much harder to present him as worthy of leniency. The solicitor blames her client's behaviour on his drink problem and suggests that as he has taken steps to bring his drinking under control he will no longer trouble the court. But Ms Burke's admission that her client still has 'an occasional drink' puts the credibility of this suggestion in doubt. The defendant's impecunious situation effectively makes the imposition of a fine pointless. Therefore, the custodial sentence imposed was probably not unexpected.

The Different Roles of Solicitors and Barristers

Section 17 of the Courts Act, 1971 provides that a solicitor acting for a party shall have a right of audience in any court. In practice, most solicitors do not act as advocates for their clients in the superior courts, but it is usual for defendants in the District Court to be represented by solicitors. Barristers who act as advocates for defendants in the District Court do so on the instruction of a solicitor; solicitors are the legal representatives on record. Barristers are independent advocates whose relationship with the defendant is indirect in that the solicitor selects and agrees payment terms with the barrister. Contact with the defendant prior to the court appearance is likely to be minimal. Some barristers are well briefed by their instructing solicitors and are able to craft remarkably skilful presentations in court after a very short consultation with their client. However, it appears that instructions are often very limited and the quality of representation in such instances can appear desultory and formulaic.

Particular Issues for Defence Counsel Representing Foreign Nationals

Immigration Charges

Those charged under immigration legislation are almost exclusively foreign nationals.[30] In many instances such charges are not contested and solicitors are not required to have a detailed knowledge of immigration law. However, in some instances the personal circumstances or residency status of a defendant may provide grounds for a defence against immigration charges and the ensuing contest in the court may centre on relatively complex immigration law issues. To provide their foreign national clients with the optimal defence, solicitors may at times require a detailed knowledge of immigration law.

Communication Difficulties

Communication with clients who are foreign nationals may be problematic in many instances. Solicitors need to evaluate their client's fluency in English and ensure that interpreters are available for consultations with LEP clients. If solicitors overestimate their client's fluency in English, misunderstandings can arise and solicitors may not interpret their client's instructions correctly. When legal aid has been assigned by the court, the costs of providing an interpreter for consultation with LEP clients will be met by the CS (DJELR, undated) but consultations must be certified by the court.

As there is no professional accreditation system in place for court interpreters in Ireland, and the standard of interpreting is uneven (Waterhouse, 2009; Irish Translators' and Interpreters' Association (ITIA), 2008; Bacik, 2007), defence counsel cannot assume that the court-appointed interpreter will always be competent and must exercise some vigilance in this regard.

Limited Social Rights

Foreign nationals do not enjoy the same social rights and may not be able to access the same services and benefits as Irish nationals. This can mean that some foreign criminal defendants are especially vulnerable, and is especially likely to be the case for non-EU defendants. At times, defence counsel may seek to assist their clients to access services, particularly medical services. On some occasions, as in the case set out below, solicitors may ultimately have to appeal to the court to assist them.

> Mr Kumar is African in appearance and is middle aged. This man was in custody prior to the court proceedings and the court was told that the Gardaí had no objection to bail but Mr Kumar refused to sign the discharge papers. Mr Kumar sat during the court proceedings holding his head in his hands. His solicitor, Ms Murphy, told the court that her client is suffering from depression and is homeless. He doesn't have access to the treatment or the medication he needs. His solicitor commented: '. . . he doesn't have a medical card and it is important that something is done to address his difficulties.' Judge Power noted that Mr

Kumar had already appeared before him and a psychiatric report had been requested. The solicitor said there had been no progress regarding the report. Judge Power asked Ms Murphy whether representations had been made on behalf of Mr Kumar regarding a medical card and he was told that representations had been made but had not been successful. In the end, Judge Power decided that Mr Kumar should be remanded in custody until Friday and requested a psychiatric report and medical treatment. It seems that the decision to detain Mr Kumar was made on the basis that prison might be the only place where he would receive free medical treatment (FN25).

Legal Aid

Frequently a defendant will not have legal representation for his initial appearance in court. If the judge considers that the gravity of the offence, or any 'exceptional circumstances' (Criminal Justice Legal Aid Act, 1962;[31] Department of Justice, Equality and Law Reform (DJELR), undated; Irish Criminal Law Journal (ICLJ), 2007a), are such that the defendant should be legally represented, he may question the defendant regarding his personal circumstances and if he is not considered to be a 'person of means' he will be assigned legal aid.

In practice, when legal representation is considered desirable, a defendant in receipt of social welfare will be routinely assigned legal aid unless there is a suggestion that he has undisclosed means. The judge will normally ask the arresting Garda if there is any objection to legal aid and if an objection is raised a statement of means may be requested by the court. Some judges routinely request a statement of means before assigning legal aid to defendants facing certain charges. Defendants in employment may qualify for legal aid particularly if their earnings are low, they have dependants or they have fixed outgoings such as rent or mortgage repayments. Defendants whose means are such that they do not qualify for legal aid may be offered an adjournment to obtain legal advice. Defendants may also appear in court having already secured legal representation, and normally when this is the case an application will be made for legal aid.

The assessment of the gravity of an offence and 'exceptional circumstances', if any, may depend crucially on the attitude of the presiding judge. Some judges assign legal aid if the defendant is considered to be 'at risk' (see ICLJ 2007b). 'At risk' is usually understood to mean that the defendant is at risk of receiving a custodial sentence. However, 'at risk' may also be understood to mean that there is a probability, rather than a possibility, of a custodial sentence. This is illustrated by the following field note extract:

> Edgar B faces charges of drunk-driving and driving without insurance. A 'Gary Doyle' order was made, to be complied with by a date some two weeks hence and the defendant was remanded for a period of three months to Court 52. The solicitor representing Mr B in court made an application for legal aid, noting that his client works as an agricultural labourer. Judge Power said that he would not approve legal aid as the defendant was not 'at risk'. The solicitor said: 'In the context of no insurance and drunk-driving travelling together, he might well be at risk on a bad day.' Judge Power did not waiver and refused legal aid (FN35).

The solicitor's assertion that his client might be at risk 'on a bad day' suggests that he considers the risk that his client may face a custodial sentence to hinge crucially on the attitude of the judge who imposes sentence. Judge Power, however, made the decision not to grant legal aid based on his assessment that it was not probable, rather than not possible, that the defendant would ultimately face a custodial sentence.

While some judges may assign legal aid when a custodial sentence is possible and others only when a custodial sentence is probable, still other judges may assign legal aid for all but the most minor of offences. The inconsistency of judicial attitudes towards legal aid was evident in the views expressed by the two District Court judges interviewed prior to the commencement of fieldwork. Judge Sheerin asserted during interview that he considered that 'the ability of the person to conduct the case and to understand the processes' should be taken into account when assigning legal aid, and commented that many migrants who found themselves as defendants in the District Court were simply not in the same position as 'articulate English-speaking people', and consequently should be assigned legal aid in some circumstances when an Irish defendant would not deserve legal aid. Contrast this with the view of Judge Doyle who said that he only assigned legal aid when a custodial sentence was likely, rather than possible, and noted: 'In Ireland we don't normally imprison people for drunk-driving unless it's a third offence. So normally I would refuse an application for legal aid and the defendant pleads guilty. But if you grant legal aid the first thing that will happen is the number of "not guilty" pleas will increase.' Judge Doyle went on to link the higher number of foreign defendants with extra claims on the legal aid system and with a higher proportion of 'not guilty' pleas.

Core Courtroom Work Groups

Courts are organised in a different manner to most bureaucratic organisations in that courtroom actors enjoy considerable discretion in carrying out their duties and share a common professional bond and orientation towards the law with most other courtroom actors. This results in a unique reward/punishment system which is based on tacit informal norms and is undocumented and generally unacknowledged. It may be that defence lawyers who employ tactics that result in unreasonable adjournments may be sanctioned by having cases listed late in the proceedings or by being excluded from information shared with other courtroom actors. Eisenstein and Jacob (1977) identified four key characteristics of courtroom workgroups: speed, guilt, cohesion and secrecy. Speed refers to a desire to dispose of cases rather than dispense justice. Guilt refers to the assumption that defendants in court are de facto guilty and that therefore a finding of legal guilt is routine. Cohesion refers to the acceptance that all courtroom actors, even nominally adversarial ones, should co-operate. Finally, secrecy refers to the fact that most major decisions are negotiated outside the public realm in hallways or side rooms. The courtroom work groups observed in the Irish District Court are described below.

In the Dublin area a number of larger firms of solicitors which specialise in criminal law have a regular representative in each busy courtroom. Smaller firms tend to locate in a limited number of courts and assign barristers to deal with clients who appear in other court locations.

Hence, in CCC and SDC a core group of solicitors deal with a large proportion of the cases before the court. This core group is augmented regularly by solicitors who only deal with occasional criminal cases; solicitors who handle all matters for specific clients; and barristers assigned cases by various solicitors.

In NEC there is also a core group of regular solicitors attached to local firms. Occasionally reference was made during courtroom observations to solicitors handling cases for Dublin-based firms of solicitors. NEC has a much more tightly-knit work group than the other courts observed, with fewer 'visiting' solicitors and only rare appearances by solicitors from the local State Solicitor's or DPP's Office. In NEC the probation officer is included within this core work group whereas in other courts the probation officer is very much a peripheral figure who only has a very formal relationship with other courtroom professionals. The nature and extent of the inter-group ties in NEC are highlighted in the field note extract below:

> At the commencement of today's court session Judge O'Higgins said that he had a sad announcement to make. I immediately thought that the death had occurred of a judicial colleague,[32] but in fact the sad announcement was the retirement of Ms Henderson, a probation officer who has worked in the NEC district for eight years. Judge O'Higgins said that the importance of the work of the probation service is often overlooked. He described it as 'silent work'. He described Ms Henderson as 'scrupulously fair' and a 'formidable' woman. He said it was a shame that she was retiring and that he would greatly miss her. When he expressed his regrets about her retirement, the man sitting on the bench beside me said: 'It's a pity he wouldn't fuckin' retire.' After Judge O'Higgins concluded his remarks they were followed by remarks in a similar vein by the court presenter on behalf of An Garda Síochána, and by a solicitor on behalf of all the solicitors who work in NEC. The registrar then paid quite an emotional tribute to Ms Henderson on behalf of the CS and then Ms Henderson thanked everyone. It seemed extraordinary that this should take place in a busy court full of defendants and members of the public. Certainly the various representations sent a very strong message that the courtroom insiders operate as a closely-knit team and that they view each other as colleagues rather than adversaries (FN80).

On another occasion observed, a new solicitor was formally introduced to Judge O'Higgins in NEC by one of the resident solicitors, who recited at length details of the schools and university the solicitor had attended, and the tutelage and guidance he had received from another highly esteemed solicitor. This was followed by welcoming remarks by Judge O'Higgins, the court presenter, the probation officer and the registrar (FN78).

Competition and Co-operation between Defence Solicitors and between Barristers

Solicitors in the District Court have a rather unusual relationship. They are competitors vying for the same business but they are also professional colleagues. Solicitors are allowed to advertise their services subject to regulations which prohibit advertisements in 'inappropriate locations', or on any form of transport, and prohibit a solicitor from making claims to have specialist knowledge superior to other solicitors.[33] The regulations also state that 'an unsolicited approach may not be made where it is likely to bring the profession into disrepute. In particular, approaches at an "inappropriate location", or at or adjacent to a calamitous event, a Garda station, courthouse or prison, shall not be made' (Law Society of Ireland, undated). Solicitors are therefore quite constrained in the efforts they can engage in to secure clients. Solicitors working in criminal law get new business when they are assigned under the legal aid scheme to defendants in the District Court or when defendants seek them out either because they have previously represented them or because they have heard of them by word of mouth. Some solicitors can build up a substantial number of clients within particular communities in this way. This was confirmed during interview by solicitors Keane and Hanly.

> KEANE: . . . I don't know how we first started but we have a lot of Romanian clients and that's because they are a close-knit community . . . so once you advise one you end up advising their friends, and so on . . .

> HANLY: Yeah, I have loads of nationals from Iran and Iraq . . . and again it's word of mouth . . . I mean, I had five clients from Iran, say, a year-and-a-half ago and now I have more than a hundred . . .

The competition between solicitors is real but is cloaked by professional etiquette and controlled by regulations. In court many solicitors co-operate with one another as if they were part of the same team. Solicitors normally deal with a number of cases during any given court session. This means that they will sometimes leave the body of the court to consult with their clients and may be absent when some of the cases they are dealing with are called. Normally if this happens, another solicitor will play a sort of holding role by noting that 'Ms X appears in that matter', and ask for the matter to be put back to a second calling.

However, tensions between solicitors can arise, particularly when defendants opt to change their assigned solicitors. When judges assign legal aid cases they usually ask defendants if there is a particular solicitor they wish to represent them. If the defendant does not nominate a solicitor, the judge will usually try to assign cases to solicitors in court on the legal aid panel as fairly as possible. Defendants may, however, subsequently decide that they do not wish to be represented by the solicitor initially assigned to them. This can cause tension among solicitors, but not normally the kind of behaviour that occurred in the following case:

> Ali P was assisted in court by an Arabic interpreter. The solicitor for this man told the court that his client is in custody on 'an identity matter'. He added that this man's identity documents were sent to the original solicitor on record, who refused to send them on to his office and instead sent them back to Iran. The court presenter asked for a further remand for two weeks to 'give everyone a chance'. The solicitor asked that the prosecution note the position regarding the documents. Judge Sweeney asked for the name of the solicitor who returned the documents to Iran and the solicitor said: 'I'm not going to say that at the moment.' (FN59)

Barristers operate as independent agents and often handle only one or a small number of cases in a District Court session. This means that they often drift in and out of the courtroom with limited interaction with other barristers or solicitors. However, in RC where barristers deal with much of the business, it was evident that most of the regular barristers had a collegial relationship and would step in to assist colleagues when they were temporarily out of the court. On one occasion in RC, a female barrister came to court without her robes and another female barrister came to her assistance by sharing her robes. This created a kind of comical tableau in which one barrister shrugged off the robes as required, and the other quickly donned them. The whole performance was repeated several times and was entirely visible to the judge, who made no comment.

RC is unusual in that the resident group of legal representatives in this court is smaller than usual and consists in the main of barristers rather than solicitors. This may be because most defendants who appear before RC already have legal representation, and it is quite unusual for legal aid to be assigned in RC. Most defendants are not remanded in custody without being assigned legal aid or given an opportunity to consult a legal advisor. Therefore, there is almost no 'new business' to be picked up in RC. Accordingly, as the extract set out below shows, when a defendant is assigned legal aid in RC the court may have to handle the matter somewhat more delicately than usual to ensure all proprieties are addressed. The issue of assigning arose when a defendant indicated that he did not wish to be represented by the solicitor originally assigned to him. After Judge O'Toole advised him that it would be wise to have legal representation, the defendant agreed and Judge O'Toole then had to assign the matter. He dealt with it as follows:

> Judge O'Toole addressed one of the regular barristers in court and said: 'Mr Deegan, who do you represent?' Mr Deegan seemed to find this a difficult question to answer and after an initial hesitation said: 'A number of solicitors, Judge'. Judge O'Toole then said: 'Yes . . . well . . . maybe you would name them . . . perhaps alphabetically?' The barrister then listed a string of solicitors and Judge O'Toole picked a firm of solicitors. He advised Mr Deegan as follows: 'I think it best if you consult with the defendant and explain matters to him . . . he's seeking trial on indictment for the theft of a bottle of wine'. Judge O'Toole also added: 'Professionally, Mr Deegan, perhaps you might call Mr X [the solicitor] to let him know he has been assigned.' (FN73)

Co-operation between Prosecution and Defence

There is a significant amount of behind-the-scenes co-operation between the prosecution and defence in District Court cases, and most judges seem to expect them to work together almost in a spirit of partnership. This is consistent with the principle of *audi alterem partem* which requires both sides to be heard before a matter can be adjudicated upon. It is also consistent with an orientation towards streamlining courtroom procedures.

Judges expect defence lawyers to know when bail is being objected to and similarly expect the prosecution to be made aware that a bail application is to be made. It is also considered unreasonable to indicate that a guilty plea is to be entered in court without notifying the prosecution in advance.[34] When the necessary pre-court arrangements have not been put in place, judges frequently put matters back to 'second calling', which can mean a delay of a matter of minutes or a matter of hours. Even when the prosecution application is to amend a charge, the judge may expect the defence to be notified in advance. When Judge Williams found that the defence was not alerted in advance to a prosecution application to amend one of the charges, he told the court presenter: 'You can't ambush him with these requests', and put the matter back to a second calling (FN40). The following extract illustrates how a defence solicitor can work behind the scenes with the prosecution to secure the best outcome for her client and to simplify court proceedings:

> Before the commencement of the afternoon court session Ms Murphy, one of the most experienced solicitors in CCC, explained to the court presenter that Jerzy R, who appeared before the court that morning and was remanded on continuing bail, was also on the court list for the previous day and failed to appear. A bench warrant was issued due to his non-appearance. Ms Murphy managed to convince the court presenter that the failure to appear by her client on the previous day was a genuine mistake. Later, the court presenter rather than the defence raised the matter with the judge, noting that a bench warrant had been issued on the previous day and stating that he was happy that it was a genuine mistake. Judge Power cancelled the warrant and re-instated bail. (FN30)

Similarly, the field note extract set out below highlights how the defence may seek the assistance of the prosecution to secure bail on terms that the defendant can meet. The accommodation reached in this case involved a degree of compromise on the part of the defence but crucially succeeded in mollifying a judge who had adopted an intractable approach in the matter.

> Robert A was produced for the second time from the cells in the afternoon. This time he was in court long enough to be assisted by a Polish interpreter. The charge before the court is one of criminal damage. The arresting Garda indicated that there was no objection to bail subject to a cash lodgement. The defence solicitor indicated that her client is a man of very limited means. His income consists of jobseekers' allowance and he is living in a hostel. Judge Sweeney simply said: '€200 . . . cash.' The matter was put back for a further 'second' calling at the request of the defence. It was some time later before Robert A was again called and again produced from the custody cells. His solicitor

attempted ito impress upon the judge her client's very limited means but Judge Sweeney simply said: 'I'm here 'til 6 o'clock.' The solicitor was clearly frustrated but court etiquette dictates that there can be no direct display of dissent so she simply said: 'May it please the court.' Later the solicitor approached the interpreters' bench and spoke to the Polish interpreter and said: 'Could you tell him if he agrees to stay in prison 'til Tuesday the Garda will let him out with €100 bail. He should be able to get someone to come up with that'. The interpreter later accompanied the solicitor to the custody cells. When Robert A was called for the fourth time the solicitor told the court that there was consent to a remand in custody until Tuesday with consent to bail on a cash lodgement of €100. Judge Sweeney noted the terms. (FN51)

Here the requirement by the arresting Garda that a cash lodgement be made to secure bail seemed at first to present an insurmountable roadblock to the release of the defendant. Many defendants would not have difficulty in lodging a cash amount of €200 to secure bail, but in this instance the solicitor was aware that if bail was set on these conditions her client would continue to be remanded in custody. She therefore sought the assistance of the prosecution to secure the release of her client. The 'deal' was not reached without the prosecution extracting a few ounces of flesh, however, in that the cash amount was reduced on condition that the defendant was remanded in custody for a number of days.

The Voice of the Defendant

As his demeanour is always deferential, polite and refined, judges seem to infinitely prefer to 'do business' with the legal professional rather than with the defendant, who effectively does not speak the same language as the judge. Solicitors and barristers try as far as possible to secure the silence of their clients during court proceedings, but not all clients are co-operative. Some of them get visibly frustrated when they feel their solicitor or barrister is not doing their job properly. They may tap the advocate on the back in the hope of gaining their attention, or if that does not succeed in getting the attention of their lawyer they may seek to bypass them by calling out, 'Judge, Judge, can I speak?' Such interjections are not welcomed by the court, or by defence lawyers, but sometimes, as can be seen

from the extract below, the opportunity to speak seems to provide
the defendant with a certain degree of personal satisfaction.

> During a bail application today a defendant took the stand to
> testify on his own behalf. The defendant, Mr Buckley, insisted
> on testifying even though it was clear that the barrister repre-
> senting him was not keen that he should do so, and tried several
> times to dissuade him. Mr Buckley's testimony was rambling but
> he addressed the substance of the objection to bail, which was
> based on his history of bench warrants, by saying: 'Judge, Judge,
> I never ever, ever in my life, Judge, meant to take a warrant,
> never Judge . . . Judge, it's just the drugs, Judge'. He also stressed
> that he did not wish to go to prison saying: 'I'm locked up since
> I was twelve . . . I just want help . . . prison has ruined me . . . it's
> ruined me . . . it's worse in prison . . . it's worse.'[35]
>
> Mr Buckley referred to himself as drug-free. This was some-
> what surprising as his speech was slurred and his movements
> were deliberate rather than fluid. He certainly gave the impres-
> sion that he was under the influence of drugs. The arresting
> Garda asked him was he really drug-free, noting that Mr Buckley
> had told him that he had four or five 'benzos' the other day.[36]
> Mr Buckley did not dispute this claim and the following
> exchange ensued:
>
> MR BUCKLEY: 'Yeah, because me head was wrecked.'
>
> GARDA: 'But you'd still describe yourself as drug free?'
>
> MR BUCKLEY: 'Yeah, yeah . . . I'm drug free and I want to stay
> that way (turns to judge with hands together as if in prayer) . . .
> Judge, prison is going to ruin me . . . prison is going to ruin me.'
>
> Mr Buckley's barrister addressed the court and explained that
> her client's understanding of drug-free was free from heroin and
> methadone. Mr Buckley was not granted bail. When Judge
> Power announced his decision, Mr Buckley simply shrugged his
> shoulders and turned to the public gallery and said: 'What can
> you do?' (FN33)

Mr Buckley was clearly a seasoned campaigner in the court, and
despite his impassioned pleas he does not seem to have had an unre-
alistic expectation of the likelihood of his being granted bail. It was
clear by his reaction to the judge's decision that at least some of the
distress he displayed was contrived; he was essentially delivering a
performance. He seemed to enjoy his time in the witness box and
was quite aware that for a few moments he had secured the attention

of the whole court. So many times the defendant is effectively written out of the script and must accept his barrister or his solicitor as his voice. On this occasion Mr Buckley's voice was heard in the court. His barrister, however, did not want to irritate the judge by taking up too much court time, or have a situation arise in which her client might be held to have lied under oath. Hence, she felt it necessary to explain her client's understanding of 'drug-free'.

Conclusion

This chapter focused on the key courtroom actors in the Irish District Court and on the day-to-day work of the court. This non-partisan sociological account of District Court proceedings erases some of the inscrutability that has surrounded the work of the court. Drawing on extensive observations of courtroom proceedings, it provides an authentic description of courtroom argot, etiquette and procedures, and so reveals a wealth of information that would be impenetrable to a casual observer.

The chapter reveals that sittings of the Irish District Court often lack the solemnity one might imagine a criminal courtroom warrants, and can even at times comprise elements of farce, disarray and confusion. There is a lack of separation between the investigation and prosecution of the majority of matters that come before the District Court. Most charges are ultimately not contested and interactions between key courtroom actors are mainly co-operative rather than adversarial in nature. Much of the communication between courtroom actors takes place 'off-stage'. This 'off-stage' communication is necessary to allow the court to deal with its dauntingly long caseload. Despite the relatively straightforward nature of most matters, adjournments are common and add greatly to the workload of the court. Many of those that appear before the court do so without legal representation, with the allocation of legal aid being largely determined by judicial discretion. Defence lawyers are rarely required to launch a defence against the charges faced by their clients; rather, their role is often limited to securing adjournments which defer sentencing, and ultimately presenting the defendant in the best possible light to the court. The chapter points to specific issues which may impact the work of the defence lawyer representing foreign defendants, who may be especially vulnerable due to their immigration status, language difficulties, or their limited access to social supports.

The defendant, who is after all most impacted by the decision of the court, is expected to be present but is usually strongly discouraged from speaking. The courtroom is a forum for the educated and the articulate; the voice of the defendant is seldom heard, and when it is, it often seems as if it is afforded little consideration. As the chapter highlights, the opportunity to be heard in court may be important to some defendants, and may even be central to their perception of the fairness of the court process. Despite the volume of cases disposed of by the court, the cast of courtroom regulars is quite small. Even for many solicitors and higher-tier judges, the world of the District Court is quite alien. This chapter opens up that world to a wider audience. Its central contention is that by understanding the context in which the work of the court is carried out, we can better evaluate the decisions of the court and criticisms thereof.

Chapter 2 describes the defendants observed during the course of the fieldwork undertaken, and compares and contrasts Irish and foreign defendants. A number of different categories of foreign defendants are identified and the scale of the presence of foreign defendants in each location is detailed.

Chapter 2

Ordinary Crimes and Ordinary Criminals
DISTRICT COURT DEFENDANTS

Introduction

In 2010, the Irish District Court disposed of 428,472 (2009, 451,280; 2008, 482,203) summary offences and 70,200 (2009, 69,778; 2008, 68,491) indictable offences summarily (CS, 2011:62; 2010:56; 2009:64). The volume and varied nature of the cases dealt with by the District Court ensures that defendants from all sections of society appear before the court. Although many defendants will be charged with multiple offences, and many may also appear before the court on a regular basis, and in a number of different locations, others will only ever appear before the court once. Collectively, District Court defendants consist of a very large and diverse mass of people. Included among the ranks of defendants are people with a long criminal history and people with no previous convictions. Some defendants will be very familiar with court processes, others will find them bewildering. Defendants include articulate, well-educated persons as well as persons with very little formal education for whom the formal language of the court may be quite alien. Many of those who appear before the court will consider themselves to be law-abiding citizens and respectable members of the community. They will not consider themselves to be criminals and may have no difficulty asking advice from court officials or Gardaí. Others will be reluctant to approach such persons.

In recent years the court has also had to deal with a sizable proportion of foreign nationals, some of whom have limited or no English. Some of these foreign nationals will be resident in Ireland and are well embedded in Irish society; others will never have been resident and may never have intended to be resident in Ireland.

This chapter draws on observations of District Court sittings to present a picture of defendants who appear before the District

Court, with particular emphasis on foreign defendants. Initially it presents an overview of Irish defendants observed, describing the stereotypical young male offender and then looking at some of the deviations from this stereotype. Attention is drawn to the presence of defendants with mental health issues and substance abuse problems, and the disproportionate presence of Travellers.[1]

The chapter then examines the profiles of national groups resident in Ireland compiled from Census 2006 and points out that key differences in these profiles suggest that offending rates of foreign national groups resident in Ireland are likely to vary significantly. While it is not possible to present a detailed analysis of the nationality of District Court defendants observed during the course of fieldwork, the information compiled suggests that key features of foreign national groups such as age, sex and socio-economic class only partially predict offending rates. Observations indicate that the level and pattern of alcohol consumption is also a critical predictor of differences in offending rates among foreign national groups. In addition, as a proportion of the foreign nationals who appear before the District Court were not previously resident in Ireland, statistics concerning the resident population of foreign nationals have a limited predictive value. The chapter highlights that the presence of some of the foreign defendants who appear before the Irish District Court stems from transitory movements which are commonplace in modern life. Like other national criminal justice systems, the Irish system must now dispense justice within its boundaries to many who are not citizens, and to some persons who were never resident in Ireland. Finally, the chapter presents an outline of the scale and proportion of foreign defendants observed in each location.

Expanding Diversity

Although there is now a far greater breadth of diversity among the defendants who appear before the District Court, it should be acknowledged that diversity is not new to this particular court. While District Court defendants include a preponderance of young working-class men, men and women from all social classes and across all age cohorts have always appeared before the court. Drink-driving is an example of an offence which is not confined by gender or class; one finds men and women, young and old, unskilled and professional among those charged with this offence. Motorists who commit speeding offences also appear to be spread across all socio-economic classes, although the incidence of some motoring offences (such as driving without insurance) appears to be closely correlated with low levels of income. Domestic disputes which give rise to breaches of safety orders, or on occasions assault charges, also result in defendants from all socio-economic classes appearing before the court. Similarly those charged with the gravest of crimes such as murder or rape, who appear before the District Court when they are initially charged, may be middle-aged and from the middle classes and be well embedded in society, and so often do not fit with the generally accepted image of a deviant criminal. While the ethnic diversity of District Court defendants was relatively limited in the past, some diversity was provided by the presence of members of the Traveller community.

Overview of Irish Defendants

Young Working-Class Men

Observations indicate that a very large proportion of defendants of all nationalities who appear before the District Court are young men from lower socio-economic backgrounds. The bulk of foreign defendants observed were aged twenty or older, whereas many young Irish defendants were aged only eighteen or nineteen and often looked even younger. Sometimes the defendants appeared in court carefully dressed in clothes that looked as if they had been specially bought for their court appearance, but for the most part they wore casual clothes such as tracksuits and jeans. A smartly dressed defendant may indicate a middle-class background or may indicate that the defendant is particularly concerned about the charge he faces and is especially anxious to give a good impression in court. Despite their young age, many defendants were veterans in court and had progressed to the adult court from the children's court. It was rare to hear that these young men were in employment or attending school or college. A number were involved in youth out-reach programmes but the majority of them had no work or study to occupy them, and with little or no educational qualifications their prospects of gaining employment are very poor. Learning difficulties, early school leaving, a history of alcohol and/or drug abuse, parents absent or ineffective due to incarceration/sickness/death/mental health issues/substance abuse, were all common motifs in the life histories of defendants who were presented in court.

Substance abuse

The physical appearance of defendants was often testament to their substance abuse. A sickly pallor, an unsteady gait, slurred speech and uninhibited behaviour are suggestive of substance abuse and were frequently displayed by District Court defendants. Some defendants struggled to stay awake for their court appearances. A few were almost in a catatonic state. One such defendant observed was Karl Fowler.

> This morning Karl Fowler was barely conscious during his court appearance. He sat on the bench with his eyes closed and when his case had been dealt with one of the custody Guards had to rouse him so that he left the courtroom. When I left the court complex shortly after 1pm Mr Fowler was sitting on the pavement, in a stupor, about twenty feet away from the Luas stop[2]. He was still there at 2 p.m. when I returned to the court complex. When I left the court at 3 p.m. he was also there but he now only had one shoe on, and had an unlit cigarette in his mouth. His eyes were still closed. (FN43)

Although some defendants faced charges that directly stemmed from drug possession, most offending by substance abusers was indirectly related to their substance abuse. Persons who are addicted to drugs often steal to get money to buy drugs, but the effects of the drugs they take make them more liable to be apprehended (Furey and Browne, 2004, cited in Connolly 2006:77). Similarly, those who abuse alcohol often simply try and steal alcohol. If they do this when they are drunk, they stand little chance of getting away with their crime.

Mental health difficulties

Sometimes the behaviour of defendants while in court suggested that they had mental health difficulties. Some sat holding their head in their hands, others wept, while a few called out or laughed inappropriately, or seemed dazed, confused, and uncomprehending of the court processes. Solicitors on occasion referred to difficulties taking instructions from clients with mental health difficulties, or requested psychiatric reports when defendants were remanded in custody. On other occasions the court was presented with reports detailing the psychiatric history of defendants. A small number of defendants observed in RC were detained in the Central Mental Hospital.

Although mental health difficulties were often presented by solicitors as a mitigating factor, not all judges seemed to accept them as such. The field note extract set out below provides an example of this.

> One of the Irish defendants in court today pleaded guilty to a criminal damage charge. The amount of the damage was €6,000 and Judge O'Toole made it clear that in his view, jurisdiction should have been refused. The defendant is a 38-year-old man with no previous convictions. It was admitted in court that he broke twenty-four windows in a building using a sling shot and marbles. He had no connection with the institution which uses the building. A detailed psychiatric report was submitted to the court outlining the current psychiatric difficulties of the defendant. Despite this, Judge O'Toole sentenced the man to six months' imprisonment and in addition ordered that he pay compensation of €6,000 and a fine of €1,000 within six months and specified ninety days in default. He recommended that the man be detained in Wheatfield prison, commenting that Mountjoy[3] would be unsuitable, and further noted that the man should be considered for possible admission to a secure psychiatric unit. Efforts by the defence barrister to get Judge O'Toole to reconsider the order for compensation and the amount of the fine were unsuccessful. (FN64)

Family Support

Defendants did not always have a disadvantaged background or a dysfunctional family; references to 'respectable' and 'hard-working' families were presented by defence lawyers in an effort to convince judges that defendants were not likely to re-offend. Some parents accompanied their adult children in court and their presence was often noted by defence lawyers, presumably as evidence that the defendant would receive some form of ongoing familial support and control. In SDC three brothers from the same family were observed in court on several different occasions. The mother of these three young men was always present; her face quickly became very familiar to the researcher due to the frequent court appearances of her sons. She was very thin and looked completely worn out and on a number of occasions she was in tears in court. She was known to Judge Murray, who commented once: 'I see his mother in court today . . . every time he was in Court 55 she was in there with him and she is still here (FN17).' Clearly, in this instance at least, parental support was not effective in preventing re-offending.

While familial support may help some offenders to desist from criminal behaviour, sometimes family ties seem to enmesh people in such behaviour rather than encourage them to desist. In CCC a mother and her adult son regularly appeared, both separately and as co-accused, before the court and on several occasions it was noted that the partner of a defendant also had court appearances or was in prison.

Wide Variety of Defendants

Although it is possible to point to the young, poorly-educated male from a low socio-economic background as a stereotype of a District Court defendant, it is also important to recognise the diversity of defendants and the different circumstances that can lead to their presence in the District Court. In addition to those who get involved in brawls outside nightclubs, or who refuse to pay the taxi driver who has brought them home, there are persons such as the sixty-year-old grandmother charged with fraud because she continued to cash her aged mother's pension after she died. There are people before the court who repeatedly drive without insurance, or while under the influence of alcohol, and also those who find themselves before the court because they forgot to pay a speeding ticket. Courtroom demeanour of defendants can also be misleading. The defendant charged with assaulting a barman after a day of binge drinking may present in court as a calm, demure, middle-aged woman who looks altogether unthreatening when she is sober. The frail elderly man who seems somewhat dazed and confused may be facing multiple charges of child sexual abuse. The appearance of those charged with particular crimes may also not match our expectations. It was surprising to learn that a female defendant who appeared in CCC 'wearing stiletto heels, an off-the-shoulder figure-hugging top and a surfeit of gold coloured jewellery' (FN28) faced burglary charges. This and other instances observed made it clear that stereotypical images of offenders may simply not fit those who appear before the court.

Travellers in the District Court

Census 2006 indicated that the population of Travellers in Ireland only amounted to 22,435, or just over 0.5% of the total population

(Central Statistics Office (CSO), 2007). If Travellers appeared before the District Court in proportion to their presence in the population, Travellers would only account for roughly one out of every 190 defendants who appear before the District Court.[4] The fieldwork conducted, however, suggests that the presence of members of the Traveller community among District Court defendants is not in proportion to their presence among the general population, but rather is far in excess of that. If one looks at indices of employment (CSO, 2004, 2007), education (NCCRI, 2004) or health (Pavee Point, 2005), the Traveller community can be quickly identified as being a severely disadvantaged group in Ireland. Anti-Traveller sentiment among the general population can also result in discrimination and generate animosity between the Traveller community and the general population. These factors are likely to contribute to the presence of Travellers among criminal defendants.

Travellers often appeared before the court in groups rather than as individual accused persons. Indeed, during the course of the fieldwork it was not unusual to see several members of the same family before the court as co-accused. In such instances the charges usually arose out of public order incidents. As with all other defendants, public order charges faced by Travellers often stem from the consumption of excessive alcohol, but they can also arise as a result of disputes between Traveller families, or between members of the same family. When Travellers appear as defendants it is common for several, and sometimes a large number of family members to be present in court. This increases their visibility in the courtroom.

Travellers were among the most truculent defendants who appeared before the court, and it seemed that at least some of those observed felt that the criminal justice system played an inordinate and inappropriate role in regulating their life. Their attitude suggested at times that they did not fully accept that it was legitimate for the state, through the criminal justice system, to intervene in Traveller matters. Solicitors were sometimes instructed to characterise incidents which gave rise to arrests as family disputes which the family should be allowed to resolve without interference. Such efforts were not normally successful, particularly when weapons such as hammers and machetes were involved.

The presence of Travellers and Traveller families in the Irish District Court can be best illustrated by pointing to one of the families observed during the course of the fieldwork. On the first day of fieldwork two members of a Traveller family, a mother and daughter, were observed in court. Neither woman had any shoes on her feet and the older woman seemed to be wearing pyjamas (FN1). It became apparent in court that both women had been arrested at their home earlier in the day. Both seemed very angry at being arrested and struggled to maintain their composure in court. It was revealed in court that these women, and everyone else in their house, were arrested after a family dispute became violent.

During a subsequent court appearance it was noted that Kathleen, the eighteen-year-old daughter, who had a number of previous convictions, had recently got married. As the fieldwork continued, the father, two brothers and husband of the younger woman were observed in SDC on a number of occasions when they appeared on various charges. Kathleen and her mother were also observed in both SDC and CCC several times when they were in court to answer charges or to support one or other of their relatives. On one occasion Kathleen and her mother were granted a lengthy remand by the court because they had to travel to England to give evidence in a court case. Kathleen's husband was also observed in RC, where he appeared before the court on bail charged with criminal damage. He secured a six-week remand when the court was told that his wife was pregnant and expected to give birth shortly (FN57).

The fieldwork highlighted that Kathleen's early married life, and the life of her family, was punctuated by frequent entanglements with the criminal justice system which were clearly greatly resented. Many of the features of Kathleen's life were very ordered and traditional. She had married at a young age, and was expecting her first child. She clearly had strong family ties, and appeared to have a good support system within the Traveller community. But her life was very much marred by her family's involvement with the criminal justice system, which largely stemmed from violent intra- and inter-family disputes.

Resident Foreign Nationals

Census 2006 provides the most detailed source of information available regarding the population of foreign nationals resident in Ireland. Examining Census 2006 statistics regarding Ireland's resident non-Irish population not only provides us with a picture of the origins of the resident population of non-Irish nationals in Ireland in 2006 but also enables us to evaluate which national groups have features which make their members more or less likely to appear before the District Court as defendants.

The 2006 census reveals how remarkably diverse the resident population of Ireland has become. The census shows that in 2006 non-Irish nationals accounted for just over 10% of the resident population, while the proportion of resident foreign nationals was 7.4%.[5] Persons from 188 countries were resident in Ireland in 2006. However, citizens from over forty of these countries only totalled between one and ten persons, thus merely constituting small family-sized groups. While there were many small aggregations of nationals from a wide range of countries, only eight national groups numbered in excess of 10,000 (CSO, 2008).[6] In 2006 more than two out of every three non-Irish nationals resident in Ireland were citizens of just ten countries; these were the United Kingdom (112,548); Poland (63,276); Lithuania (24,628); Nigeria (16,300); Latvia (13,319); United States (12,475); China (11,161); Germany (10,289); Philippines (9,548); and France (9,046). The Irish population could therefore be said to be sprinkled with a great variety of nationalities of which just a small number have amassed to a substantial magnitude.

Diversity in Composition of Non-Irish Resident Population

Aggregate statistics indicate significant differences in the sex and age profile of the non-Irish population compared to the Irish population. The proportion of males in the migrant population was greater than in the Irish population, and the age profile of non-Irish nationals resident in Ireland in 2006 was heavily concentrated in the twenty to forty-four age cohort, with far fewer persons in the older or younger age categories than was the case for the Irish resident population (CSO, 2008). However, if we look at the profiles for each of the largest ten national groups resident in Ireland we see a far more varied picture. Among the Polish population the male/female ratio was the highest at 64:36 (CSO, 2008:29). In contrast, females significantly outnumbered males in the Filipino population, where the male/female ratio was 41:59 (CSO, 2008:57). The age profile of UK nationals resident in Ireland did not differ substantially from the Irish resident population (CSO, 2008:25).

US and Nigerian persons resident in Ireland in 2006 included a higher proportion of children under the age of fifteen than the general population (CSO, 2008:37, 45). Among some other national groups there was a very marked age clustering. More than seven out of ten Chinese nationals resident in Ireland in 2006 were aged in their twenties (CSO, 2008:49), and seven out of ten Poles were aged between twenty and thirty-four (CSO, 2008:29).

There were also very significant differences in levels of participation in the workforce by the different national groups, and the area and type of employment. Very high workforce participation was recorded for Filipino, Polish, Lithuanian and Latvian nationals resident in Ireland in 2006. For each of these national groups, over 80% of persons resident in Ireland in 2006 and aged over fifteen were employed. The highest level of employment recorded was 85% for Filipinos (CSO, 2008:58). In contrast, only 38% of Nigerians were employed in 2006, and at 31% Nigerians also had the highest level of unemployment (CSO, 2008:38).

While high proportions of Poles and Lithuanians were employed in construction and manufacturing, Chinese workers were very heavily concentrated in the hotel and restaurant industry. The working population of Filipino nationals was heavily concentrated in the health sector, with seven out of ten female and four out of ten male Filipino nationals employed in 2006 working in this sector (CSO, 2008:58).

The proportion of Polish, Lithuanian and Latvian workers in the higher socio-economic classes only ranged between 4% and 9% (CSO, 2008:30, 34, 42). This contrasts with the very high proportion of US, German and French nationals employed in Ireland in managerial or professional occupational groups. Indeed, over half of US nationals at work in Ireland in 2006 were in managerial or professional occupations (CSO, 2008:46).

The proportion of non-Irish nationals who described themselves as students also varied very considerably by national group. The highest proportion of students in any national group was 43% of Chinese nationals (CSO, 2008:50). Just over one in six of both US and Nigerian persons aged over fifteen and resident in the Ireland were also students. However, only a very small proportion of Lithuanian (3%), Latvian (3%) and Polish (2%) persons aged over fifteen and resident in Ireland in 2006 were students.

The spatial concentration of national groups also varied. Nigerians were the most urbanised of all national groups profiled, whereas UK nationals were most likely to be living in a rural location. In 2006, some national groups seemed to be much more integrated with the native Irish population than others. While a high proportion of both UK and US nationals lived with an Irish partner in 2006, just 1% of Lithuanians aged over fifteen had an Irish partner (CSO, 2008:34). It seems likely that the especially low level of integration between the Lithuanian and Irish populations was chiefly because most Lithuanians had only recently arrived in Ireland in 2006. The resident Lithuanian population in Ireland increased nearly twelve times between 2002 and 2006 (CSO, 2008:32), which means that the vast majority of Lithuanians living in Ireland in 2006 arrived during the four-year period from 2002–06.

Risk of criminal offending

This brief comparison of the largest non-Irish national groups resident in Ireland in 2006 highlights their diversity. Non-Irish nationals living in Ireland are not a homogeneous group, and the differences already pointed to strongly suggest that the risk of non-Irish nationals engaging in criminal behaviour will vary between nationalities. Criminal offending is likely to be higher among national groups that are heavily concentrated in the twenty to thirty-four age cohort and which have a high proportion of males. Factors which are likely to reduce the probability of criminal offending are high proportions of females, more diffuse spread of ages, and higher socio-economic status. One would therefore expect, given the features of the resident population in Ireland in 2006, that Polish, Chinese, Latvian and Lithuanian nationals would be more likely than US, UK, French, German or Filipino nationals to engage in criminal behaviour and to consequently appear in the Irish District Court. While some features of the Nigerian resident population suggest that offending is less likely (sex and age distribution), the very high level of unemployment among Nigerian nationals resident in Ireland in 2006 may be suggestive of a higher risk of criminal offending (see Smith et al., 1992).

Overview of Foreign Defendants

As the nationality of defendants is not recorded by the CS and nationality is not routinely mentioned in court, it is not possible to present a breakdown of the defendants observed by nationality. However, it is possible to present an overview of the foreign defendants observed. This overview corresponds in some respects with the expected profile of foreign defendants based on the analysis of the results of Census 2006, but there are also some unexpected findings.

Due to the sizable presence of Polish, Lithuanian and Latvian nationals in the Irish population, it was anticipated that they would also feature commonly among District Court defendants, and this was found to be the case. They most commonly faced public order or motoring offences such as drink-driving or driving without insurance. Heavy alcohol consumption seems to greatly contribute to the presence of Polish, Lithuanian and Latvian nationals in the District Court.

Chinese nationals were less commonly observed among District Court defendants than expected given the size of the Chinese resident population. Indeed, a sizable proportion of those who appeared before the court were charged with breaches of immigration legislation, and the majority of these had not been previously resident in the state. Observations indicate that Chinese nationals are very seldom charged with breaches of public order legislation. Cultural influences may result in Chinese nationals carefully regulating their public behaviour. Chinese nationals were also rarely observed in the District Court charged with motoring offences. This may indicate lower levels of alcohol consumption by Chinese nationals. It is possible also that the level of car ownership among this group is lower than average as Chinese nationals resident in Ireland in 2006 were overwhelmingly resident in urban areas (CSO, 2008:48) and included the highest proportion of students of any national group.

With the exception of UK nationals, defendants from other EU-15 countries were rarely identified. This is consistent with the high education levels and socio-economic status of EU-15 nationals living in Ireland. It may also reflect the strong social support systems in these countries, which may make EU-15 nationals more likely to return home if they face unemployment or health difficulties.

No Filipino or US nationals were identified during the course of the fieldwork. The high employment level enjoyed by Filipino nationals combined with a preponderance of females may account for their absence. More US nationals than any other national group were employed in managerial and professional occupations. The high socio-economic status of this group may contribute to a low level of offending.

Despite the favourable sex/age distribution of the resident Nigerian population, Nigerian nationals were frequently observed among District Court defendants during the course of the fieldwork. However, like Chinese nationals, Nigerian nationals were rarely charged with public order offences and tended to appear before the court in relation to motoring offences, theft charges, and breaches of immigration legislation. Offending rates may be impacted by the very high unemployment rates experienced by this group.

Romanian nationals were observed among District Court defendants in greater numbers than would be expected based on Census records of resident foreign nationals. This was particularly the case in SDC and CCC. Almost all of the Roma who appeared before the District Court were Romanian nationals. The frequent presence of Roma among District Court defendants in SDC and CCC therefore greatly contributed to the disproportionate number of Romanian nationals observed.

Mobility, Irregular Migration and Foreign Defendants

While the recorded population of non-Irish nationals resident in Ireland in 2006 gives us some basis for anticipating the likely profile of non-Irish nationals who will appear in Irish courts charged with criminal offences, it must be remembered that not all foreign nationals before the courts will have been previously resident in Ireland, and not all foreign nationals previously resident in Ireland may be enumerated in Census 2006.

During the course of the fieldwork conducted, many foreign nationals were observed subsequent to failure to produce satisfactory documentary evidence of their identity. Such persons were charged under the provisions of s.12 of the Immigration Act, 2004. In SDC, most persons charged under the provisions of s.12 had been detained at Dublin airport while attempting to gain entry to the country. Almost all of these had never been previously resident in Ireland. All persons observed who had been arrested under the provisions of s.12 at a point of entry to the state were non-EU nationals. Persons observed in SDC following arrest at Dublin airport were mainly either Chinese or from one of a number of different African countries. In CCC, many of those arrested and charged under the provisions of s.12 had previously been resident in Ireland but it is not clear whether all such persons would have been captured by Census 2006. The origins of those charged with immigration offences in CCC were more diverse than those in SDC. A large proportion of those charged were Europeans from non-EU countries, but persons from Africa, Asia, and members of the Roma community who were EU nationals were also observed in court facing charges under the provisions of s.12. In RC, a high proportion of foreign nationals of very diverse origins were observed who appeared before the court on immigration charges. These charges had arisen in a wide variety of circumstances and the persons charged were a mixture of persons never previously resident in Ireland and persons previously resident in Ireland. Immigration charges were very rare in NEC.

A small number of persons never resident in Ireland were also observed in court on non-immigration matters. Some of these people faced very serious charges in relation to the possession and importation of drugs of significant value. A number had been arrested at Dublin airport and one man observed was arrested at Rosslare port. If convicted they were likely to face very lengthy prison sentences; they were also likely to be deported at the end of their prison sentence. All they may ever have seen of Ireland were Garda stations, courts and prison cells.

Persons who come to Ireland for a short visit can also find themselves before the District Court. As the field note extracts set out below highlight, sometimes the visit may be motivated by entirely legitimate reasons, and on other occasions it may be triggered by criminal machinations.

> Robert Krzynska was produced from the custody cells for his court appearance. His appearance was noteworthy because his ruddy fresh face and strong muscular build suggested robust health, in contrast to the pale, wan and often sickly appearance of many of the defendants in the District Court. A Polish interpreter was provided for this man and he also had a solicitor. This man was charged with offences under sections 4 and 6 of the Public Order Act. The charges arose from an incident in Dublin airport where he was drinking while waiting for his flight. He also faces charges arising from the alleged burning of a mattress in a Garda station. The court hearing essentially only dealt with an application for his bail. The prosecuting sergeant

indicated that bail would be subject to a cash lodgement of €1,000. Judge Murray was surprised and asked: 'Why is that?' The sergeant replied: 'Judge, he's of no fixed abode in this country.' The sergeant also went on to stipulate that the defendant be required to reside at an apartment adjacent to the IFSC. The matter was relisted to await DPP's directions. The judge asked: 'Is it a legal aid matter?' and the defence solicitor replied: 'No Judge, it is not.' (FN20)

This man came to Ireland on a visit with no expectation of appearing before a court. It seems that his drinking got out of hand just as he was about to leave the country, and he made matters substantially worse for himself by behaving badly while in Garda custody. Nowadays it is commonplace for people, particularly people from wealthy developed nations, to make frequent trips overseas. Increased international travel will inevitably lead to a greater incidence of foreign nationals among those charged with criminal offences.

Other visitors come to Ireland with less benign motives. Examples of such visitors are the four Romanian nationals[7] who appeared before SDC as co-accused (FN13). The four were charged with the theft of a woman's handbag in the short-term car park of Dublin airport. Bail was initially objected to by the court presenter because the defendants were unable to provide an address in the state. Their solicitor noted that they had been living out of a car since their arrival in the country and described them as being 'on a short stop-over in Ireland' (FN13). He also described them as having come to Ireland to look for work. On hearing this, Judge Murray said: 'They mustn't be listening to the radio so, or reading the newspapers' (FN13). When Judge Murray established that each of the defendants had either a passport or national ID card he granted bail on condition that a €100 cash bond was lodged by each defendant. The defendants were remanded on bail, to appear in SDC two weeks later. On that date none of the defendants appeared in court, although at least one of the defendants was still in Ireland as it was noted that he was in custody in Cloverhill prison (FN19).

Judge Murray's decision to release these offenders on bail seems to have been driven by pragmatism. He may well have assessed that there was a high probability that they would fail to turn up for their next scheduled court appearance but perhaps he hoped that they would leave the jurisdiction in the intervening period. By granting bail subject to a cash bond he ensured that the cash bond would be retained by the state if the defendants failed to appear in court as directed.

Roma Defendants

Roma defendants were common in CCC and to a lesser extent in SDC. Many members of the Roma community adopt a peripatetic lifestyle and move frequently between Ireland and their country of origin. It is difficult to know how many of the Roma observed in court considered themselves to be resident in Ireland or how many would have been enumerated in the 2006 census. When defendants move frequently between jurisdictions this inevitably results in them failing to appear in court on some occasions. One Roma man arrested on foot of a bench warrant explained his failure to appear in court by saying simply: 'I had to go home' (FN32). Another man similarly arrested claimed he had left the country owing to the death of a family member. He was released on his own bond (FN42).[8] A history of bench warrants makes it more likely that bail will be objected to by the prosecution. A number of judges seemed to allow Roma defendants more latitude than is normally shown other defendants when they failed to appear in court. Explanations presented by solicitors for the non-appearance of their Roma clients such as 'he's rung us from France' (FN 46) and 'he's actually in Romania and is returning tomorrow' (FN38) succeeded in securing adjournments when one might have expected bench warrants to have been issued. On other occasions the court was requested to schedule dates to take account of the defendant's travel arrangements.

Variations in Scale and Characteristics of Foreign Defendants

The proportion and composition of foreign defendants observed was not consistent, and varied in each court location. The highest proportion of foreign defendants observed was in RC, where foreign defendants accounted for 26.2% (209/798) of defendants on court lists for court sittings observed. A significant proportion of the foreign defendants observed in RC were charged under the provisions of s.12 of the Immigration Act, 2004. Persons charged under these provisions are routinely remanded in custody until they can produce proof of their identity.

In CCC, almost a quarter of the defendants on court lists for the proceedings observed were foreign (24.5%: 413/1688). However, CCC dealt with a large number of defendants who were not on the court list and therefore the court lists do not provide a complete picture of defendants who appear before the court. Most persons who are arrested and taken into custody to a Garda station are later released on 'station bail' which is set by the Garda in charge of the station. Those not granted station bail must make an application for bail before the District Court. CCC is a custody court and during the court sittings observed the court frequently dealt with persons not granted station bail following their arrest; such persons are required to be brought before the next available sitting of the District Court; consequently it was not unusual for persons, both Irish and foreign, to appear before the court who were not on the court list. This happened to a much lesser extent in SDC and NEC and almost never happened in RC.

The foreign defendants who appeared before CCC were very varied in every respect. Some defendants were not living in or near Dublin's city centre, and appeared before CCC because they had been charged with theft or public order charges while they were shopping or socialising in the city centre. Some seemed to have a network of social ties and support and were in employment. However, a proportion of foreign defendants in CCC lived very precariously on the margins of Irish society. The combination of unemployment, homelessness, substance abuse and limited proficiency in English (LEP) makes a defendant exceptionally vulnerable. Very few female defendants were observed with all of these characteristics. Most exceptionally vulnerable defendants were single foreign men, usually of Eastern European origin, with very limited social ties in Ireland. Unemployment can leave foreign defendants without any income if they do not have the work history or the required period of residency to qualify for social welfare payments. A few defendants who had only recently come to Ireland seemed to have arrived with little means of supporting themselves, and with very little in the way of a support network. It was not unusual to hear that such defendants were homeless, living in hostel accommodation, or 'semi-homeless', which equated to relying on a friend or friends to provide a couch to sleep on. It was also not uncommon to hear stories of mental illness, alcohol and drug addiction. LEP often further isolated many of these vulnerable defendants.

In SDC, just over a fifth (21.3%: 222/1040) of all defendants were foreign. While many of the foreign defendants before SDC had problems controlling their use of alcohol, drug abuse and especially homelessness were not commonly attributed to foreign defendants in this court. Most defendants were employed or had only recently become unemployed after a history of employment since their arrival in Ireland. Many defendants were living in family units and indeed several foreign male defendants were observed in SDC as a result of charges arising from domestic disputes. The proportion of female foreign defendants (31.1% of all foreign defendants) was unusually high in SDC. This was because a significant proportion of foreign defendants who appeared before SDC were charged with breaches of immigration legislation. While males on immigration charges were remanded to appear before RC, females facing immigration charges were remanded in custody to appear before SDC. As defendants on such charges typically appeared before the court on multiple occasions, the different treatment of male and female defendants remanded in custody resulted in SDC dealing with an unusually high proportion of female foreign defendants.

The lowest proportion of foreign defendants observed was in NEC, where this cohort accounted for just 13.8% (136/989) of all defendants on court lists of court sittings observed. Only a handful of foreign defendants appeared before NEC on immigration charges and many of the foreign defendants who appeared before NEC had lived in the environs of North Eastern Town (NET) for some years and were embedded in the local community.

The proximity of NET to the border with Northern Ireland means that UK nationals frequently appear before NEC, most commonly in relation to motoring offences or minor public order offences. During the court sittings observed, when residents of Northern Ireland appeared before the court the court was often told that the defendant 'lives outside the jurisdiction'. It was also not unusual to hear references to defendants who were resident in or near NET but who were employed in Northern Ireland or who perhaps were absent from court because they were attending job interviews or hospital appointments in Northern Ireland. It was very clear that there is a great deal of cross-border movement, with many of those living close to the border with Northern Ireland living lives that are partially played out in both jurisdictions. It was noted that UK nationals were normally required to lodge a cash sum before being granted bail, and when the court imposed a fine they were directed to pay the fine before leaving the court. They were therefore treated in quite a different manner to defendants resident in Ireland.

African defendants constituted a substantial proportion of foreign defendants in NEC. As Nigerians form one of the largest groups of resident non-nationals in NET, this was not unexpected.

Overall, the proportion of foreign nationals observed in each location was in excess of the proportion of resident foreign nationals. However, it should be borne in mind that the presence of foreign nationals in SDC and RC was particularly impacted by the high numbers before the court on immigration charges, and indeed if those on immigration charges were excluded in SDC, the proportion of foreign nationals would be roughly consistent with the resident foreign population.

Foreign Defendants and 'Not Guilty' Pleas

It has been suggested that non-Irish defendants are more likely to plead 'not guilty' than Irish defendants (Riordan, 2007). This is of concern to the court because when charges are contested they can take up a considerable amount of court time. The District Court simply would not be able to process the large volume of cases it currently handles without a very high proportion of guilty pleas. Matters listed for hearing in CCC are listed separately, and it was therefore an easy matter to establish whether there was a disproportionate number of hearings scheduled in respect of foreign defendants. In fact, during the period when fieldwork was conducted, 22.7% of hearings scheduled were in respect of foreign defendants in CCC. During the same period, 24.5% of defendants listed to appear before CCC were foreign nationals. This finding does not lend support to the contention that foreign defendants are more likely to plead 'not guilty' than Irish defendants. It should be remembered that most of the cases listed for hearing do not proceed because the matter is either struck out or a late guilty plea is entered.

Authenticity of Documents

There were occasions when charges were contested by foreign defendants when it seemed that there was little or no prospect that the court would not find the charges proven. A number of instances were observed when foreign defendants charged with using or being in control of a false instrument contested the charges even though they admitted that they had obtained the false instrument, normally a passport or a driving licence, in a manner that had in some way circumvented the official channels. One such defendant observed was a man who faced a criminal charge after the Romanian driving licence he produced to Gardaí was found to be false.[9] He contested the charge even though he readily admitted that he had not obtained the licence through official channels. He was found guilty. The defendant told the court that he had gone to a policeman with his driving instructor and his documents and money to get his licence. When asked if it was normal procedure in Romania to get a driving licence from a police officer he answered: 'No, but I wanted to save time.' The prosecution then suggested that by going to a policeman rather than the usual channels for his licence he must have realised that there was a risk that the driving licence was fake. The defendant's reply was: 'No, I'd no reason to believe it was a fake' (FN43).

It is difficult to understand the defendant's claim that he believed the driving licence was an authentic document, and even more difficult to understand why he would continue to contest its authenticity despite evidence to the contrary from documents experts in An Garda Síochána. It seems that while in Ireland there may be an acceptance that there is only one valid source for important documents, such as driving licences or passports, in some other societies there may be a belief that one can obtain authentic identity documents through unofficial sources.

Trust in Criminal Justice Process

It is possible that sometimes 'not guilty' pleas may be entered because foreign defendants are especially fearful of the penalties that may be imposed by the court if they are found guilty. This may be particularly likely for defendants who come from countries where trust in criminal justice procedures is low. On two occasions observed during the course of the fieldwork, African defendants who were found guilty after contesting s.12 immigration charges sank to their knees before the judge when they realised that they were free to leave the court. It may also be that this overt expression of relief and gratitude is expected from a defendant in some societies when the court has shown leniency.

Mr Odunayo was sentenced to one month's imprisonment in respect of a section 12 charge but as he had already served three months and twenty-four days in Cloverhill prison while held on remand in respect of this charge he does not have to serve any further time in prison. Judge Byrne said to Mr Odunayo: 'You're free to go.' On hearing this, Mr Odunayo sank to the floor on his knees, bowed his head and put his hands together as if in prayer. Judge Byrne looked quite startled and uncomfortable by Mr Odunayo's reaction. (FN38)

Conclusion

Foreign defendants have greatly contributed to the diversity of District Court defendants, but diversity is not new to the court. The wide range of offences disposed by the District Court ensures that District Court defendants are a heterogeneous aggregation which includes persons from all social classes, and increasingly in recent years, persons of diverse national origins and ethnicity. However, the bulk of defendants, and in particular persistent offenders, both Irish and non-Irish, are young men from a low socio-economic class. Persistent offenders of all nationalities tend to be vulnerable individuals encumbered with a range of social problems such as substance abuse, mental health issues, unemployment and homelessness. LEP adds to the vulnerability of foreign nationals who are persistent offenders.

The age, sex and occupational profile of foreign residents living in Ireland varies significantly by national group, and the differences in the demographic profiles of resident national groups suggest that offending rates are likely to vary between such groups. The fieldwork conducted found that offending levels and patterns of offending varied considerably by national group, with nationals from EU-12[10] countries and African nationals over-represented and EU-13,[11] US and Chinese nationals under-represented among District Court defendants observed. While demographic differences largely account for the variations observed, cultural influences also appear to partially explain the observed pattern of offending. It is also possible that some national groups may be the subject of greater Garda surveillance than others (see European Union Agency for Fundamental Rights, 2009), which may contribute to their presence in the District Court.

Not all foreign defendants are resident in Ireland prior to their arrest and it is not clear if all foreign defendants with an irregular residency status are recorded among the resident population. Comparing the scale of foreign defendants in the District Court to the recorded foreign resident population is therefore problematic. The fieldwork conducted did not find any evidence to support the claim that levels of 'not guilty' pleas are higher among non-Irish defendants.

In Chapter 3 sentencing decisions in the District Court are explored. The chapter details the absence of any presumptive sentencing philosophy or sentencing guidelines and considers issues which impact the sentencing of both Irish and foreign defendants.

Chapter 3

The Punishment of Minor Offences
SENTENCING IN THE DISTRICT COURT

Introduction

The sentencing decisions reached in our criminal courts can have a significant impact on the lives of individual offenders, and on victims of crime, while also being of significant import to the wider Irish society. From the perspective of individual offenders, a criminal conviction can derail career plans or result in the loss of employment; it can place limits on foreign travel or plans to emigrate; it can prevent an individual from adopting or fostering a child; it carries a significant social stigma and it can result in any future breaches of the criminal code being penalised more severely. Criminal convictions leave a tarnish that can be life-changing, and in Ireland a tarnish which is life-long as criminal convictions imposed upon adults cannot as yet be expunged (Spent Convictions Group, 2009; IPRT, 2008).[1]

Convictions which attract custodial sentences are likely to have the greatest impact on the life of individual offenders. Even short custodial sentences can result in a major disruption to an offender's life; not only do they result in a loss of liberty, they may give rise to collateral consequences such as the loss of employment, eviction and loss of personal belongings, and the break-up of relationships. By placing an individual proximate to drug users and drug taking, a custodial sentence may even result in a previously drug-free individual experimenting with illicit drug use. The impact of a custodial sentence is not limited to those directly affected; it causes ripples of effects among prisoners' families and communities (Murray, 2006; O'Donnell et al., 2007; Codd, 2008). Unduly lenient sentences may leave victims feeling unsafe, or be contrary to the public interest by undermining public confidence in the fairness and legitimacy of the criminal justice system (LRC, 2004). Sentencing those convicted of criminal offences is therefore an onerous task which may be subject to a great deal of public scrutiny and criticism.

This chapter begins by detailing the objectives that are generally understood to underlie the imposition of criminal sanctions and examining the case for and against sentencing guidelines and regulations. The international prominence of a 'just deserts' sentencing approach is outlined, as are the recommendations of the Law Reform Commission (LRC) (1996) in this regard. The LRC's emphasis on the importance of consistency in sentencing is contrasted with the reported views of the judiciary on this issue. The chapter discusses the absence of sentencing guidelines in Ireland and the recent increased regulation of sentencing.

The chapter then considers sentencing in the Irish District Court. Irish District Court judges, a relatively small group of men and women, have to decide on the appropriate form and severity of punishment for a very large volume and wide range of criminal offences. They make these decisions with very little in the way of legislative direction, or information about court-wide sentencing patterns, but subject to the constraints of the limited sentencing power of the court. Courtroom observations are used in this chapter to probe the rationales which guide sentencing decisions and to consider what factors, legal and extra-legal, impact sentences imposed. After considering the factors that influence all sentencing decisions, the chapter examines variables which may influence the sentencing of foreign offenders. The sentencing of immigration offences is examined separately in Chapter 4.

The chapter outlines the key role played by the District Court in terms of the volume of offenders sentenced and the impact of sentences imposed on the Irish penal population. Sentencing decisions in the District Court are analysed using examples of sentencing decisions reached during courtroom observations. While the sentencing decisions explored relate to foreign defendants, many of the issues discussed have a wider relevance and should help to shed light on sentencing decisions for all offenders convicted of minor offences. Courtroom observations point to the lack of a coherent court-wide approach to sentencing and the prominence given to previous criminal convictions, a prominence which at times seems inappropriate given the minor nature of the offences before the court. The chapter contends that the relevance of previous convictions for minor offences should be re-examined if proportionality is to be maintained in sentencing decisions.

How Should We Understand Criminal Sanctions?

There is no unanimity about the purpose of criminal sanctions or indeed their impact on levels of crime or public safety. However, criminal sanctions are generally understood as serving a number of key purposes. These comprise punishment, deterrence, incapacitation, rehabilitation and reparation (DJELR, 2010). In some jurisdictions, such as England and Wales, the purposes of sentencing have been formalised and are set out in legislation.[2] This is not the case in Ireland where in general there has been a marked reluctance to introduce legislation which could be viewed as encroaching on the independence of the judiciary. The rationale which guides sentencing decisions and the relative importance of the various, and at times competing, purposes which criminal sanctions serve may depend on factors relating to the offence and the offender, the penal philosophy of the individual sentencer, and the legislative framework within which sentences are imposed.

It should be noted that criminal sanctions are now shaped by a legislative framework which extends beyond national boundaries and which seeks to ensure that the human rights of persons within the criminal justice system, and in particular those subject to incarceration, are adequately and appropriately protected. While only the human rights protections offered by the Irish Constitution and the European Convention on Human Rights have direct effect on Irish law, criminal sanctions are also monitored by bodies such as the International Convention on Civil and Political Rights and the Council of Europe. The monitoring role played by such bodies constitutes a form of non-direct enforcement, and provides avenues of complaint to aggrieved individuals who consider their human rights to have been infringed (DJELR, 2010). The authority of the state to impose criminal sanctions is therefore limited, and must be exercised with restraint. This is particularly the case in relation to the use of incarceration.

Sentencing Guidelines and Regulations

Sentencing guidelines provide frameworks which assist judges in deciding on the appropriate criminal sanction to impose. They are a means of promoting sentencing coherence and reducing sentencing disparity. Sentencing guidelines can vary from statements of best practice, which are voluntarily applied, to statutory provisions, which compel adherence. Sentencing guidelines set out the rationales and principles that should be adopted by judges and may encompass sentencing regulations which stipulate mandatory and or presumptive sentences in respect of specific offences. Regulations which provide for mandatory or minimum sentencing only allow for judicial discretion to be exercised in imposing a sentence in excess of the minimum. Those which provide for presumptive sentencing establish a legal presumption that a specified sentence will apply but also provide for certain exceptional circumstances when the presumptive sentence will not apply. Presumptive sentences therefore encroach on judicial discretion to a lesser extent than mandatory sentences. The principal advantage of sentencing guidelines is that they result in more consistent and predictable sentences. Consistency will stem in particular from prescriptive sentencing guidelines. Consistency and predictability in sentencing may promote public confidence and trust in the judiciary and in the criminal justice system.

Mandatory sentences are associated with a number of significant disadvantages. It is argued that mandatory sentencing cannot reflect the range of circumstances pertaining to individual offences and offenders that should be taken into account in deciding on the appropriate sentence and consequently may result in unduly harsh sentences. Another objection to mandatory sentences is that they are not an effective deterrent. Mandatory sentences appear to have little influence on crime rates (Tonry, 1996) and may be considerably less effective in lowering crime rates than other alternatives (Greenwood et al., 1996). A further argument against mandatory sentences is that they succeed in shifting rather than eliminating discretion so that the reduction in judicial discretion leads to an increase in 'plea bargaining' and greater discretion on the part of non-judicial criminal justice actors. The downward shift in discretion results in less transparent decision-making and, it is argued, may weaken the integrity of the criminal justice system. Mandatory sentencing may also result in greater arbitrariness in sentencing rather than increased consistency if judges seek to avoid imposing sentences that they consider to be unjust. Finally, mandatory sentences may also lead to a higher proportion of contested cases and a greater number of trials (IPRT, 2009).

'Just Deserts' and Monitoring of Sentencing Practices

Sentencing models are systems of sentencing which are oriented towards a particular rationale or adopt a particular philosophy, such as a rehabilitative model of sentencing. Sentencing models may be incorporated into sentencing guidelines and regulations.

Internationally, there has been a shift towards a 'just deserts' (Von Hirsch, 1993; Von Hirsch and Ashworth, 2005; Von Hirsch, 2009) model of sentencing, which is primarily oriented towards retribution. Such sentencing models seek to assess the severity of an offence based on considerations of harm and culpability, with limited adjustment of penal tariffs for aggravating and mitigating factors. A 'just deserts' model of sentencing is consistent with a legal-rational model of justice which focuses chiefly on the offence rather than the offender. Proponents emphasise that punishment must be proportionate to the gravity of the offence. Critics contend that 'just deserts' sentencing models are associated with more punitive sentencing practices and place an unreasonable restraint on judicial discretion. Studies suggest that in some jurisdictions such models can result in a shift of discretion away from the judiciary to the prosecution through plea bargaining practices, which can be difficult to monitor or regulate (Tonry, 1981, 1982; Remington, 1993; Dickey, 1993). In the United States, Australia, Canada, England and Wales, Sweden and Finland the sentencing guidelines or reforms which have been introduced have largely been influenced by 'just deserts' principles (LRC, 1996).

The move towards the regulation of sentencing points to an increased emphasis on procedural rather than substantive justice, which may be linked to an escalation in the monitoring of sentencing practices and a concomitant heightened awareness of sentencing disparities. Unduly high levels of sentencing disparities can lead to criticisms of sentencing decisions and their characterisation as whimsical, arbitrary and even discriminatory. In modern, complex societies which are culturally diverse and multi-ethnic, members of minority groups often have higher levels of contact with criminal justice processes than the general population, and claims of inconsistency and unfairness in sentencing decisions tend to focus

on the treatment of minority group members. Such claims, if uncontested, can ultimately erode perceptions of the legitimacy of the
criminal justice system.

Sentencing models which emphasise the offence rather than the
offender may make sentencing decisions more transparent, and hence
raise perceptions of fairness. However, the increased emphasis on consistency and accountability in sentencing, and the use of actuarial
devices such as statistical models to measure individual offenders' risk
of re-offending, has led some critics to claim that there is a shift
towards a technocratic model of justice which results in judges being
deskilled, and sentences being formulaic and homogenised, rather
than being devised and scripted on the basis of individual welfare and
a substantive notion of justice (Franko-Aas, 2005).

Sentencing Guidelines and Regulations in Ireland

In Ireland, the question of the appropriate sentencing rationale has
been examined by the LRC (1993, 1996). The members of the
Commission were unanimous in their view that any guidelines
issued should be on a non-statutory basis. However, the
Commission members failed to reach a consensus regarding an
approach to sentencing and the views of both the majority and the
minority were published in the report issued.

The majority supported a 'just deserts' approach to sentencing
which was based primarily on considerations of retribution and
involved the assessment of the seriousness of the offence by reference to the harm caused or potentially caused and the degree of
culpability of the offender. The approach recommended also
allowed for limited recognition of aggravating and mitigating
factors. The minority rejected this approach, arguing that judicial
discretion should be maintained as this provides the best means of
ensuring that sentences imposed take account of both the offence
and the individual offender. Given the lack of unanimity among the
Commission members it is perhaps not surprising that the 'just
deserts' policy recommended by the majority has not resulted in sentencing guidelines being issued.

While sentencing guidelines have not been introduced, proportionality has in general been endorsed by the Irish courts (O'Malley,
2006), and O'Malley claims that 'Irish courts have shown little incli-
nation to depart from proportionality as the dominant distributive

principle of sentencing' (2009:107). It should be noted that the Irish interpretation of proportionality is that a sentence should be proportionate to the gravity of an offence and the personal circumstances of an offender (O'Malley 2009:118). Proportionality need not be incompatible with the aim of rehabilitation, and indeed O'Malley states that, wherever possible, sentences should be both proportionate and rehabilitative (2006).

Consistency in sentencing: a realistic aspiration?

The LRC has stated that it is 'important for the public to perceive that there is consistency in sentencing, and that offenders in similar circumstances who have committed like offences should be sentenced in a like manner. Any public perception that there is inconsistency, or worse, inequality, in the criminal justice system should thus be avoided' (LRC, 2004:90:6.33). The 'largely unstructured sentencing system' (O'Malley, 2006) which operates in Ireland, and the lack of an adequate statistical database about sentencing decisions, make it difficult to promote a public perception of consistency in sentencing. Indeed, one might question whether such a perception would reflect sentencing practices. The LRC, however, believes that sentencing 'is in fact more consistent than its portrayal in the media would suggest' (LRC, 1996:4.25).

The Commission's concern with consistency does not seem to be fully shared by the Irish judiciary. The LRC reported that the judiciary indicated in consultations regarding sentencing that judicial inconsistency was 'an indication of health in the system' (LRC, 1996:4.23). It would seem therefore that the judiciary may value the ability to tailor sentences according to individual circumstances, and perhaps individual penal philosophies, above the need to preserve public confidence in the criminal justice system.

One means of promoting consistency in sentencing without impinging on the much-prized and guarded independence of the judiciary is through a sentencing information system that could provide a range of both quantitative and qualitative information on sentencing practices, key judgements and legislative changes. In preparing the *Report on Sentencing* (1996), the LRC canvassed the judiciary about proposals regarding a sentencing information system. While High Court and Circuit Court judges indicated broad support for such a system, District Court judges were less enthusiastic. The LRC noted that:

> ... the judges of the District Court felt less need for information,
> firstly because their sentencing jurisdiction was limited and, sec-
> ondly, because in Dublin at any event they have little difficulty in
> keeping up with the sentencing norm for different offences. The
> Commission felt that this was perhaps a very Dublin Metro-
> politan perspective. (LRC, 1996:4.22)

This suggests a particular lack of appetite on the part of District
Court judges to promote a court-wide approach to sentencing. It
should be noted that statistics regarding the sentencing practices of
individual judges are not published by the CS; this means that it is
not possible to point to patterns of disparity which are linked to specific judges. We are also unable to state whether or not the decisions
of individual District Court judges are more or less likely to be over-
turned on appeal as verdicts appealed to the Circuit Court result in
a full rehearing of the case and the outcome of such cases are not
separately identified or analysed.

A steering committee established to plan for and provide information on sentencing, designated the Irish Sentencing Information
System (ISIS), has undertaken a number of pilot projects in various
tiers of the criminal courts (see Conroy and Gunning, 2009). The
information compiled by the ISIS can be accessed at www.isis.ie.
The database compiled aims to provide a descriptive information
source on sentencing. Following a pilot project undertaken in
selected Dublin District Courts in 2009 a database of 121 cases was
compiled. The database provides information about the offender,
including details of nationality.[3] Although the database is modest in
size, it is a welcome initiative.

Until recently there were only a small number of offences in Ireland
which resulted in mandatory sentences. Murder, aggravated murder
and treason attract a mandatory life sentence while drunk-driving
attracted a mandatory disqualification from driving until recent legislative changes.[4] The Criminal Justice Acts of 1999 and 2006
introduced presumptive sentences for a number of drug and firearm
offences. However, with the introduction of the Criminal Justice Act,
2007 there has been a 'major shift towards presumptive and mandatory sentencing' (IPRT, 2009:3). Those convicted of a second or
subsequent 'serious' offence within seven years following the first
serious offence now face a presumptive sentence of three quarters of
the maximum sentence or a sentence of ten years if the maximum is

life imprisonment. The expansion of presumptive sentences has been criticised (IPRT, 2009) but the restrictions on sentencing that have been introduced only apply to serious offences and hence do not affect sentencing decisions in the Irish District Court.

Sentencing Decisions and Previous Criminal History

Before considering how sentences imposed by the District Court shape the Irish penal population, it is appropriate to reflect on the role that previous criminal history should play in sentencing. The weight afforded to previous criminal history can significantly influence the sentencing of minor offences and this issue is therefore a key factor to consider in assessing District Court sentencing.

There is some debate regarding the influence that previous criminal convictions should have in the sentencing of criminal offences. Certain commentators argue that taking account of previous convictions in sentencing is essentially a form of double punishment (Bagaric, 2000). However, previous criminal history is considered a legally relevant factor in deciding sentence in most jurisdictions, and most studies indicate that previous criminal history can be a key influence on the form and severity of sentence. Roberts argues that 'considering previous misconduct is an inescapable element of contemporary penalty' (2008:228). The key question is perhaps not whether, but to what extent, criminal history should impact sentence.

A 'just deserts' approach to sentencing seeks to ensure that the sentence is proportionate to the gravity of the offence. Such an approach would only allow previous convictions to play a limited role in determining the appropriate sentence. However, in some jurisdictions sentencing guidelines dictate that the severity of punishment is linked to the number of previous convictions. The habitual offender laws or 'three strikes' rule in certain American states provide that a third felony conviction, even if it is in respect of a minor offence, can attract a very lengthy and even at times a life sentence. This can mean that proportionality is entirely jettisoned in favour of punitiveness and incapacitation (see Bagaric, 2000).

As previously noted, the treatment of minor criminal convictions in determining sentence is of particular relevance in examining sentencing practices in the Irish District Court.[5] O'Malley notes that Irish statute law provides little guidance on the issue of previous convictions and authoritative direction from the courts is limited (2009:113). Criminal history does not influence the sentence which attaches to the most serious of offences – those that carry a mandatory life sentence – and neither does it impact the sentence for the most minor of offences – those punishable by fixed penalty charges (O'Malley, 2009). The majority of offences before the courts are subject to maximum rather than fixed penalties, and there is therefore room for judicial discretion in deciding what weight, if any, should be afforded to previous criminal convictions. There are, however, a number of statutory provisions stipulating higher sentences for persons reconvicted of the same offence (O'Malley, 2009:112).

The approach adopted by Irish courts corresponds for the most part to a progressive loss of mitigation for previous criminal convictions. This approach affords a person without previous convictions a certain amount of mitigation for their previous good behaviour. This mitigation is reduced with increases in the offender's criminal history. O'Malley points out, however, that in certain instances Irish courts have found previous criminal history to be an aggravating factor which effectively increased the gravity of the offence and hence increased the appropriate sentence (2009:115–18).

This brief review of sentencing models, guidelines and regulations and the treatment of previous criminal history demonstrates that the discretion afforded to the Irish judiciary is significantly more generous than that enjoyed by many of their international counterparts. The chapter now turns to the importance of District Court sentencing decisions before considering the manner in which sentences are reached and the key factors which influence sentences imposed.

Understanding the Importance of and Influences on District Court Sentencing

District Court Sentences and the Irish Penal Population

As the District Court is the lowest tier of the Irish court hierarchy, it might be thought that it does not have a significant impact on the Irish penal population. In fact, sentences imposed by the District Court play a major role in shaping the Irish penal population. CS statistics indicate that the District Court imposed terms of imprisonment on 12,979 offenders in 2010 (12,411 in 2009; 11,747 in 2008) for the principal offence categories (CS, 2011:62; CS, 2010:56; CS, 2009:64).

The disposition of offences in the 'other' category is not analysed. The almost 13,000 terms of imprisonment imposed by the District Court compares to the 1,906 (1,991 in 2009; 2,326 in 2008) terms of imprisonment imposed by the Circuit Court in 2010 (CS, 2011:61; CS, 2010:55; CS, 2009:63). O'Malley notes the difficulty of calculating how many offenders go to prison on foot of District Court sentences because of the automatic right of appeal to the Circuit Court but concludes that 'a very considerable number of offenders sentenced to terms of imprisonment by the District Court go to prison' (2010:3).

In 2010, 12,487 (10,865 in 2009; 8,043 in 2008) persons were committed under sentence to Irish prisons (IPS, 2011:15, 2010:19, 2009:18) and it seems clear that the majority of persons committed to Irish prisons are sentenced by the Irish District Court (O'Malley, 2010). Therefore, the decisions of District Court judges dictate to a very large extent the flow of persons into the Irish penal population. This is borne out by an examination of the sentence length of persons committed to prison. In 2010, just over 91% (2009:89%, 2008:87%) of persons committed to Irish prisons were committed in respect of a sentence of less than two years. Over 87% (2009:85%, 2008:80%) were committed in respect of a sentence of less than one year, while 75% (2009:70%, 2008:62%) were committed in respect of a sentence of less than six months (IPS, 2011:16, 2010:22, 2009:22). So, despite the limited sentencing powers of District Court judges, their sentencing decisions are a key determinant of the Irish penal population.

Overview of Courtroom Observations

Before presenting reflections on District Court sentencing based on courtroom observations, it is useful to consider the speed with which District Court sentences are reached and the individualised sentencing yardsticks used by judges.

Although the decisions made by Irish District Court judges carry great import and are often difficult and onerous, District Court judges normally do not retire to consider their verdicts[6] and pronounce sentence immediately after hearing the 'facts'; the defendant's criminal history if any; and the defence's presentation of mitigating factors. District Court judges usually therefore have little opportunity to reflect before reaching their decisions. A request for a report from the probation services creates a hiatus between conviction and sentencing and also provides judges with an independent assessment of the offender. The rate of referrals to the probation services varied considerably between the court locations observed. Referrals were common in NEC, but in SDC and CCC they were considerably less common. No probation officer was in attendance in RC and referrals to the probation services were rare.

The speed with which many decisions are reached suggests that a lot of decisions are arrived at in a relatively formulaic fashion with judges using an individualised yardstick to measure the seriousness of an offence and to weigh up aggravating and mitigating factors. Individual judges routinely use standard fine amounts, and they also routinely specify a standard number of days imprisonment in default. The 'standard' is, however, an individualised standard rather than a court standard. So Judge X may routinely apply a fine of €100 for offences which are very minor, and routinely specify three days' imprisonment in default. Judges Y and Z, on the other hand, may routinely apply fines of €200 and €500 respectively for the same offences and specify seven, ten, or even forty-five days in default.

The individualised approach adopted by District Court judges can create an impression of an arbitrary system of justice in which outcomes crucially depend on the attitude of the presiding judge. Sentences can appear to be more dependent on who is imposing sentence than the offence that has been committed. The progress of cases may also depend on the presiding judge as defence lawyers may decide to seek adjournments when appearing before a judge considered to be punitive, or alternatively may seek to bring matters to a conclusion when appearing before a judge who is normally lenient.

During the course of the fieldwork conducted, foreign defendants charged with a wide range of offences were observed in District Court sittings. The most common offences faced by foreign defendants were section (s.)4 (intoxication in a public place) and s.6 (threatening, abusive or insulting behaviour in a public place) public order offences; s.4 theft offences; and various RTOs, with drink-driving and driving without insurance being particularly common. It was also not unusual to see foreign persons charged with offences such as burglary, criminal damage, assault, possession of a controlled substance, fraud, or being in possession of a false instrument. These charges are also habitually faced by Irish defendants although charges in respect of false instruments were more commonly faced by foreign defendants. Foreign defendants observed also frequently appeared before the District Court charged with an offence under the provisions of s.12(1) of the Immigration Act, 2004 which required non-Irish nationals to produce on demand documents to verify their identity; such charges cannot arise in the case of an Irish defendant.[7] As explained in Chapter 4, this legislation has now been amended.

Only one foreign defendant charged with sexual assault was observed, and he successfully contested the charge against him. A number of foreign defendants charged with very serious offences including rape and charges in relation to the importation and possession of illicit drugs for supply or sale were observed in the District Court, but these defendants were sent forward for trial to the Circuit or Central Criminal Courts.

Many defendants appeared before the court with no previous criminal history. Others had what could be described as an intermittent or occasional pattern of offending, having accumulated a small number of convictions at intervals over a period of time. Still others were persistent offenders who had amassed very large numbers of convictions and who frequently had very significant issues around alcohol and or drug abuse. Overall, the fieldwork provided opportunities to observe the sentencing of a comprehensive range of offenders charged with a large and diverse selection of charges.

Gravity of the Offence

All of the offences dealt with by the District Court are considered minor offences. During the course of the fieldwork, persons charged with offences ranging from murder and rape to parking offences appeared before the court. Those charged with serious indictable offences were sent forward for trial by indictment. Normally when the DPP directs that an indictable charge be dealt with summarily, District Court judges accept jurisdiction. However, judges may decide that the gravity of the offence warrants trial by indictment, and they may overrule the directions of the DPP and refuse jurisdiction.

The gravity of the offences dealt with varied in each of the courts observed. The composite case mix of NEC was the least serious. A significant volume of the cases dealt with in NEC were very minor RTOs which would not have necessitated a court appearance if the fixed penalty charge had been paid. A considerable portion of persons summonsed to court on such charges did not appear. When defendants failed to appear in court, the fines imposed were much greater than the fines imposed on those who did appear in court. Fines imposed on foreign nationals in such circumstances may prove particularly difficult to collect as at least some offenders may have left the jurisdiction. SDC, CCC and RC did not deal with very minor RTOs and overall dealt with more serious offences than NEC.

The gravity of an offence is a key determinant of sentence but the assessment of offence gravity varies from judge to judge. Some judges may consider drug offences to be especially serious while others may adopt a more benign view towards the same offences. Even when relatively serious charges are brought and prosecuted with vigour, as in the case set out in the field note extract below, the assessment of gravity will crucially depend on the presiding judge.

> Lech K was represented by a solicitor but was not assisted by an interpreter. He faces a charge of endangerment under s.13 of the Non-Fatal Offences Against the Person Act, 1997.[8] The facts of the case are presented to the court as follows. On 14/03 a shop assistant at the Esso garage on Whiterock[9] Road was threatened by the defendant. Two photographs were presented as exhibits. One showed damage to a sign and the other was a picture of the defendant at a counter in the shop attached to the petrol station. The court was also told that after threatening the shop assistant the defendant went to a petrol pump and put petrol on himself. His solicitor commented: 'I think Mr K was under the influence of alcohol at the time of this incident.' Mr K has one previous conviction for a s.4 public order offence. His solicitor told the court that his client is Polish and has lived in Ireland for three years. He works in a restaurant near St Stephen's Green and has worked there for eighteen months. He admits he has a drink problem and asks for leniency given the very early guilty plea. The sentence imposed by Judge Whelan was two months imprisonment suspended for twelve months. (FN42)

One solicitor expressed the view to the researcher that the critical factor in determining sentence in this case was not the gravity of the offence but the attitude of the presiding judge, whom he described as 'pathologically disinclined to commit anyone to prison'.

Proportionality is understood to be the central principle which guides Irish judges. This means that the gravity of the offence should always be a key determinant of sentence, but this may not always be the case in the sentencing of minor offences. For summary offences the absence of the defendant may greatly impact the penalty imposed, and the attitude of the presiding judge may also have a crucial impact on sentence.

Guilty Pleas

The overwhelming majority of defendants in the District Court plead guilty to the offences they are charged with. An early guilty plea is normally viewed by the court as a mitigating factor as the defendant's acceptance of his wrongdoing suggests that he is truly contrite and therefore is less likely to re-offend. Early guilty pleas also assist the court by truncating the pre-sentence court process. However, when, as is often the case, guilty pleas are entered when a hearing date has been sought and granted, the mitigation which normally attaches to a guilty plea may be lost. As the field note extract set out below highlights, when a defendant has no previous convictions this can mean the difference between having the charge dismissed under the provisions of the Probation of Offenders Act, 1907 and leaving the court with a criminal conviction.

> Matthias Z looked as if he had dressed carefully for his court appearance. When his case was called he removed his rain jacket, revealing his neat shirt and tie. This case was in for hearing but Mr Z's solicitor indicated that his client was pleading guilty. The charges faced by Mr Z relate to an incident some months previously when he was drunk in O'Connell Street. He initially left the area when instructed to do so by Gardaí but later returned and became confrontational. A small knife was later found in Mr Z's backpack and in addition to public order charges he is charged with carrying an offensive weapon. The explanation given by Mr Z at the time was that he carried the knife because he felt he needed to have it to protect himself from danger. Mr Z's solicitor noted that his client was very drunk at the time that he gave this explanation. He now claims that he bought some fish and the knife was lent to him by a friend. Following this explanation the judge was obviously puzzled and said: 'Sorry, could you just run that by me again?' The solicitor explained that the knife was to be used to prepare the fish. Judge Power didn't really seem too convinced by the fish story and said: 'What was said to the Garda at the time seemed to suggest that he was carrying it for protection', but the solicitor again asserted that his client had a valid reason to have the knife.

The solicitor noted that at the time of the incident his client, who had previously been employed, was refused social welfare because of the income of his girlfriend. This caused friction between the couple. The solicitor noted that his client has no previous convictions and that the incident was a 'one-off'. He produced a letter which indicated that Mr Z is now on a FÁS course. Judge Power indicated that he was going to convict and fine and asked how much Mr Z earns. He was told that Mr Z is in receipt of €204 per week. His solicitor made a last attempt to prevent his client being convicted and said: 'I wonder if you would consider giving him the Poor Box?' Judge Power said: 'There was a plea of not guilty . . . it's put in for hearing.' The solicitor noted that his client had changed his 'not guilty' plea to 'guilty', but Judge Power was not impressed and said: 'Sure isn't that where you come into play, Mr O'Sullivan . . . he's taken up court time.' Mr O'Sullivan replied: 'He hasn't taken up much court time, Judge.' Judge Power replied: 'He has . . . the time for a hearing has been allocated.' Judge Power then ended this debate and announced his sentence, which was a conviction and fine of €150. He ordered that the knife be destroyed. (FN28)

The extract shows that, despite the guilty plea, the solicitor tries to construct a credible reason why his client was found with a knife on his person. It seems almost as if he is suggesting that the defendant is actually not guilty of the charge, but is willing to plead guilty. He then tries to cast the defendant's behaviour as being out of character by pointing to tension between him and his girlfriend at the time of the incident. Judge Power's comments seem to suggest that the key factor which influenced his decision to convict and fine rather than apply the Probation Act was the late guilty plea. The extract also reveals that Judge Power views the late guilty plea as being at least partially attributable to the defence solicitor.

Previous Convictions

No previous convictions

Observations indicate that previous criminal convictions, and indeed previous forms of sentences imposed, can critically impact sentencing decisions in the District Court. The standard practice in sentencing first offenders is to dismiss the charges or discharge the offender conditionally under the provisions of section 1(1) of the Probation of Offenders Act, 1907. The application of the Probation Act means that although guilty, the offender will not have a criminal conviction. Judges typically apply the Probation Act saying, 'I find the facts proven, dismissed under the Probation of Offenders Act', or 'DPOA s.1(1)', or simply 's.1(1)'. Judges will often then issue some kind of caveat to the offender such as 'don't do anything like that again', or 'remember, I won't be so lenient if you come before me again', or 'keep the peace in future'. Some will despatch the offender saying, 'the best of luck to you'.

The legislative provisions and the attitude of the court clearly suggest that the agreed protocol is not to burden most people who commit one offence, subject to its gravity, with a criminal conviction. The courts therefore frequently adopt an assumption that many first offenders will not progress to be troublesome repeat offenders and the requirement for them to appear in court before a judge may be sufficient to deter them from further offending. This assumption is supported by the lower recidivism rates found for first-time offenders (O'Donnell et al., 2008).[10]

Defence lawyers will often make it known to the court that their client has 'a sum of money' in court which they are prepared to pay into the Court Poor Box on application of the Probation Act. On occasions such as that set out in the field note extract below, when a judge indicates that a sum of money is to be paid into the Court Poor Box but the defendant does not have the money in court, the judge may stipulate that if an offender fails to pay the Poor Box 'donation' by a stated future date that he be convicted and fined, with the amount of the fine often being higher than the requested Poor Box donation.

> The solicitor for Mr Yuri K told the court that his client is a thirty-year-old Ukranian national who has been in Ireland for ten years. He has recently found himself unemployed for the first time in his life. He is eligible to apply for citizenship this year and is anxious about the possible effect a criminal conviction would have on his application. The solicitor concluded by saying: 'I would ask the court to look on it as leniently as possible.' Judge Austen then said: 'I do take into account all you say, counsel, I do take into account how you have outlined all your client's circumstances, I also take into account your client's plea and his co-operation with the Gardaí. If he makes a €300 donation to Temple Street Children's Hospital I will apply s.1(1) of the Probation Act. If this amount is not paid by 21/06 I will convict and fine €500.' The defence solicitor then asked that his client be

excused attendance in court to pay the contribution to charity
and the judge agreed, indicating that a receipt from the court
office would be acceptable. (FN39)

In some instances, it was observed that persons who make a contribution to the Court Poor Box have the charges against them
struck out (FN51). This is contrary to the recommendations of the
LRC (2005).

Offenders with previous convictions

Sentencing becomes more problematic when an offender has a
history of criminal offending. Prior to sentencing, judges ask the
prosecution, 'any previous?' or 'any previous convictions?' The
court presenter will then normally first indicate the total tally of previous convictions, if any, before going on to detail individual
convictions. If an offender has amassed an unwieldy number of convictions,[11] the court presenter might use his judgement to shorten
the process by saying something like, 'they're mainly RTOs', or
'most of them relate to public order offences', but most judges like to
be presented with details of the most recent convictions and sentences imposed, and some will seek a very complete history of
convictions.

Given the weight afforded to previous convictions in the sentencing process, it was surprising that during court sittings observed,
only one instance was recorded when a foreign offender's convictions were entered into evidence in court. During interview, when
asked about her experience of foreign criminal convictions, Ms
O'Brien, a solicitor, commented as follows:

> It would be quite rare actually to hear them recited, I've heard
> them certainly brought up and probably in more serious cases,
> when the case has taken longer to process and the Garda has had
> the time then to go to the trouble of making more far-reaching
> enquiries, and has established that the person has overseas con-
> victions. It's rare enough but I have heard them brought up in
> the District Court.

This comment and observations of court proceedings suggest
that the investigation of criminal convictions outside the state may
be conducted in a discretionary manner. However, EU legislation
directs that member states take account of previous convictions in
other member states of the European Union in the course of new

criminal proceedings (Council Framework Decision 2008/675/JHA, 24/07/2008). It seems that this requirement may not always be complied with in the prosecution of minor offences.

An episodic pattern of criminal charges may indicate that the offender engages habitually in criminal activity but is often able to avoid detection. Gaps in a criminal history can also emerge during periods of incarceration. If there is a very large hiatus between charges and the new offence is a very minor offence, it may be treated as if it is a first offence. In other instances the pattern of charges may mirror the pattern of offending.

Periodic offending may be driven by circumstantial factors. Heavy alcoholic binges or periods of drug abuse may trigger offending behaviour in some people who would otherwise not come into contact with the criminal justice system. Loss of employment or delays in accessing social welfare support can also trigger offending. If previous criminal convictions relate to minor road traffic infringements, they will not usually result in a more severe penal tariff being imposed (unless the defendant faces similar charges), and some judges will treat such an offender as if they have no previous convictions. Previous criminal convictions make it more likely that legal aid will be granted and may also influence the form and severity of the sentence imposed.

> Stefan W, a Polish man, came before the court in relation to theft charges. He was assisted by an interpreter but initially was not represented by a solicitor. Judge Murray spoke slowly and carefully to the interpreter, saying: 'This gentleman is charged with stealing a bottle of vodka from Lidl in Whitetown.[12] Is he pleading guilty or not guilty?' The interpreter conferred with the defendant and answered: 'I'm pleading guilty.' Judge Murray then asked the court presenter: 'Anything previous?' The court presenter said: 'Yes Judge, three previous', and began to detail the previous convictions. Judge Murray interrupted and said: 'All right, I'm going to stop you there, Sergeant . . . Mr Fagan.' So, with a nod from the judge in the direction of Mr Fagan, a solicitor, the defendant was assigned legal representation. The case was put back to a second calling, with Judge Murray noting that he would allow the man to vacate his guilty plea if he so wished. When the case was recalled, Mr Fagan told the court that the defendant 'wishes to progress with his plea of guilty'. The solicitor told the court that all three previous convictions were

> alcohol-related. The defendant is thirty-nine years of age. He works in a printing company but work is scarce and his hours have been cut. He has problems with alcohol and has no recollection of the incident but he accepts that he stole the vodka. Judge Murray pronounced sentence, saying: 'Convict and fine . . . I'll just fine him €20 . . . have you €20 on you?' The solicitor consulted with the defendant, who did not have any money on him. The judge said: 'Ok, seven days to pay.' Legal aid was applied for and granted. (FN16)

In this case when the judge realised that the defendant had three previous convictions and that therefore he might be 'at risk', he immediately decided that it was inappropriate to proceed with matters until the defendant had legal representation. He also made it clear that the guilty plea entered by the defendant before consultation with a solicitor could be vacated. This defendant's offending seems to stem from his misuse of alcohol, which is serious enough for him to have no recollection of events but not serious enough to prevent him from working. The fine imposed suggests that Judge Murray considered the offence to be petty and he appears to have given little weight to the offender's previous convictions. It also suggests that the defendant was not really at any risk of facing a custodial sentence. The amount of the fine imposed is unusually small and may have been influenced by the recent cut in the offender's income.

In addition to criminal history impacting the form and severity of sentence, the extract below highlights that previous penalties imposed on the defendant constitute another critical factor. Once a custodial sentence, including a suspended sentence, has been imposed, judges may feel that their choice of penal tariff is limited.

> Maciej R was called a few minutes before three. He is a tall, heavily built man with tightly cut fair hair and a large, angry-looking scar on his face. He pleaded guilty to a s.4 theft charge and his solicitor asked if the judge might hear the facts as his client was anxious to have the matter settled. Judge Moore asked: 'Does he have previous?' and was told: 'Yes, Judge.' Judge Moore indicated that he would hear the facts. The theft charge relates to goods valued at €10.28. The defendant has five previous convictions, including a suspended sentence which has expired. When Judge Moore heard that the defendant had previously received a suspended sentence he got quite irate and said:

'You didn't tell me he already has a suspended sentence . . . he's looking at a custodial sentence next given that he's already got a suspended sentence . . . what do you think I'm going to do . . . go backwards rather than forwards? I have a heavy caseload and it's Friday evening . . . you know as well as I do the way the system works . . . now if he's ready for a sentence I'll give him one.' The solicitor consulted with his client and said: 'We're seeking a further remand,' to which Judge Moore rejoined: 'Hopefully I won't be here.' (FN37)

Here we see that despite the very minor nature of the offence, Judge Moore's comments suggest that a critical factor likely to impact sentence in this matter is the suspended sentence previously imposed on the offender. His comments further suggest that a progression up the penal ladder is inevitable for a repeat offender. The phrase 'hopefully I won't be here' suggests that he finds the imposition of custodial sentences onerous and burdensome, and something he would rather avoid. It would seem, therefore, that even if individual judges are oriented towards rehabilitation, their decisions will be influenced by the previous decisions of their fellow judges. Hence, a number of judges imposing harsh sentences, or quickly resorting to custodial sentences, can raise the level of custodial sentences imposed by less punitive judges on repeat offenders.

A repeat conviction for a similar offence makes it more probable that a more severe form of punishment will be imposed. It may not result in the imposition of a custodial sentence but judges will often issue a warning to offenders such as, 'she had a previous conviction for a similar offence . . . we're getting closer to a custodial sentence' (Judge Moore, FN36), if they feel the risk of a custodial sentence has heightened. When the time between a repeat conviction for a similar offence is short, it is particularly likely that this will be viewed negatively by the court as it suggests that the previous punishment imposed was not sufficient to deter the offending behaviour, and it also suggests that there is a lack of a will to reform on the part of the offender.

Persistent offending and proportionality

Those that persistently offend, particularly if there is an escalation in the seriousness of the offending, may be more likely to have the charges against them dealt with at Circuit rather than District Court level. Persistent offenders dealt with by the District Court usually have engaged in low-level offending such as breaches of public order legislation or theft. The persistent offender before the District Court can often be described as a public nuisance rather than a public danger; it is common for his offending to stem from alcohol or drug abuse and to be unplanned and impulsive, and therefore more likely to be detected.

In each court location where District Court sittings were observed, the researcher quickly came to recognise by name and face the 'local', both Irish and foreign, regular and persistent offenders. While many offenders may only engage in offending behaviour within a limited geographic area, normally close to where they live, others adopt a more peripatetic style of offending. A number of offenders were observed in more than one court location, and one was observed in three of the four courtroom locations where sittings were observed. It was also not unusual to hear references to court appearances in other locations when court dates were being scheduled. It seems likely therefore that many judges will recognise at least some persistent offenders, and will be aware before they ask, 'any previous convictions?' that the defendant has a long history of offending.

Judges in the Dublin Metropolitan Region are moved regularly to different courts so their exposure to the same repeat offenders is reduced. In courts outside Dublin, judges may be permanently assigned to a specific location, with movable judges being assigned as required to cover for judges absent on leave or due to sickness. This is the case in NEC, where the familiarity of the judge with offenders was particularly evident.

At times judges display impatience and frustration dealing with persistent offenders; they may well have sentenced the offender leniently in the past and may express annoyance that the offender has not taken steps to modify their lifestyle. Roberts (2008) notes that a tendency to attribute offending to internal characteristics of the offender rather than external circumstantial factors increases with the rate of offending. So, in the mind of a judge, the offender may move from being a young man from a dysfunctional family who has developed an unhealthy dependence on alcohol which results in offending behaviour, to an unruly drunk, or an inveterate thief. This shift in perspective may make the decision to sentence persistent offenders more harshly seem fitting and logical.

However, most persistent offenders observed were vulnerable

individuals with chaotic lifestyles characterised frequently by homelessness, drug and alcohol abuse, mental health issues and low levels of education. Their criminal behaviour is inextricably linked to their web of problems, and they may need ongoing assistance in a number of different areas of their lives before they will desist from offending. Persistent offenders with LEP are especially vulnerable, and on a number of occasions judges made comments such as, 'Would he not consider going home? He's wandering around here like a lost soul' (Judge Murray). Judges, however, normally react to persistence by imposing more severe penalties.

It was not unusual for a persistent offender to fail to appear in court, thus adding to their already lengthy criminal records. On other occasions one heard that the defendant was absent because he was in another court, in a Garda station, or in prison. One could not help but conclude that the accumulation of a very high tally of criminal convictions, particularly in a short period of time, was usually evidence of rampant substance addiction and/or psychiatric illness in tandem with fragile or absent social support networks, and not indicative of serious or organised criminal activity. Despite this, those who persistently offend typically receive harsher penalties in the District Court. The field note extracts set out below provide some examples of how persistent offenders are sentenced by the District Court.

> Andrei K was in custody prior to his court appearance. He looks as if he is aged forty to forty-five, is of slim build and is European in appearance. He was assisted by a Polish interpreter. His solicitor, Ms McCabe, told the court that her client was entering a guilty plea in respect of all charges. The matter was put back to a second calling. It was after lunch before this matter was recalled. The facts were presented by the prosecuting Garda. Mr K is charged with theft and failure to appear. Judge Williams asked: 'Any previous convictions?' When he was told fifteen previous convictions, he said: '*Fifteen!*' as if this was a startlingly high number of convictions. Ms McCabe told the court that her client is a 44-year-old Polish man who has been in Ireland for three years. He hasn't worked for most of his time here and has resided in various hostels in the city centre. He is in the grip of a serious alcohol addiction. Judge Williams said: 'He has learned absolutely nothing from his previous court appearances.' Ms McCabe asked Judge Williams to deal with the matter leniently. Judge Williams said: 'How can I?' Ms McCabe tried to secure

some leniency by presenting her client as a redeemable character. She told the court that her client was hoping to get on a FÁS course. Judge Williams asked: 'What has he done to assist himself in the last three years . . . has he gone to the AA, to the HSE?' Ms McCabe said any courses have been in relation to learning English. Then, after Mr K conferred with the interpreter who in turn conferred with Ms McCabe, she added: 'I understand he is attending AA meetings.'

Judge Williams sentenced the defendant to two terms of imprisonment. The first term was for two months and the second for seven months, both sentences to run concurrently. The severity of the sentence seemed to result in a sort of stunned silence settling on the court. Ms McCabe went to the custody cells with the interpreter and Mr K. When the interpreter returned she said: 'Seven months, can you believe it?' (FN46).

This extract highlights the expectation of the court that the defendant should be able to take steps himself to improve his life and the judge's impatience that the defendant had not taken measures which he considers he could, and should, have taken. The appeal for leniency is responded to by Judge Williams saying, 'How can I?' which illustrates that the judge feels an obligation to deal with the matter by imposing a harsh sentence. The late assertion by the defendant's solicitor that he is attending AA meetings is not very credible, and the defence solicitor distances herself somewhat from it by saying, '*I understand* he is attending AA meetings.' The severity of the sentence seems to breach accepted norms and suggests that there are courtroom 'going rates' (Eisenstein and Jacob, 1977) or expectations as to the 'worth of the case' (Feeley, 1979).

Some judges clearly recognise the need for offenders to receive assistance with rehabilitation but are still mindful of a responsibility to punish indiscretions. This is illustrated in the extract set out below.

Grzegorz A has accumulated a large number of charges. Fifteen turns are listed on today's court list but Judge Butler indicates that she has thirty sheets before her. He is represented by both a solicitor and a barrister and assisted by an interpreter. When his solicitor indicates that he wishes to enter pleas in respect of the charges, the matter is put back to a second calling. Mr A is recalled at about 1.20 p.m. The facts are given by the court presenter in respect of the bulk of the charges. The majority of the charges are s.4 theft charges and there are a number of s.13 charges which 'speak for themselves'.[13]

It appears that Mr A had been stopped after taking goods without paying for them from a number of shops. Judge Butler reviewed the charge sheets before her and commented aloud on the goods stolen and the shop from which they were taken. In one case the goods stolen included smoked salmon and caviar, which brought a smile to Judge Butler's face. On a number of occasions Mr A was found in possession of a tinfoil-lined bag and a pair of pliers, which indicate that the theft was planned rather than opportunistic.

Mr A has eight previous convictions. The court is told that the defendant is a 32-year-old Lithuanian man who has also lived for a while in the Ukraine. His family are still living in Lithuania. He has had a number of jobs but has been unemployed for some time and fell on hard times and became homeless. With the help of the social welfare services he obtained a place in a hostel but unfortunately then developed an addiction to heroin. His heroin use escalated and his offending was driven by the need to fund his habit. Prior to his arrest he had secured an address in Newtown[14] and had decided to seek medical help for his addiction. His solicitor said: 'He knows he's staring down the barrel of a gun today.' The solicitor reminded the court that the property had been recovered in all cases.

Judge Butler noted that given the number of sheets, and that the defendant was habitually committing offences, the minimum sentence she could impose was five months' imprisonment. She noted, however, that the sentences would be concurrent and not consecutive. She also noted that she was requesting that the defendant receive medical treatment for drug addiction. I over-heard the solicitor tell the defendant in English: 'You've done very well . . . if you'd gone back to the Bridewell before Judge X . . . (shrugs his shoulders) you'd be looking at a lot longer of a sentence.' (FN58)

In this instance, although Judge Butler feels obliged to impose a custodial sentence because of the habitual nature of the offending she does it somewhat reluctantly, and indicates that she is imposing what she considers to be the minimum sentence given all the circumstances. Her request that the defendant receive medical treatment for drug addiction recognises that the defendant's offending behaviour stems at least in part from his drug abuse.

However, despite this, there is no suggestion that the custodial sentence can be waived. The defence solicitor clearly assesses the sentence to be as lenient as could be hoped for and points out to the defendant that he would have received a harsher sentence if the matter had been handled by a different judge.

Sometimes those who appear before the court are so vulnerable that punishment and sentencing may be a secondary consideration. The field note extract set out below provides an example of two particularly vulnerable offenders who the court recognised primarily needed assistance rather than punishment.

> Andrzej K and Mantas S were dealt with jointly as co-accused. Both men were in custody prior to their court appearance. Andrzej K is a tall man with grey hair; Mantas S is smaller but heavier in stature and has a shaved head. Both men appeared to be about fifty years old and both looked weather-beaten as if they spend a lot of time outdoors. Mantas S had several cuts and abrasions on his face and the area around Andrzej K's left eye was bruised. Both defendants appeared before the court on public order charges. Andrzej K also faces a s.13 charge arising from a failure to appear in court. It was noted in court that both men are Latvian nationals. They were assisted in court by a Russian interpreter and were represented by a solicitor, Mr Fagan. The s.13 charge was contested on the basis that Mr K was actually in prison on the date that the bench warrant was issued. The matter was put back to a second calling to allow the dates of Mr K's incarceration to be confirmed. When the defendants were recalled it was confirmed that Mr K had been in Mountjoy on the date of the bench warrant and the warrant was cancelled.
>
> The men were arrested after they became aggressive and abusive to Gardaí when they were asked to move on (they were apparently sitting under an ATM machine at the time). Both have a very lengthy list of criminal convictions. Andrzej K has eighty-two previous convictions and Mantas S has forty-three previous convictions. Their solicitor told the court that the men have been in Ireland for four to five years and the offending behaviour of both men stemmed from their chronic alcohol abuse. He noted: 'If they have money they go to hostels, but mostly they're on the streets.' The court was told that the men do not have any qualifications but did work as labourers at one stage. Judge Power asked if they had done anything to address their alcohol addiction. Mr Fagan said that Mr K had gone to an AA meeting at one point but as it was in English it was of no

value to him. He also noted that in prison the lack of English resulted in the men being left largely on their own. Judge Power then turned to the probation officer and asked her if Mr K could be visited in prison to try and set up some support structure when he gets out. The judge noted that this would depend on the co-operation of the defendant and asked the defendant if he would be willing to co-operate with the probation services. The defendant indicated that he was willing to co-operate with the probation services. It was agreed that the probation services would prepare reports in respect of both men. The probation officer indicated that normally it would take two weeks to prepare reports on persons in custody but the reports for these defendants might take a little longer because of the need for an interpreter. Judge Power commented: 'On purely humane grounds something should be done . . . if it doesn't work out . . . (shrugs) . . . but we should try.' Both men were remanded in custody for one week. (FN28)

In the space of the four or five years that these men had been living in Ireland they had amassed a very large number of convictions. They had both received a number of custodial sentences that total to several years but it seems that when committed to prison they had been released on several occasions after only completing a short portion of their sentence. Judge Power could have imposed sentence immediately, and if he had it seems likely that he would have imposed a custodial sentence. However, he probably anticipated that given the minor nature of their offending these men were likely to secure temporary release from prison and be back on the street within a short time with the same lack of support. By remanding them in custody pending the preparation of a probation report he ensured that they would not be released until the probation report was prepared and therefore created the opportunity for support structures to be put in place, which may help to stop the cycle of re-offending.

Extra-legal Factors and Sentencing

Criminal sentences should be decided on the basis of all legally relevant factors. Factors which are legally irrelevant or extra-legal such as race, gender, religion or sexual orientation should not influence criminal sentences. Sentencing decisions are discriminatory when they are affected by legally irrelevant factors. A number of key extra-legal factors are considered below in relation to the sentencing decisions of the Irish District Court.

Race/Nationality

Internationally, a great deal of research has been directed at the impact of race on sentencing decisions (see Hagan, 1974; Kleck, 1981; McConville and Baldwin, 1982; Hagan and Bumiller, 1983; Zatz, 1987; Hudson, 1989; Hood and Cordovil, 1992; Brown and Hullin, 1992; Chiricos and Crawford, 1995). The research has been driven by the disproportionate presence of minorities among those processed by many criminal justice systems and a widespread perception that minorities are unduly targeted and unfairly treated by criminal justice processes. Research results have not been conclusive and suggest that the impact of race on sentencing decisions may depend on a variety of factors including local area features, gender of offender and victim, and type of crime. The interaction of several variables may also increase the pertinence of race in sentencing decisions. This means that a constellation of factors, which include ethnic minority status, male gender and unemployment, when combined, may result in individual defendants being considered particularly troublesome, and increase the likelihood that a custodial sentence will be imposed (Spohn and Holleran, 2000). Chiricos and Crawford found that race directly affected decisions to imprison and that non-whites faced a particular disadvantage when there was a large minority population and high levels of unemployment. They suggest that the combination of a large minority population with high levels of unemployment may be regarded as potentially destabilising and so threatening as to engender a 'moral panic' (1995:301), which would influence sentencing decisions.

Concern about the presence and treatment of minorities within the Irish criminal justice system has previously focused on the Traveller community. In Ireland there is anecdotal evidence to suggest that Irish Travellers have for many years faced a greater likelihood of being involved in the criminal justice system than the general population. Although the inadequacies of our statistical database do not allow us to chart the presence of Irish Travellers within the criminal justice system, there is a widespread perception that they are disproportionately represented at all stages of the criminal justice process (see Linehan et al., 2002; Drummond 2006, 2007).

Certainly the courtroom observations of this researcher indicate that Travellers are over-represented among those who appear before the District Court. It is possible that their presence in the criminal justice system is partially attributable to prejudicial attitudes held by members of the wider community and by some persons working in the criminal justice system.

As has been highlighted already, details of the nationality/race of accused persons are not recorded by the CS. District Court judges use cues such as appearance, level of proficiency in English, accent and name to assess whether or not a defendant is non-Irish. While on most occasions it may be possible to identify foreign defendants in this manner, it is often impossible to attribute nationality or indeed race without specific information. One may be able to say that a defendant appears to be foreign, but is he Algerian, Italian, Syrian, Mauritian or perhaps Iraqi? Is the Portuguese speaker from Portugal or Brazil? Similarly a French interpreter may be required for a defendant from the Democratic Republic of Congo or Sierra Leone.

Race and nationality may also intertwine in a variety of ways. No definitive racial image is linked, for example, to Brazilians or South Africans. Judges often ask questions such as, 'Where is he from?', 'Does he speak English?', 'What language does he speak?', or 'What is his residency status?' Those who do not ask may make assumptions that may not always be accurate. Information regarding the nationality/residency status and English proficiency of the defendant may be relevant to court processes, or to the substantive charge before the court in the case of an immigration offence, and it seems more appropriate that it should be recorded and made available to judges rather than judges making enquiries in court.

There have been occasions when the reported comments of District Court judges regarding immigrants who appear before them as defendants have been criticised (Lally, 2003; Pope, 2003; Joint Committee on European Affairs, 2009; Carbery, 2012). It would seem therefore that we cannot assume that all judges will consider foreign nationals who appear before them on criminal charges in the same light as they would Irish defendants.

Courtroom observations did not reveal any instances of overtly inappropriate racial comments on the part of any persons involved in the courtroom process. At times it did seem, however, that some foreign nationals were treated with a degree of impatience which verged on discourtesy; this was particularly the case when defendants with LEP required interpreters. Observations indicate that at times efforts to ensure that foreign defendants with LEP are provided with interpreters are prompted by concerns that the absence of an interpreter might provide grounds for appeal rather than a real concern that fair procedures be applied. On one occasion when a Garda disputed a solicitor's assertion that his client had no English and required an interpreter, Judge O'Higgins interjected in an impatient tone and said: 'Oh look, he'll be off to the European Court of Justice if we go ahead without the interpreter' (FN80).

Solicitors Keane and O'Brien indicated that they were concerned at times about the attitude of judges towards foreign nationals. Ms Keane pointed to an instance when she felt a foreign national client had been unfairly refused legal aid. She claimed that some judges displayed racist attitudes and commented: 'I see it every day with District Court judges, no question.' Ms O'Brien, however, pointed to more subtle differences in the way foreign nationals are treated by the court. She said:

> Well, I think there is a casual kind of disrespect that comes out, where there is no serious attempt to pronounce their name properly, for example, where there is a presumption that their English may be better than they're letting on . . . I mean I've seen terrible examples of that over the years, there's just a kind of an expectation that it's going to take a bit longer than is convenient sometimes, there is a weariness that sometimes you see the judges approach the case with . . . it's certainly not true of all of them, and I think it's an easy attitude to slip into but it's not desirable really.

This 'casual disrespect' may not be consciously or actively displayed but it is nevertheless evident at times, as the following field note extract shows.

> When Aleksandr S was called, his solicitor Mr Kelly told the court: 'He is in the confines of the court, I have spoken to him.' Two separate charges are listed against this defendant. I understood that one of the charges is a drink-driving charge. The matter proceeded even though it seemed that the man was not actually in the courtroom. Mr Kelly said: 'My problem with this client is his English is atrocious – I'm having great trouble taking instructions.' Judge O'Higgins said: 'Is it his English that's the

problem?' and Mr Kelly replied: 'Well he has other problems, Judge.' Both men seemed to think this exchange was very humorous (FN81).

After this exchange, Judge O'Higgins directed that the defendant be provided with an interpreter. In this instance the defendant's LEP was used as a bargaining tool by his solicitor and seemed to provide a source of amusement to both his solicitor and the judge. Even when the defendant is provided with an interpreter an adjournment is sought, and it is clear that this was the desired outcome all along.

Casual references to someone having 'atrocious English' may not seem to be a matter for concern but they attest to an attitude which views LEP defendants as being somehow inferior and something of a nuisance. Comments such as these can amount to a subtle form of discrimination and detract from the general respect and courtesy that is normally afforded by the court to defendants. However, we cannot infer that the attitude that gives rise to such comments would necessarily translate into discriminatory sentencing practices.

The Irish District Court now processes defendants from very diverse origins. While it continues to deal with local offences the offenders have become global in character. There is a danger that the sentencing discretion enjoyed by the judges of the District Court could be recast on occasion as discriminatory sentencing practices. The field note extract set out below highlights how such a claim could arise. The defendant in the case was an African woman. Nothing in the proceedings in court suggested that this factor influenced the decision in this case. But the sentence was perceived by courtroom regulars as being harsh, and one cannot rule out the possibility that the offender, or her legal representatives, might consider that race influenced the sentence imposed.

> When Destiny B was called, she was not in court. Her solicitor asked for the court's patience as he believed his client to be on her way. The matter was put back to a second calling. Later, when the case was recalled, Ms B was present, but with a young child in a pushchair. She initially stood at the back of the court beside her child but moved to the front of the court when indicated to do so by her solicitor. The child had already complained intermittently but when she lost sight of her mother she launched into a full-pitched screeching. A male Garda approached the buggy tentatively and the child cried even more ferociously.

Reinforcements arrived in the form of a female Garda, who removed child and buggy to the courtroom foyer. This at least muted the sound of the child's cries for those in the courtroom. Judge Gilligan commented dryly: 'The fact that she has brought a baby to court does not in the slightest impress the court.' I wondered if the woman had thought the presence of the child might ensure that the judge would treat her more leniently, or if she simply had no-one she could ask to mind the child for her.

While the rumpus with the baby was taking place, the arresting Garda gave evidence that the charge arose out of a burglary and the theft of a suite of furniture. Ms B was observed committing the burglary. Judge Gilligan clarified with the Garda that the residence was vacant at the time of the burglary. The Garda confirmed that it was, noting that the defendant had moved out of the residence six days prior to the burglary, during which time the landlord had changed the locks. When the Garda called to the home of the defendant, she admitted the theft and showed him the furniture.

The defence solicitor valiantly ploughed on with the case; he and everyone else in court was aware that the disturbance caused by the baby was irking the judge. He indicated that his client was pleading guilty to the charge, noting that she accepted that her actions were wrong, and then began to present her personal circumstances. He told the court that his client is a 39-year-old Nigerian woman who has lived in Ireland for the last twelve years. She has five children. The solicitor told the court that the furniture was taken from a residence at which the defendant had resided for six years. He said that there was an issue with a deposit and his client was pursuing this through the PRTB.[15] At this a solicitor from the State Solicitor's Office stood up[16] and said that as the defence had raised the issue of the deposit she felt it appropriate to advise the court that the landlord was in court and was prepared to testify about the condition in which the apartment had been left. The defence solicitor looked like he wished he had never mentioned the deposit. Judge Gilligan did not call the landlord and after establishing that the defendant had no previous convictions he proceeded to pronounce sentence. He noted that the maximum sentence permissible is a twelve-month term of imprisonment but in light of the defendant's guilty plea he would reduce this to nine months. There was a slight pause, during which I saw that a number of solicitors and Gardaí looked a bit taken aback. Judge Gilligan then continued and said that the lack of previous criminal convictions warranted a further

reduction in the sentence to six months and in light of the mitigating circumstances put before the court he would suspend this
sentence for a period of two years. He commented to the defence
solicitor: 'You might advise your client of the consequences of a
suspended sentence.' (FN19)

The body language of the courtroom regulars made it clear that
this sentence was viewed as being harsh. Judge Gilligan started at
the maximum sentence possible and reduced this to take account of
mitigating factors. The circumstances in this case suggest that the
maximum penalty might not have been an appropriate departure
point for this sentencing decision. The practice of using the
maximum allowable penalty as a starting point for sentencing decisions seems likely to result in harsher sentencing decisions than
might otherwise be made.

While no system can be put in place that will eliminate claims of
discrimination, perceptions of discrimination might be avoided if sentences for minorities could be shown to be in line with those for the
general population. This would require the collection and reporting
of more detailed statistical information about defendants and convicted persons and the sentences imposed by the court. It would also
require the monitoring of sentencing decisions of individual judges.

Gender

A number of studies have sought to explore the impact of gender on
sentencing decisions (see Lyons and Hunt, 1988; Dowds and
Hedderman, 1997; Hedderman and Gelsthorpe, 1997). Research
findings have not been conclusive but offer tentative support for the
thesis that female offenders are sentenced more leniently than male
offenders. During the course of this research, 14.2% of the foreign
defendants observed were female. This proportion varied significantly by location, with no foreign female defendants in RC and
31.1% in SDC. A large proportion of foreign female defendants in
SDC appeared before the court on immigration charges whereas in
NEC most foreign female defendants faced charges in respect of
RTOs or theft. Foreign female defendants in CCC most commonly
appeared before the court on theft charges, although many also
faced immigration charges. In this court the profile of defendants
was especially vulnerable and a small number of foreign female
defendants were homeless and/or struggling with substance abuse.

Overall, however, foreign female defendants differed from their male counterparts in the type and frequency of their offending behaviour.[17] Observations indicate that foreign male defendants often appear before the District Court on public order offences. This is especially the case for male defendants from EU-12 countries. Observations indicate that African and Asian males rarely face public order offences. Likewise, foreign female defendants hardly ever appeared before the court on public order charges during the course of the observations conducted. It was also unusual for Irish female defendants to be charged with public order offences. Foreign female defendants also rarely faced charges of assault or criminal damage.

The rate of offending of males and females also differed. Most foreign defendants before the court had no previous convictions but those with a previous criminal history, especially persistent offenders with lengthy criminal histories, were overwhelmingly male.

In summary, the vast majority of foreign female defendants observed appeared before the court on minor offences with little or no previous history of offending. Consequently, they were normally dealt with very leniently by the court. Given the differences in offending patterns of foreign male and female offenders, it is not possible to conclude that the leniency shown to foreign female defendants was related to their gender. It was noted, however, that the caring responsibilities of female defendants of all nationalities were commonly mentioned in mitigation and it was therefore easier perhaps for the court to view them as persons more worthy of leniency than young men with no dependants.

Income/Employment Status

A number of studies have examined the relationship between income and employment status and the sentences imposed by criminal courts (see Chiricos and Waldo, 1975; Clarke and Koch, 1976; Crow and Simon, 1987; McCullagh, 1992). The findings have varied and do not chart a clear relationship between income/employment status and the sentences imposed.

A significant proportion of the criminal charges dealt with by the Irish District Court are RTOs. Persons from all socio-economic classes are charged with RTOs. Those charged with other offences are, however, overwhelmingly persons of lower socio-economic class, dependent on social welfare or with low levels of earned income.

Observations indicate that foreign defendants before the District Court are more likely to be in employment, or to have had a recent history of employment, than Irish defendants. Many foreign defendants who were working indicated to the court that they were earning very low weekly wages. It is difficult to assess the accuracy of such representations; defendants may be reluctant to reveal their true earnings if they think they will receive a higher penalty. The weekly wages revealed to the court tended to range from €250 to €400 per week. Very occasionally a defendant would indicate that he earned a 'significant' income, the amount of which was left ambiguous. A number of those who appeared before the court were asylum applicants in receipt of a weekly allowance of €19.10, or no allowance at all when they were not living in Direct Provision Centres. Others were described as having no income as they were not in employment and did not qualify for social welfare. Such persons were often said to be relying on the goodwill of friends. When a defendant has no income or a very low level of income, as in the case set out below, a financial penalty may not be considered appropriate by the court.

> The solicitor indicated that his client was pleading guilty and the arresting Garda presented the facts of the case. Mr Gariashvilli was stopped in TK Maxx after he had passed the last point of payment with a bag containing more than €900 worth of goods. The property was recovered. The solicitor told the court that his client is twenty-nine years of age and comes from Georgia. He is an asylum applicant who has opted to stay with friends rather than in designated refugee accommodation and consequently does not receive the €19.10 payable to asylum seekers in accommodation centres. The solicitor noted that the Georgian community in Dublin are a close-knit community who look after new arrivals as best they can but Mr Gariashvilli was naturally frustrated by his lack of means and inability to work. His solicitor claimed that the crime was motivated by poverty and frustration. He asked that the judge give his client the benefit of the Probation Act. Judge Murray commented: 'I think that €19 is appalling . . . I've seen highly qualified people who are not allowed to work and end up before me . . . OK, s.1(1) . . . and I've certified for your interpreter as well.' (FN10)

Although the defendant in this case had no previous conviction the value of the goods stolen is not insignificant and therefore the offence may well not have been viewed as 'trivial' and warranting dismissal under the provisions of the Probation Act, 1907. Certainly, the defendant could not assume that the Probation Act would be automatically applied. It would seem that the defendant's lack of material means may in this case have been interpreted as 'exceptional circumstances' which did then warrant the dismissal of the charges.

However, as the field note extract set out below highlights, a lack of means does not always mean that financial penalties will not be imposed.

> Omar Presensingh is a man I have observed in court on several occasions previously. He is Asian and of slim build and appears to be aged thirty-five to forty. Today his solicitor indicates to the court that his client is pleading guilty. This man is before the court on two separate charges of theft; the second charge arose about three weeks after the first. His solicitor told the court that he has lived in Ireland for a number of years working as a kitchen porter and studying English. He hasn't worked for six months and the college he was attending has closed down. Judge Williams asked why he had committed the thefts and the solicitor replied that they were committed out of desperation. The man was convicted on both charges and fined €150 in respect of the first offence and €400 in respect of the second offence with seven days imprisonment specified on default for each fine. (FN41)

In this instance there can have been no expectation that the defendant would be able to pay the fines imposed. The defendant had no income and was in receipt of no support from the state and seemed to have been living precariously, as on each successive court appearance that he was observed, his physical appearance was increasingly dishevelled. Effectively the fines imposed would almost certainly translate into a custodial sentence unless this man left the jurisdiction.

Offences by New Arrivals

In a number of instances, when offences were committed within a short time after arrival in Ireland this was treated by the judge as an aggravating factor in deciding on the sentence to be imposed. The rationale for this seems to have been that the short interval between arrival in the country and offending was indicative of a likely future offending trajectory. In the cases observed, suspended sentences were imposed for first offences when one might otherwise have anticipated that the Probation Act would be applied. As the extract set out below shows, the choice of sentence in such matters seemed to be primarily influenced by a desire to send a message to the offender that he would be wiser not to remain in Ireland.

> Marius R was recalled after the solicitor assigned by the court had an opportunity to consult with him with the assistance of an interpreter. At the first calling of this matter an objection to bail was raised by the prosecution as no satisfactory address was available for this defendant who only arrived in the country some days previously. Now the solicitor indicates to the court that his client is pleading guilty. Evidence is given that this man was caught by a Garda stealing a wallet with €180. The defendant is described by his solicitor as a 28-year-old married man with three children. His wife and children are in Romania. He came to Ireland to stay with friends. Judge Power asks: 'Is there some talk about him leaving?' The solicitor looks at the judge rather blankly as the judge notes that the defendant told the arresting Gardaí that he would be returning to Romania shortly. Judge Power asks again: 'When is he due to leave?' The solicitor then consults with his client and replies: 'He's going to stay about a month.'
>
> Judge Power indicates that it is of concern to him that this offence occurred within days of Mr R arriving in Ireland. He imposes a three-month suspended sentence on the condition that the defendant leave the jurisdiction within four days and stipulates that he is not to return for one year. (FN29)

The practice of imposing a custodial sentence suspended on condition that the defendant leave the jurisdiction has been noted elsewhere (Riordan, 2007). In this case, given that the defendant was an EU citizen, it is not clear whether the sentence imposed is in keeping with EU law. This practice is a curious variation on the previous habitual 'banishment' of Irish offenders, who were often 'encouraged' to take the boat to England with the alternative being a custodial sentence in Ireland (Russell, 1964).

Sentencing Decisions and Foreign Nationals

Similar penalties will not impact all offenders equally. Periods of incarceration may result in vulnerable offenders suffering particular hardship. The characteristics of a foreign national may render them especially vulnerable so that certain penalties will have an untypically harsh impact. Irish courts have found that the vulnerability of foreign nationals should be considered a mitigating factor when imposing a custodial sentence. McEvoy's review (2005) of the sentences imposed on persons convicted under the provisions of section 15(a) of the Misuse of Drugs Act, 1977 (as amended) highlights that in certain circumstances the Circuit Court found that a term of imprisonment was more difficult for a foreign national than for an Irish national and this warranted shorter terms of imprisonment being imposed on some offenders. This approach was also adopted in a number of decisions by the Court of Criminal Appeal.[18] McEvoy explains that:

> The rationale behind this approach is that a foreign national (1) is separated from family and friends and would not have the benefit of visits and other contacts that an Irish prisoner might have, (2) may have socialisation difficulties where, for example, he cannot speak English which might prevent him communicating with other prisoners, (3) may encounter various cultural difficulties in custody (for example difficulties with the food, religious practices, racism and so on). (2005:5)

McEvoy's review makes it clear that custodial sentences are not considered to be particularly burdensome for all foreign nationals, especially those who are well educated and reasonably able to communicate, and that the relevance of a person's status as a foreign national will therefore depend on the particular circumstances of each case. It is perhaps surprising that during the course of the District Court sittings observed, although many foreign nationals received custodial sentences, no judge indicated that they had considered the person's status as a foreign national as a mitigating factor. Mitigation statements by defence lawyers frequently made reference to the foreign nationality of defendants. The court was often told, 'My client has lived here for three years and is from Poland', or 'My client is an asylum applicant and is from Zimbabwe'. However, such statements never made explicit reference to a custodial sentence being potentially more onerous for their client than for an Irish national.

Conclusion

This chapter has pointed to the comparatively unfettered judicial discretion granted to Irish judges and the absence of sentencing guidelines, either descriptive or prescriptive. The chapter has noted that proportionality is understood to be the dominant rationale which guides the sentencing decisions of Irish judges. Efforts to establish an Irish sentencing information system have been noted, but as yet the information compiled has been very limited. In the District Court, the girth of discretion afforded to judges, combined with the absence of court transcripts or audio recordings, very limited statistics about sentencing patterns, and no requirement for judges to provide reasons when imposing a custodial sentence, results in the sentencing decisions of the court having a somewhat impenetrable quality. In this chapter courtroom observations were used to probe sentencing decisions of District Court judges and to consider the factors which influence them.

All of the offences dealt with by the District Court are minor offences.[19] The maximum term of imprisonment that can be imposed for a minor offence is twelve months, although the District Court can impose a period of imprisonment up to twenty-four months for multiple offences. Despite the limited sentencing powers of the District Court, it is responsible for the majority of committals to Irish prisons. In 2008, a term of imprisonment was imposed by the District Court in 13% of all cases not dismissed (DJELR, 2010). As all the cases dealt with by the District Court are minor, one must question whether imprisonment is truly being used as a punishment of last resort.

The offences dealt with by the District Court range in gravity from petty offences, which only attract a financial penalty, to offences which, if tried by indictment, could potentially attract lengthy custodial sentences. Non-custodial sentencing options other than financial penalties are limited and observations indicate that they are only used for a small proportion of offenders. Proportionality in sentencing requires that the gravity of the offence is a key determinant of the sentence imposed. While some guidance on the gravity of an offence can be gleaned from the maximum sentence which is stipulated by legislation, by and large District Court judges have to assess the gravity of offences using personal indices which measure harm and culpability. Gravity is therefore not an objective, externally measurable characteristic but a dimension which is subjectively evaluated. Inevitably, as such indices of gravity will vary from judge to judge, this means that sentences are very much dependent on the individual

presiding judge. Inconsistency in the sentencing decisions of District
Court judges and the awareness of this inconsistency among courtroom regulars are highlighted in the chapter.

The issue of previous criminal convictions is also addressed in
this chapter. It is noted that foreign criminal convictions are rarely
presented to the court. Overall, previous criminal convictions are
shown to have a profound influence on the sentences imposed for
minor offences. This influence is contrary to the recommendations
of the Council of Europe (1993) and at times threatens the proportionality of sentences.

The chapter explores the impact of a number of extra-legal
factors. Observations indicate that familial responsibilities were
more likely to be recited as mitigating factors for female defendants,
but the different offending pattern of females made it impossible to
reach any conclusion regarding the impact of gender. Some, but not
all, judges took account of the very low income levels of some
foreign defendants. Observations indicate that criminal offending by
newly arrived foreign nationals is treated by some judges as an
aggravating factor in imposing sentence. Although Circuit Court
decisions have alluded to the greater penalty that certain vulnerable
foreign nationals may face when serving custodial sentences, no evidence was found that this factor was taken into account by District
Court judges. While there was no evidence of overt discrimination
in the treatment of foreign nationals by the court, at times a certain
amount of impatience and disrespect was displayed. Inconsistencies
in sentencing patterns can create a perception that sentences are
influenced by the race/nationality of the defendant. Without court-
wide robust statistics regarding sentencing patterns, such claims
cannot be easily refuted.

We entrust the onerous task of criminal sentencing to our judges.
We can expect our judges to carry out this task responsibly and diligently, but we should not assume that they will have extraordinary
levels of wisdom or benevolence. At present, District Court judges
are expected to make sentencing decisions with little or no time for
reflection, and with little or no support or guidance. It is expected
that judges will very quickly be able to assess the gravity of an
offence; will be able to take account of an offender's criminal
history, and fairly assess the personal circumstances as presented;
and then without hesitation pronounce a sentence which takes all

these factors into account. Current arrangements ignore the possibility that judges may be influenced by 'situational' factors such as a very busy caseload; a noisy and crowded court; the demeanour of an offender; a personal friendship/dislike for an individual Garda or defence lawyer; or even a crying child.

Despite the LRC's assertion regarding the importance of consistency in sentencing, the current arrangements suggest that consistency in the sentencing of minor offences is not promoted or valued. This seems regrettable. A mechanistic, technocratic, grid-determined sentencing approach is not advocated, but a more appropriate balance between affording judicial discretion and endorsing consistency in sentencing is surely possible.

In Chapter 4, immigration offences disposed of by the District Court are considered. The chapter addresses a range of issues, including the criminalisation of breaches of immigration legislation, the scale of offences, the circumstances in which offences arise and the origins and treatment of those accused of immigration offences.

Chapter 4

Immigration Offences

Introduction

Immigration legislation is, for the most part, introduced to regulate the movement and right to work of non-citizens. When immigration legislation provides for criminal sanctions, the immigrant population is more likely than the native population to have greater contact with the criminal justice system. Immigrants are more likely to be stopped by the police, to appear in court on charges and to be detained in prisons if immigration breaches are subject to criminal sanctions. Some breaches of immigration legislation in Ireland are punished by criminal sanctions. As this chapter shows, criminalising breaches of immigration legislation can result in the differential policing of the immigrant population. This may corrode social cohesion and efforts to integrate immigrants into the wider community. It also results in the detention of irregular immigrants in prison, which in the Irish context adds to overcrowding in prisons and may create an impression in the wider community that criminality is more widespread among the immigrant population.[1]

The chapter begins by considering the different issues which modern states have to consider in formulating immigration policies and the impact of EU enlargement on migration patterns. It notes the lack of unanimity within the EU about sanctions for breaches of immigration legislation, and provides details of the various alternative approaches adopted. Irish immigration legislation is detailed and particular attention is drawn to s.12 of the Immigration Act, 2004 as the majority of the foreign nationals observed who appeared before the District Court in relation to immigration offences were charged under the provisions of this legislation.

The chapter draws on courtroom observations to highlight the variety of circumstances in which immigration offences are detected.

114

The chapter also points out that pre-trial detention has been a routine feature of immigration charges, and at times the period of pre-trial detention has been extensive. The attitude of judges to those before the court on immigration charges is explored, and the use of immigration legislation in relation to the Roma population and those claiming asylum is also considered. Procedures in relation to persons detained under the provisions of s.9(8) of the Refugee Act, 1996 are also outlined.

The chapter notes that following a judicial review, the High Court has found s.12 of the Immigration Act, 2004 to be unconstitutional and it outlines amendments to the Act introduced by the Civil Law (Miscellaneous Provisions) Act, 2011. It then discusses the effect of this change.

Policy Challenges Posed by Immigration

Modern states must grapple with a number of complex, and at times competing, issues when it comes to immigration and border controls. Considerations of national security, national identity, supranational agreements and allegiances, human rights, and economic imperatives all impact on immigration policies and the type of measures used to deal with irregular immigrants detected at points of entry to the state, and within the state. While robust border controls are imbued with symbolic value, the borders of modern liberal democracies are in practice porous and the state's ability to control who moves in and out of its borders is limited.

Border controls are used as a means of preserving national security and controlling access to states. The state exercises its sovereignty by allowing or refusing access to its territories. An individual's nationality has a major influence on how easily he can embark on international travel. States may require citizens of certain countries to apply for a visa before granting them access to their territories and may waive visa requirements in respect of citizens of other countries. Therefore, an individual's freedom to travel outside his country of origin may be constrained because of inter-governmental issues rather than individual characteristics. Citizens of countries in conflict and without a recognised government may have no legitimate means of travelling outside the boundaries of their state.

Border security measures and immigration policies are also shaped by economic considerations. The significance of revenue from overseas tourists means that immigration controls cannot be so stringent as to unduly discourage short-term visitors. They must also be flexible enough to accommodate foreign students, investors and business travellers, as all of these visitors provide a positive stimulus to the domestic economy. Some immigration may also be needed to meet labour shortages in the domestic economy. Immigration policies therefore have to balance a number of often competing objectives and, perhaps not surprisingly, are often the subject of criticism and debate.

Immigration and the EU

The commitment of EU member states to the free movement of EU citizens[2] (and their family members of any nationality) within the Union has meant that border controls at EU states differentiate between EU and non-EU citizens, and controls are primarily directed towards non-EU citizens. Within the 'Schengen' area,[3] internal border controls have been removed and freedom of movement is a reality for most EU citizens.

The EU objective of creating an area of 'freedom, security and justice'[4] has been criticised by some commentators who claim that it will contribute to the creation of 'Fortress Europe' and make the borders of the EU almost impenetrable to immigrants and asylum seekers from non-EU countries. The substantial enlargement of the EU in 2004, and the further enlargement in 2007, has provided an impetus for movement between East and West in the European continent (Alscher, 2005). Migration from EU accession states accounted for the biggest source of inward migration to Ireland between 2005 and 2008 (CSO, 2009), although the pattern of inward migration reversed in 2009 (CSO, 2009, 2010).

As intra-EU migration has increased, efforts to curb migration by third-country nationals[5] have been introduced. Within the EU, tougher asylum policies (Lavenex, 1999; Hatton, 2005) and the introduction of measures to secure the co-operation of sending and transit countries (Boswell, 2003; Alscher, 2005) are linked to a substantial fall in asylum applications. In 2006, asylum applications to EU-27 countries were only half the level they were in 2001. Since 2006, however, the downward trend in applications has reversed (Eurostat, undated; Eurostat, 2009).[6] EU expansion has also been associated with restrictions on employment opportunities for non-EU citizens.

In Ireland, as in the wider EU, asylum applications have declined in recent years, but unlike the composite EU-27 asylum application trend, there has been no recent increase in applications. First-time asylum applications peaked in 2002, and after an initial rapid decline they have steadily decreased since then. This pattern is generally attributed to a number of key policy changes, outlined briefly below, in particular the change in citizenship rights introduced by a constitutional amendment in 2004 which removed an automatic right to citizenship to children born in Ireland (Garner, 2007). Provisions making carriers liable for transporting unauthorised migrants, and the implementation of a 'safe country of origin' concept whereby applicants from countries designated as 'safe' are *prima facie* presumed not to be in need of protection (Ruhs and Quinn, 2009), are also associated with a decline in asylum applicants. Increased restrictions on the right of asylum applicants to social welfare support and the use of Direct Provision Centres (FLAC, 2010; Ugba, 2007), and the policy of fingerprinting resident non-EEA[7] nationals (Ring, 2008), have also been linked to the decline in asylum applications. Despite this decline, however, asylum applications in Ireland remain substantially above the EU average (Cahill, 2009).

While the Irish government opened its labour markets to EU-10[8] nationals in 2004, it also introduced restrictions on occupations eligible for work permits, thus limiting job opportunities for non-EEA nationals (see Employment Permits Act, 2003, 2006). The thrust of the policy changes introduced has been to restrict employment opportunities for non-EEA nationals to highly skilled individuals. A significant reduction in the number of work permits issued and renewed has been observable since 2003 (Ruhs and Quinn, 2009). The effect of efforts to reduce asylum applications and to make the asylum process less attractive, and reductions in employment opportunities for non-EEA nationals, is unclear. It is possible that reduced access for non-EEA nationals through regular immigration channels may have increased levels of irregular migration.

Sanctions for Breaches of Immigration Legislation

Despite common EU policies on many aspects of border and immigration control (see European Commission (EC), 2006), there is no unanimity among EU member states regarding the appropriate form or severity of sanctions which should be imposed on irregular immigrants. EU legislation requires member states to apply criminal penalties to persons involved in smuggling, trafficking or, in serious cases, employing third-country nationals with irregular immigration status. EU law does not oblige member states to provide criminal penalties in relation to third-country nationals who enter or stay in the country in contravention of immigration regulations (European Migration Network (EMN) 2009).

Many argue that such breaches should be viewed as administrative offences sanctioned by fine. Others consider that the importance attaching to immigration and border control warrants the criminalisation of irregular immigration. In countries such as the Netherlands, Bulgaria, Hungary, Portugal, Slovenia and Spain, breaches of immigration legislation by third-country nationals are not criminalised (EMN, 2009). In Finland, irregular immigrants from third countries are subject to a criminal sanction but punishment is limited to a fine. In Latvia, criminal penalties are reserved for those who repeatedly illegally cross the national border (EMN, 2009). In other countries such as the UK, Luxembourg, Poland and Ireland, criminal sanctions, including terms of imprisonment, may be imposed on irregular immigrants.

Concerns about criminalising irregular immigration

The practice of criminalising irregular immigration contravenes the stance of the Council of Europe: Commissioner for Human Rights (COECHR), which has stated that 'criminalisation is a disproportionate measure which exceeds a state's legitimate interest in controlling its borders' (Hammerberg, 2008). The COECHR also notes that, 'the adoption of criminal laws establishing offences which can only be committed by or in respect of foreigners presents important challenges for human rights norms' (COECHR, 2010:6–7). The Commission is especially concerned about the effect of the criminalisation of breaches of immigration legislation on asylum seekers and contends that, 'governments appear to have invested too much political capital in "being tough" on asylum seekers' (COECHR, 2010:20).

Irish Immigration Legislation and Immigration Offences

Current Irish immigration legislation is set out in an array of Acts, including Aliens Act, 1935; Aliens Order, 1946 (as amended); Refugee Act, 1996 (as amended); Immigration Act, 1999; Illegal

Immigrants (Trafficking) Act, 2000; Immigration Act, 2003; Employment Permits Act, 2003; Immigration Act, 2004; and Employment Permits Act, 2006 (Becker, 2008). The most recent amendments to immigration legislation are contained in the Civil Law (Miscellaneous Provisions) Act, 2011. The primary focus of these Acts are persons who are not citizens of Ireland who are variously described as 'aliens' and 'non-nationals'. Offences under the Acts arise from the failure to present to an immigration officer; the failure to possess a visa; the failure to report to the relevant immigration registration office; the failure to produce documentation or to provide information; the failure to leave the state; and the breach of conditions of a permission to enter and be in the state. In addition, offences may arise from landing at unapproved ports, or the unauthorised engagement in a business profession or employment (Becker, 2008). The Immigration Residence and Protection Bill, 2008 was withdrawn in 2010 after hundreds of amendments were scheduled (O'Halloran, 2010). A new Bill the Immigration Residence and Protection Bill 2010 was published in July 2010 but the combination of financial crisis, economic recession, a change of government and a return to net outward migration has meant that immigration legislation has not figured prominently on the legislative agenda and some three years later the Bill has not yet been enacted.

Immigration Offences and the Irish District Court

During the period that courtroom observations were conducted, the overwhelming majority of those charged with breaches of immigration legislation in the Irish District Court were charged under the provisions of s.12 of the Immigration Act, 2004. Following a judicial review, the High Court found in March 2011 that the provisions of s.12 are unconstitutional. The findings of the High Court and the subsequent legislative amendments are discussed later in this chapter. For now it is useful to review the position prior to the judicial review.

S.12 of the Immigration Act, 2004 provides that:

(1) every non-national shall produce on demand, unless he or she gives a satisfactory explanation of the circumstances which prevent him or her from so doing, (a) a valid passport or other equivalent document, issued by or on behalf of an authority recognised by the government which establishes his or her identity and nationality, and (b) in case he or she is

registered or deemed to be registered under this Act, his or her registration certificate.

(2) a non-national who contravenes this section shall be guilty of an offence.

'On demand' is explained in Section 12(3) of the Immigration Act, 2004 as 'on demand made at any time by any immigration officer, or a member of An Garda Síochána'. A person found to be in breach of this legislation was subject to arrest without warrant, and on summary conviction was liable to a maximum fine of €3,000 and or a maximum term of imprisonment of twelve months. The provisions of section 12 applied to all non-Irish nationals, including EU citizens.

Variation in Incidence of Immigration Offences Observed

The scale and pattern of immigration offences varied very significantly in each of the four court locations observed. Immigration offences were very rare in NEC. It had been anticipated that the proximity of NET to the border with Northern Ireland would result in irregular immigrants being detected and charged, but this was not found to be the case.

In SDC, immigration charges were common. In the majority of instances the charges arose after a foreign national was arrested and detained at Dublin airport. It seemed that such persons almost invariably made an application for asylum as the practice of defence lawyers was to inform the court that an asylum application had been made. The stated policy of the Garda National Immigration Bureau (GNIB) is to facilitate asylum seekers and it may be that many, and perhaps most, of those who claim asylum at a point of entry to the state are not arrested but are directed to the Office of the Refugee Applications Commissioner (ORAC). It was not always apparent why the decision had been made by a GNIB officer to arrest persons observed in court under the provisions of s.12 of the Immigration Act, 2004. It seems that the decision to charge irregular immigrants who present at ports of entry may crucially depend on the attitude of individual GNIB officers, and on such factors as the timing of asylum applications and the discovery of false documents.

In CCC, immigration charges were also not uncommon but there was far greater diversity in the type of situations which gave rise to such charges. In RC, the proportion of foreign nationals before the court on immigration charges was very high and charges had arisen in a wide variety of situations. This was the only court where persons detained under the provisions of s.9(8) of the Refugee Act, 1996 were observed (see below).

Observations highlighted that while breaches of immigration legislation may be detected at a point of entry to the state, it is also not unusual for such breaches to come to light during the course of routine Garda work. Those charged with immigration offences may never have lived in Ireland or may have lived here for some time. Some of those charged may have entered the state with all required documentation but over time their status may have changed and they may have become irregular immigrants. It is clear therefore that our border controls do not eliminate irregular immigration. It is not possible to accurately calculate the presence of irregular migrants living in Ireland (Migrant Rights Centre of Ireland (MRCI), 2007).

The Process is the Punishment

Courtroom observations indicate that many judges understood the process of charging foreign nationals under the provisions of s.12 of the Immigration Act, 2004 to be a tool used by Gardaí to allow them to detain persons until they could satisfactorily establish their identity, rather than an ordinary criminal charge which requires censure. Persons charged under these provisions were therefore by and large punished by the process of being detained until they could produce a passport or 'an equivalent document', rather than by the sentence imposed by the court. During interview, solicitor O'Brien expressed frustration at the efforts required to produce documentation for clients in custody on section 12 charges and summed up the process as follows: 'It's a saga while we try and get [ID] for them . . . and the case goes away when we get it for them . . . it's really all about nothing in my view.'

In the majority of cases observed, those charged with offences under this legislation had the charges dismissed under the provisions of the Probation Act. A small number were bound to the peace for a period of time and others had the charges struck out when their identity was established. However, it was the practice of one judge observed to routinely impose a custodial sentence in respect of s.12 charges.

Observations indicate that most of those charged under the provisions of s.12 entered a plea of guilty. The high level of guilty pleas may have been because it was often difficult to construct an effective defence to s.12 charges but may also have been affected by the knowledge that a 'not guilty' plea might risk attracting a higher penalty. However, as explained in detail below, the provisions of s.12 were challenged on a number of occasions in the District Court and a challenge arising from a case that commenced in the District Court led to a High Court ruling that the provisions are unconstitutional.

The process

Observations indicate that the accepted protocol for handling s.12 charges was not to make an application for bail or seek to enter a plea until some progress had been made in establishing the identity of the defendant. Court appearances in 'ID matters' tended to be perfunctory and last a matter of seconds rather than minutes. Typically, the defendant was produced and provided with an interpreter if necessary. The defendant was normally granted or already had legal representation. The court presenter usually indicated the nature of the case by saying, 'it's an identity matter, Judge', or 'ID is still an issue', and the defence simply sought another adjournment noting something like, 'at this stage no meaningful application can be made', or 'we haven't got ID papers as yet'. Normally the matter was adjourned for two weeks, with leave to apply for an earlier court appearance. Occasionally, the defence secured a one-week adjournment if they indicated that 'documents are on their way', or if the court was told that documents had already been submitted to the Gardaí. Court appearances were therefore usually very brief and interpreters often had little or no chance to translate what was said to the defendants.

The process of obtaining a passport or satisfying the GNIB by some other means as to the identity of an individual can take several weeks or even months. This resulted in lengthy periods of pre-trial detention for some defendants charged under the provisions of s.12.

Some judges did allow defendants to plead guilty to such charges when they had begun the process of establishing their identity. Some almost invited defendants in custody to plead guilty. When Judge Cahill commented regarding a man held on remand for two months for a minor theft and a s.12 charge, 'if he were to plead guilty today he's likely to be as free as the birds in five minutes', the man immediately entered a guilty plea and was sentenced in relation to the theft charge to a period of imprisonment equal to the period he had already been detained (which was sixty-three days), and a peace bond was imposed for twelve months in relation to the s.12 charge conditional on his supplying satisfactory ID within two weeks and co-operating with ORAC in processing his asylum application (FN67). Other judges accepted a guilty plea and noted that the defendant was entitled to plead guilty.

Some judges, however, simply would not accept a guilty plea until such time as the Gardaí indicated that the defendant's identity had been satisfactorily verified. In one instance observed, when a solicitor indicated that her client, who was in custody, wished to enter a guilty plea to a s.12 charge, Judge Foley said: 'Identity is still an issue Ms McColgan, I can't convict him' (FN57). A lengthy exchange followed, the flavour of which can be gleaned from the following field note extract.

> Ms McColgan argued at some length that her client has engaged with the asylum process and that he cannot produce documents he does not have. She claimed that it is not acceptable simply for the state to say that identity is still an issue; the onus must be on it to verify the defendant's identity. She said: 'We say who we are and the state are saying we're not who we are. He's saying he has identified himself as best he can, and it is the state's job to establish if he is someone else.' Judge Foley said with an air of exasperation: 'Ms McColgan, he is charged with a criminal offence.' Judge Foley clearly felt that there should be no question of progressing the matter when identity was still subject to verification and the defendant was unable to produce an 'equivalent document'. Ms McColgan repeated that her client could not produce what he did not have and Judge Foley suggested rather extraordinarily that he would therefore have to continue in detention, for life if necessary! (FN57)

Exchanges went on in this vein for some time, with Judge Foley's determination not to convict the defendant hardening when he learned that the man had previously been refused asylum, and that deportation proceedings were ongoing. He became a little exasperated at one point and said: 'It's quite conceivable he's from Kerry, Ms McColgan', to which Ms McColgan simply replied: 'Yes, Judge.' Matters concluded as follows:

> Judge Foley said: 'He is obliged to produce a passport or an equivalent document.' Ms McColgan rejoined: 'If he can, Judge',

to which Judge Foley retorted: 'No, there's no "if he can".' At this point Judge Foley decided to wrap up matters and announced that he was remanding the defendant for two further weeks. Ms McColgan asked: 'Would you consider marking that peremptory against the state, Judge?' and Judge Foley retorted: 'No, I would consider marking it peremptory against you, though!'

However, Judge Healy, in dealing with a young Somali man whose identity had not been established, accepted a plea of guilty after the barrister representing this man told the court that as Ireland has no diplomatic ties with the government in Somalia, and indeed for all intents and purposes there is no government in Somalia, the defendant has no prospect of being in a position to furnish the state with ID documents. The arresting Garda pointed out that the man had been able to source documents to travel half way around the world, and that as there are no direct flights from Africa to Ireland he must have travelled through at least one other EU state prior to his arrival in Ireland. The case concluded as follows.

> The barrister put forward the view that as her client was pleading guilty to the charge, he could not be remanded in custody solely on the basis of identity concerns except for sentencing. The arresting Garda pointed out that if released, the man would still be in breach of Irish law (because of his lack of a passport/ID) and he would be liable to arrest again and again. Judge Healy indicated that he was proceeding to sentence. In mitigation the court was told that the defendant is nineteen years of age and his only living relative is his mother, as his father, brother and two sisters were killed in the hostilities in Somalia. He has been unable to make telephone contact with his mother since his arrival in the state. His barrister claimed that he is not here to frustrate the system and he simply is not in a position to produce documents. Judge Healy interjected and said: 'He also knew what he was doing.' The barrister reiterated her position, saying: 'He wasn't coming here to beat the system, he came here to seek refuge.' Judge Healy imposed a three-month sentence suspended for four months and also directed that the defendant enter into a peace bond for twenty-four months. Turning to the prosecuting Garda from the GNIB, he said: 'He has to be given the opportunity to get to ORAC', and the Garda replied saying: 'Oh of course . . . I'm not going to be hiding outside in the bushes.' (FN55)

This sentence was a departure from Judge Healy's observed practice of imposing a peace bond on persons convicted under the provisions of s.12 of the Immigration Act, 2004. It could be interpreted as a penalty for effectively forcing the court to accept a guilty plea before the state was able to satisfactorily verify the identity of the defendant. Judge Healy's direction to the Garda that the defendant be given the opportunity to process his asylum application was made in recognition of the fact that in the absence of a passport the defendant would continue to be unable to comply with the requirements of section 12 of the Immigration Act, 2004 and would therefore be liable to re-arrest.

Lack of co-operation may extend period of detention

At times the actions of defendants hampered efforts to establish their identity, which lengthened the period of their detention (see Fallon, 2008). Some of those arrested at the airport were reluctant to reveal any information, such as the route by which they arrived into Ireland. This meant that it proved impossible to identify their luggage, which may have contained documents that would have allowed them to establish their identity.

> Adam Badmus was called and was produced from the custody area of the courthouse. A Garda from the GNIB told the court that a French interpreter was required. None was in court, although the Garda told Judge Gilligan that one had been requested. The matter was put back to a second calling. When the case was recalled, the interpreter was in court. The GNIB officer told the court that the defendant had been arrested at Dublin airport on the previous day. The defendant is apparently from Togo, although there is some doubt about this as the official language of Togo is French, and this man doesn't seem able to speak French. The judge asked the interpreter if the defendant understood French. The interpreter spoke to the defendant and replied: 'He indicates he understands but he can't express himself well in French.' The judge said rather acerbically: 'There will be time for expression later.' Up until this point this man had no legal representation.[9] Judge Gilligan asked: 'Does this gentleman want me to assign him a lawyer?' The defendant indicated that he did wish to have a lawyer. A solicitor was assigned and the matter was put back to allow the solicitor to confer with his client. When the case was recalled, the defence solicitor said: 'I don't think we can do anything today . . . we're

not able to progress anything today.' The solicitor indicated that his client may have some means of identification in his luggage and asked if this was in the possession of the Gardaí. The GNIB officer looked a bit exasperated as she explained that the defendant hadn't indicated where he came from, or on what airline, and they were therefore not currently in a position to redeem his luggage. Judge Gilligan noted: 'If the Garda is to assist you, he must assist the Garda.' The man was remanded in custody to Cloverhill. (FN19)

Immigration Offences at Ports of Entry

The majority of those appearing before SDC on immigration charges were persons arrested at Dublin airport who were not previously resident in Ireland. Most of those who appeared before the court on immigration charges were of Chinese or African origin. Persons charged under the provisions of s.12 of the Immigration Act, 2004 did not normally apply for bail at their first court appearance as they were unable to establish their identity to the satisfaction of the Gardaí and in these circumstances bail was almost certain to be refused.

In the Dublin Metropolitan Region, male defendants remanded in custody are normally remanded to Cloverhill prison and subsequent court appearances are in RC. Female prisoners are, however, remanded in custody to the Dóchas prison and appear before SDC, or the court where they were initially produced, for subsequent court appearances. When a man and woman travelling together are arrested they will usually be treated as co-accused, and the man will then be remanded to appear before the court where the case was first heard rather than RC. This means that in SDC and CCC one would only normally get an opportunity to see a foreign male charged under the provisions of s.12 on his first appearance in court, or if the person had secured bail when the matter had been referred back to the original court. However, it was easier to track the progress of females before the court on immigration charges. Multiple remands were not unusual in such cases.

One such case involved a young Zimbabwean couple, who were treated as co-accused. M. and D. Nwachi were observed on seven separate occasions in SDC. Both defendants lodged an asylum application after their arrest in Dublin airport. The solicitors representing this couple intimated to the court at each court appearance prior to their release on bail that documents were expected imminently, and on this basis sought and secured weekly court appearances. The delay in procuring their identity documents was attributed to problems in Zimbabwe. They were released on bail after being remanded in custody for six weeks. Ms Nwachi was pregnant during her time in custody and her solicitor requested that she receive medical attention. Neither of these defendants ever addressed the court during any of their court appearances. They normally appeared very impassive in court as if they were resigned to their fate, but Mr Nwachi did smile brightly when the court granted them bail. The following field note extract is from their last appearance in court.

> I have observed M. and D. Nwachi in court on many occasions. Although the GNIB were not fully satisfied regarding their identity, they were finally granted bail at their last court hearing. When their names were called, Judge Murray said: 'Are they here?' I wonder if he has anticipated that they will not present themselves in court. Both defendants are in the courtroom. They are represented by two separate solicitors, who enter a plea of guilty on their behalf. Garda McNulty from the GNIB tells the court that the defendants were stopped at Dublin airport on 18/10 after arriving on a flight from Geneva. They presented South African passports which were found to be false. Garda McNulty notes that as the defendants were unable to produce documents to satisfy the GNIB as to their identity, they spent a number of weeks in custody but tells the court that satisfactory documents have now been produced. Judge Murray pronounces sentence saying: 's.1(1) in both cases.' (FN23)

It is possible that the use of false passports was a key factor in deciding to arrest these asylum applicants. The timing of the application for asylum may also be crucial in that it appears that this couple only applied for asylum after their arrest and not immediately upon presenting themselves to immigration officials.

Whose children?

When adult immigrants accompanied by minor children are arrested for breaches of immigration legislation at a port of entry to the state, the children are not simply assumed to be the children of the adult with whom they arrived into the country. The possibility of human trafficking has to be considered.

During the course of the fieldwork, two African women were observed who were accompanied by minor children when they arrived at Dublin airport. One woman charged under the provisions of s.12 of the Immigration Act, 2004 was accompanied by two children, who were both initially placed in the care of the Health Service Executive (HSE). DNA tests confirmed that she was the mother of the five-year-old boy who accompanied her. She claimed that the young teenage girl who also accompanied her was her cousin but this could not be satisfactorily confirmed by DNA testing. A social worker from the HSE told the court that this older child would not be placed in the care of the defendant but the young boy would be returned to his mother's care.

This woman was released on bail after a period of thirty days in custody. She was observed in court on four occasions (FN7, 12, 17 & 18). Contrary to normal practice, bail was granted prior to this woman's identity being satisfactorily confirmed as her solicitor convinced the court that as she came from a country in conflict there was substantial uncertainty regarding how long the process of securing a passport would take and it was therefore unreasonable to detain her further. The fact that her young child would be re-united with his mother also seemed to influence the decision of Judge Murray to grant bail (FN18). Due to the lack of a conclusive DNA link between this woman and the young girl who accompanied her, the girl was to remain in the care of the HSE while enquiries regarding her identity were pursued. A doubt remained as to the motivation of the defendant in bringing the girl to Ireland. It is possible that she would remain in the care of the HSE until she reached the age of eighteen.[10]

In the second case observed, the female defendant, Kerina Mwake, was accompanied by three minor children on her arrival at Dublin airport (FN13). She appeared in court charged with being in possession of a false instrument as she presented a false passport at Dublin airport. A social worker gave evidence in court that the defendant was not believed to be the mother of any of the three children, two boys aged five and ten and a twelve-year-old girl, who accompanied her. All three children were placed in the care of foster parents on their arrival in Ireland. Prior to the court hearing, contact had been made with the putative mother of these children, an asylum applicant in the UK. A GNIB officer told the court that DNA testing had been undertaken to confirm the identity of the children's mother.

It appeared that Ms Mwake cared for the children after their parents moved to the UK. She was sent money to purchase tickets for herself and the children and she also had a substantial sum of money on her person that had been provided to her as a means of proving that she had independent means and would not be seeking any support from the state. The GNIB officer indicated that this woman was being refused permission to land and would be detained in custody until arrangements for her departure could be put in place. Judge Murray applied the Probation Act in relation to the charge before the court. In this latter case the woman accompanying these children could be construed as being involved in human trafficking, or alternatively could be seen as having been manipulated by the parents of these children.

Unaccompanied minors

Once immigration officers have identified an unaccompanied child seeking entry into the state, the provisions of s.8 of the Refugee Act, 1996 require that the unaccompanied child be referred to the HSE. However, the process of identifying unaccompanied minors is not straightforward. A large proportion of children identified as unaccompanied minors are between the ages of fourteen and seventeen. This proportion has grown in recent years (Joyce and Quinn, 2009:16). Distinguishing between children aged sixteen or seventeen and young adults can be especially difficult. In addition, some minors may initially present themselves as being over the age of eighteen, and may have travel documents which present them as adults. Others who claim to be unaccompanied minors may in fact be adults seeking to benefit from the extra protection afforded to minors. Joyce and Quinn (2009) note the absence of a written policy on age assessment and point out that a variety of approaches are adopted by different actors. They point out that:

> . . . there is an inherent tension between immigration concerns and the principle of the best interests of the child taking precedence at all times. These two imperatives may conflict, particularly at the border. The issue of age assessment at the border is crucial and certain NGOs argue that minors have been detained and/or returned due to a lack of age assessment or an incorrect conclusion being drawn. (2009:xiii)

The provisions of s.12 of the Immigration Act, 2004 only applied to non-nationals aged over sixteen. In theory, therefore, a child of sixteen or seventeen could have been charged with a breach of this legislation but the practice appears to have been to apply these provisions only to adults.

During the course of the fieldwork conducted, a young Chinese woman who had presented identity documents which gave her age as sixteen appeared in court on immigration charges. It was impossible to determine this woman's age from a cursory inspection. She was small and thin, which probably meant she was more likely to be assessed as being younger than her chronological age. However, despite presenting these documents, the woman did not pursue a claim to be a minor in court (FN11, 13 & 19). A second defendant who did claim to be a minor was, however, assessed to be an adult.

> Ahmed Awoko is a young African man who, despite wearing a hooded woollen jumper under his coat, looked as if he was very cold. This man was on bail prior to his court appearance, which is unusual for an immigration charge. The barrister representing him indicated that his client wished to enter a not guilty plea. A hearing date some three months hence was set. The barrister went on to further note that his client arrived in the country as an unaccompanied minor, and as such requests that he be placed in the protection of the HSE, who should act in 'loco parentis'. Judge Gilligan noted rather dryly as he looked at the defendant, who is of a muscular build and has a patchy beard on his face: 'Those are your instructions.' Certainly the defendant looks more like he is in his twenties than he is sixteen or seventeen but this is hardly definitive evidence that he is an adult. A Garda from the GNIB said that it is the state's belief that the defendant is over eighteen years of age. The judge asked: 'Do you know who he is?' The Garda replied: 'We do, and is he aged considerably older than eighteen, Judge.' Judge Gilligan then announced: 'I won't make any such order in those circumstances.' (FN20)

Persons Resident in the State Charged with Immigration Offences

Many persons resident in the state appeared before the court on immigration charges. The irregular immigration status of several defendants observed came to light after they were arrested in relation to other charges. In one instance a man charged with theft was also charged under the provisions of s.12 when Gardaí found him to be in possession of two sets of ID, one Polish and one Czech. The solicitor representing this man told the court that the Czech ID was in the name of a comedian, and the man's friends had got it made with his photograph as a joke. The solicitor said her client had always identified himself to Gardaí as a Polish national and had never claimed to be a Czech national. The court was told, however, that internet searches had not confirmed the existence of the Czech comedian and the assistance of Interpol had been requested. When Judge Nolan asked, 'Is he on holiday here?' he was told that the defendant had lived in Ireland for five years and had a girlfriend and child here (FN44). This man was remanded in custody pending clarification of his identity.

Two defendants observed had been arrested at social welfare offices after they represented themselves as EU nationals and produced false passports with a view to securing a PPS number. One was a Nigerian man who represented himself as a Dutch national. Within days of his arrest this man lodged an asylum application with ORAC. Judge Healy imposed a peace bond for twenty-four months and directed that he liaise and comply with ORAC (FN56). The other defendant was a Pakistani man who produced a false French passport and a false French ID document. This latter defendant had lived in Ireland for almost ten years prior to his arrest, having originally come to Ireland as a student of hotel management. Judge Power applied the Probation Act (FN29).

Immigration charges also stemmed from routine traffic checks. On a number of occasions the defendant was the driver of a car stopped at a traffic check and was arrested when he produced a false driver's licence. In such circumstances the defendants were normally charged in relation to the false instrument[11] as well as under s.12 of the Immigration Act, 2004 if they were unable to produce a valid passport.

One woman observed faced a s.12 immigration charge and a charge in relation to a 'false instrument' s.29 (see note 11). Both charges arose when she was asked to produce her passport by a Garda after a car she was a passenger in was stopped at a routine traffic check. The woman, a Nigerian national, was arrested when she was unable to produce a passport. After spending a week in custody she produced a passport and was released on bail. However, on examination the passport proved to be false. Detailed evidence was given in court by a Garda from the documents section as to the differences between a genuine Nigerian passport and the document produced by this woman. The woman, through her barrister, contested the finding that the passport was false, even though it was admitted in court that she did not apply for her passport through official channels in Nigeria but had instead paid a 'Mr Joe' a sum of money to procure a passport for her. The argument presented by the defence regarding the validity of the passport seemed to lack any substance, and as the field note extract set out below shows, only served to irritate the judge.

> Judge Murray looked exasperated as the barrister persisted in trying to make a case that this woman could have reasonably thought that the passport she got from 'Mr Joe' rather than through official channels was a valid passport. Judge Murray said to the defending barrister: 'If you needed a passport, would you go to Chapel Street for a passport, Mr Moloney?' When he didn't get an immediate reply he answered the question himself, saying: 'No you would not, and neither would any right-thinking person, and if they did they would not come into this court and try and make a case that they thought the passport was valid' (FN23). The defendant was ultimately convicted of the section 29 charge and fined €50, with the s.12 charge 'taken into consideration.' (FN24)

This woman was a passenger in a car stopped at a routine traffic check. There was no suggestion that her behaviour excited any alarm or suspicion on the part of the Gardaí conducting the traffic stop. One can only conclude therefore that she was requested to produce a passport because she does not look 'Irish'.

This woman had breached the law and was convicted, but does her arrest point to a practice of stopping people whose physical appearance suggests they are not Irish? If people are stopped in similar circumstances and arrested but are later able to produce a valid passport the charges against them may not proceed and hence the extent of this practice may not be measurable by observing courtroom proceedings.

Legislation recently enacted in Arizona requires non-citizens to carry immigration documents and gives the state police the power to detain illegal immigrants. The provisions introduced in the Arizona legislation are not dissimilar to those contained in s.12 of the Immigration Act, 2004. However, the Arizona legislation has provoked demonstrations and discussions across the US amid claims that the law is a recipe for racial and ethnic profiling by the police (Archibold, 2010). Although it is contended that s.12 of the Immigration Act, 2004 also licensed inappropriate racial and ethnic profiling by An Garda Síochána, it has not provoked widespread controversy or disquiet.

In Britain, the MacPherson (1999) report finding of institutional racism on the part of the British police has led to greater monitoring of the presence of ethnic minorities at all stages of the criminal justice process. Despite this, black, and to a lesser extent Asian, people are still disproportionately targeted by the police during stop and search exercises (Equality and Human Rights Commission (EHRC), 2010; Delsol and Shiner, 2006).[12] This potentially damages relationships between ethnic minorities and the wider community and corrodes trust in the police force.

We cannot point to similar statistics for Ireland. We do not know with certainty if those who look unlike or speak differently from a stereotypical Irish person are more likely to be targeted by An Garda Síochána. However, the role of An Garda Síochána in relation to immigration matters has been identified as a possible impediment to building positive relationships with minority communities (Ionann, 2004). The European Union Minorities and Discrimination Survey carried out in 2008 also presents findings which suggest inappropriate targeting of minorities by Irish police. The survey indicated that 59% of sub-Saharan Africans surveyed had been stopped at least once by Gardaí in a twelve-month period, and one in three Eastern Europeans had been stopped in the same period. The stop rate for sub-Saharan Africans was the highest for any ethnic minority in the EU and compares to stop rates in Malta of 8%, in Portugal of 9% and in Sweden of 19% (European Union Agency for Fundamental Rights, 2009:102). The findings of this survey were challenged by the Integration Minister, who claimed that the methodology used in Ireland differed from that used in other countries and that respondents were only based in Dublin (McCarthy, 2010).

The limited evidence available suggests that some Garda activity may have been unduly directed at ethnic minorities, and that in some instances at least the provisions of s.12 may have been interpreted as licensing Gardaí to unduly target non-Irish citizens, or those who appeared to be non-Irish citizens. This issue is explored further below in relation to the policing of the Roma community.

Immigration Charges and the Roma Population

In a number of cases observed in court no explanation was presented as to why Gardaí demanded foreign nationals to produce their passport. If a Garda formed the view that a person is a non-citizen under the provisions of s.12 of the Immigration Act, 2004, they could demand that they produce their passport or equivalent document. It would seem therefore that non-Irish nationals who speak in a foreign language, or have an obvious accent, those who dress differently, and those who are visibly different in appearance from a stereotypical Irish person were most likely to be asked to produce their passport under the provisions of s.12 of the Immigration Act, 2004. As solicitor O'Brien noted: 'The more you look like a non-national then the more likely you are to get picked up on [a s.12 charge].'

Courtroom observations indicate that most persons charged under the provisions of s.12 of the Immigration Act, 2004 were non-EU nationals. If EU nationals were charged under these provisions, it seems that the charges were usually dropped when the person's nationality was satisfactorily established. An exception to this rule was the treatment of members of the Roma community who were EU nationals. Solicitors Hanly and Keane identified as a particular matter of concern the use of s.12 of the Immigration Act, 2004 in relation to the Roma community. Mr Hanly noted that it is a 'community law' issue, and specifically referred to the EU directive on freedom of movement.[13] Ms Keane commented that s.12 was used as a means of controlling members of the Roma community and said:

> . . . it's absolutely abused, there is no question but that it is abused by the authorities . . . the way that they are noticed on the street is generally through begging . . . but because begging is no longer an offence[14] then they are no longer able to stop them from begging so . . . they can charge them with sort of jumped-up public order issues, or under the Children Act is another one, and then s.12 is another.

Later in the interview Ms Keane characterised s.12 offences as 'a sort of offence of last resort'. This description seems to imply that at times persons were charged with s.12 offences when their behaviour was considered undesirable but they had not otherwise breached the criminal code.

Spatial variations in targeting of Roma population

Observations indicate that the use of s.12 as a means of controlling members of the Roma community may have been a local rather than a general practice. No Roma defendants charged under the provisions of s.12 appeared in NEC during the course of observations. Indeed, it was unusual to see a Roma person in court at all in this location, although Roma women were visible on the streets selling copies of *Ireland's Big Issue*. In SDC most Roma appeared before the court on theft charges, and in RC no Roma were identified as being held on remand in relation to immigration charges. However, in CCC it was not unusual to see Roma defendants charged under the provisions of this Act even though they were identified as Romanian nationals. Most of these charges were essentially undefended, with the defendant pleading guilty and reference being made to a Romanian ID card having been furnished to the Gardaí.[15] The charges were usually dismissed under the provisions of the Probation Act, 1907 and effectively therefore no penalties were applied. Unlike other persons charged under the provisions of s.12, most Roma persons charged were released on bail after the lodgement of a cash sum. It seemed therefore that there were really no substantive concerns about the identity of the individuals arrested.

Challenges to s.12 Charges

Although no defence was offered to the majority of s.12 charges, not all charges went uncontested. S.12 charges brought against two Roma women, who were both Romanian nationals, were contested ardently and at length, firstly in CCC (FN34) and then in another court on three further occasions.[16] The circumstances surrounding the arrest of these women were that while begging in Dublin city centre they were approached by Gardaí and asked to produce proof of their identity. When they did not immediately produce the required documentation they were arrested and brought to a Garda station. They were searched 'for their own safety' (FN34), and were found to be in possession of Romanian ID cards. Hence, when these women were charged, Gardaí were aware that they were Romanian nationals.

Each of the two defendants had separate legal representation, and at the first hearing the two lawyers conducted a kind of legal tag game with each taking it in turn to argue their case. The first lawyer argued that 's.12 of the Immigration Act, 2004 is used by the "executive" in a discriminatory manner and in a manner which is not consistent with the EU directive on the right of movement and residence of EU citizens' (FN34). She contrasted the position in Ireland with the position in EU countries with national ID systems. Such systems effectively place the same obligation to carry appropriate ID documents on all EU citizens. However, as there is no obligation on Irish nationals to produce ID on demand, she contended that the provisions of s.12 of the Immigration Act, 2004 are contrary to the EU directive on freedom of movement because they fail to treat all EU nationals in the same manner. She further argued that the punishment specified by the legislation is disproportionate to the offence. She noted that plans to introduce a national ID system in Britain would require residents to hold a valid ID card, but not produce it on demand, and the planned penalties for non-compliance would be civil rather than criminal. She told the court, that 's.12 is frankly abused. Time and time again it is used to criminalise, particularly the Roma community which is already marginalised' (FN34). She also referred to a regular practice of the 'executive' of confiscating Romanian ID cards from Roma on the grounds that they were being verified, leaving individuals open to further charges.

The second solicitor took up the baton and argued that the provisions of s.12 were 'not really disposed towards non-nationals who are EU citizens'. He also argued that in the absence of a national identity card system it was discriminatory to apply the provisions of s.12 to EU citizens.

The prosecution for this case was handled by the solicitors' division of the DPP. The solicitor in court struggled to combat the submissions of the defence. She claimed the EU directive had no bearing on the case and referred the court to the statutory instrument which she described as a 'weaker and more limited instrument than the parent document' (FN34). This was contested by the defence, who claimed that the statutory instrument (SI) is the Irish government's attempt to transpose the directive, and it was claimed in this case that the SI is fundamentally flawed. The prosecuting solicitor claimed that the free movement of EU nationals was actually constrained by 'multiple criteria which must be fulfilled by non-nationals'. She then claimed that the Garda had to establish if the women were EU nationals and said: 'She could have been African, she could have been Indian . . . he simply did not know' (FN34). Why this was necessary if the legislation applied equally to EU nationals was not clear. The solicitor for the prosecution then made the rather extraordinary claim that in any event the defendants' free movement had not been impeded by the charge. At this Judge Power interjected and said: 'Well she was arrested, charged and brought before a court, and only granted bail subject to a cash lodgement. I think her free movement could be said to have been impeded' (FN34).

Throughout this lengthy hearing, Judge Power looked uncomfortable and ill at ease.[17] He asked a number of times whether the District Court was the appropriate place for this matter to be decided. On one occasion he said: 'I'm asking you again, is this court competent to decide the proportionality of s.12?' Ultimately he deferred sentencing, saying: 'I'm not going to determine the issue today . . . I'm not entirely clear in my own mind how it all fits together or if it fits together . . . I'm not sure if this court has jurisdiction to decide if a penalty is proportionate' (FN34).

At the next court hearing the state withdrew the s.12 charge against one of the women, with Judge Power commenting: 'Yes, there was a question as to whether she understood the charges' (FN83). Further submissions by the defence made it clear that there was no claim by the state that the defendants had entered the state illegally and what was at issue were the demands made on the defendants to prove their identity while in the state. Judge Power again stated that he did not consider the District Court to be the appropriate place to decide whether the provisions of the Act are discriminatory or provide for disproportionate punishment. The matter was again adjourned. The absence of an interpreter prevented any progress at the next hearing date (FN84) but at the final hearing the second s.12 charge was also withdrawn by the state. In effect the court was able to avoid adjudicating on the claim that the provisions of s.12 are discriminatory and provide for a disproportionate punishment.

Legislative Change

Asylum Applicants and s.12 Charges

The circumstances which impel some asylum applicants to flee their country of origin may be such that they are unwilling to seek identity documents from their country of origin. Those who originate from a country at war or without an effective government may face lengthy delays before they can procure a passport. This meant that some undocumented asylum applicants were liable to arrest and re-arrest under the provisions of s.12 of the Immigration Act, 2004.

This situation prompted the legal representatives of one such woman to seek a judicial review. This review was deferred on a number of occasions but eventually in March 2011 the President of the High Court the Hon. Mr Justice Nicholas Kearns found s.12 of the Immigration Act, 2004 to be unconstitutional. The details of the case and key extracts from the judgement are set out below.

Judicial Review: Dokie v DPP

The judicial review was taken on behalf of an asylum seeker, Ebere Dokie, who claimed to be a national of Liberia. Ms Dokie was charged under the provisions of s.12 of the Immigration Act, 2004 on her arrival at Dublin airport in 2008. She was believed to have travelled to Dublin from Lagos in Nigeria having transited through an unknown European port. On arrival at Dublin airport, Ms Dokie was accompanied by three minor children. Ms Dokie is the mother of only one of these children. She claimed that the other two children were sons of a man she met in Lagos airport who asked her to take the two boys to Ireland. She claimed to have paid an agent $5,000 to arrange for her to travel from Lagos to Dublin and to provide her with passports for herself and her daughter. Ms Dokie was aware that the passports provided were false.

Ms Dokie was in custody from 3 April 2008 until 28 May 2008 when she was released after the District Court judge took a view that the charge was null and void and made 'no order'. She was re-arrested on 29 May 2008 and again charged under the provisions of s.12 of the Immigration Act, 2004. She was granted bail on 23 June 2008 but was unable to take up bail until the terms were adjusted on 15 July 2008. Subsequent to being granted bail in July 2008 Ms Dokie initiated a judicial review. She was not re-arrested during the judicial review proceedings although she did not produce a passport or proof of identity (see www.courts.ie).

The details of this case highlight the tangled and complicated circumstances that can form the background to asylum applications and to breaches of immigration legislation. We can see from this case that at times there may be difficulties in reconciling the security of our borders and upholding immigration legislation with our obligation to offer protection to asylum seekers. It is also evident that it may be very difficult to distinguish those who are genuine asylum seekers from those who are not.

Justice Kearns' finding that s.12 was unconstitutional was largely based on the uncertainty regarding the meaning of what constitutes a 'satisfactory explanation' for failure to produce a passport or equivalent document. He noted that:

> The section as worded has considerable potential for arbitrariness in its application by any individual member of An Garda Síochána. There is no requirement in s.12 that the demanding officer should have formed any reasonable suspicion that the non-national has committed a crime, is about to commit a crime or is otherwise behaving unlawfully before he/she can require the non-national to provide a 'satisfactory' explanation for the absent documents.

He further stated:

> . . . the offence purportedly created by s.12 is ambiguous and imprecise. In my view it lacks the clarity necessary to legitimately create a criminal offence. (www.courts.ie)

However, Justice Kearns found that the punishment provided was not disproportionate because of the importance of having effective immigration control procedures.

Legislative Amendment

The Immigration Act, 2004 has been amended by s.34 of the Civil Law (Miscellaneous Provisions) Act, 2011. The amended legislation now defines a non-national as a person who is not an Irish citizen nor a person who has a right to enter and be resident in the state under EU regulations; for practical purposes this amendment ensures that there is no distinction between the treatment of Irish citizens and citizens of other EU member states. Under the amended legislation, an accused person may be able to enter a defence against a charge if at the time of the alleged offence he or she had reasonable cause for not producing a passport. Prior to amendment it was up to the arresting officer to determine if there was reasonable cause.

Anecdotal evidence has suggested that since the High Court finding in March and the subsequent introduction of amending legislation, fewer people are charged under the amended provisions of s.12. It should be noted however that while members of the Roma community are unlikely to face charges under the amended immigration legislation they may if they are begging face charges under the provisions of the recently introduced Criminal Justice (Public Order) Act, 2011.

Persons Committed to Prison in the Absence of Criminal Charges

During the course of the fieldwork, the researcher observed foreign persons who were not charged with a criminal offence but who were detained in an Irish prison. She also became aware of other categories of foreign persons who do not appear in court but are subject to detention in prison, although the detention is considered civil in nature.

Persons Refused Permission to Land

The statistics published by the IPS indicate that a very high proportion of persons detained in Irish prisons for breaches of immigration law are held for periods of less than eight days. In 2007, 55.1% (2006: 39.4%) of persons detained for breaches of immigration law were held in prison for zero to three days with a further 17.9% (2006: 22.9%) held for four to seven days.[18] These statistics highlighted an anomaly between the observed time taken to process immigration charges in the District Court and the time spent in custody as recorded by the IPS in respect of those detained for breaches of immigration legislation. As already noted, those observed in court charged with immigration offences frequently spent weeks and sometimes even months in prison in pre-trial custody. The duration of the pre-trial detention was normally determined by the length of time it takes the defendant to prove his/her identity to the satisfaction of An Garda Síochána. When identity was established defendants were granted bail. Observation of District Court proceedings and interviews with defence solicitors indicate that when a person was charged with an offence under s.12 of the Immigration Act, 2004 a period of pre-trial detention was normal, and generally exceeded eight days.

Enquiries were made with officials from the IPS in an effort to fully understand the prison statistics. These enquiries revealed that included within those detained for breaches of immigration offences are persons arrested and detained under the provisions of s.5(2)(a) of the Immigration Act, 2003 after they have been refused permission to land. Persons refused permission to land are removed from the state as soon as is practicable, and may only be detained for a maximum period of eight weeks. In many cases it may be possible to remove them on the same day, but in other instances travel arrangements may dictate that a short period of detention is necessary. Persons refused permission to land are not charged with a criminal offence and do not appear before an Irish court unless they seek to challenge their removal from the state. Such challenges are rare, but a number of high-profile cases have received media and political attention amid claims that immigration procedures are arbitrary, and rely unduly on the exercise of discretion on the part of individual immigration officers (Mac Cormaic, 2008; Joyce, 2009:16). Unfortunately, the IPS have not up to now kept records which separately identify non-Irish nationals detained in prison following refusal of permission to land, but it seems likely that a significant proportion of those detained in Irish prisons for short periods of time in relation to breaches of immigration offences are persons who have been refused permission to land.

Persons Subject to Deportation Orders

Persons subject to deportation orders may also be subject to a period of detention in an Irish prison prior to the execution of the deportation order. Such persons do not face criminal charges but are not separately identified in the statistics produced by the IPS.

Persons Detained under the Provisions of the Refugee Act, 1996

In accordance with s.9(8) of the Refugee Act, 1996 where an immigration officer or a member of An Garda Síochána, with reasonable cause, suspects that an applicant:[19]

(a) poses a threat to national security or public order in the state,
(b) has committed a serious non-political crime outside the state,
(c) has not made reasonable efforts to establish his or her true identity,
(d) intends to avoid removal from the state in the event of his or her application for asylum being transferred to a convention country pursuant to section 22,
(e) intends to leave the state and enter another state without lawful authority, or
(f) without reasonable cause has destroyed his or her identity or travel documents or is in possession of forged identity documents,

he or she may detain the person concerned under s.9(8) of the Refugee Act, 1996. The maximum period of detention is unspecified as a judge may commit an asylum seeker to successive periods of twenty-one days in detention while their application is being determined. Persons detained under the provisions of s.9(8) of the Refugee Act are not charged with a criminal offence; their detention is civil rather than criminal. Observations indicate that the provisions of s.9(8) of the Refugee Act are not widely used to detain asylum applicants. Indeed, a GNIB officer indicated to the researcher that just a small number of GNIB officers use these provisions. RC was the only location where persons detained under these provisions were observed. In the two-month period during which fieldwork was conducted in this location seven detained persons were observed; several were observed on more than one occasion. All of the detained persons were male. Of these, one man's asylum application was transferred to another country, four had been released, and two were still in detention on the date that fieldwork concluded.

Persons detained under s.9(8) can be detained for lengthy periods. One man observed was released after having been detained for sixteen weeks. Another man had been arrested and charged under the provisions of s.12 of the Immigration Act, 2004 on his arrival into the state. When questioned by immigration officers on arrival in Dublin, he initially claimed that he was here as a tourist. On cross-examination he explained that he did not lodge his asylum application immediately because he wished to take legal advice first. He was sentenced to three months' imprisonment but was released after just two weeks. On release he was immediately detained under the provisions of s.9(8) of the Refugee Act, 1996. When Judge O'Toole ordered his conditional release after a further six weeks' detention, he commented as follows:

> The applicant's asylum application is at appeal stage. No date has been set for the appeal hearing and it seems uncertain as to when this will take place. It could be July, August or September. The applicant was released on TR[20] and there was no breach of the terms of the TR. He was released on 3 June and had barely stepped out when he was re-arrested. He gave his reasons for coming here and proceeding as he did at Dublin airport. He has been in custody since 3 March, part of that on remand, and has served part of a sentence. Having regard to all of that, I have come to the conclusion that we are running into excessive delay. At this stage this delay is not the fault of the applicant. We should therefore prepare for a conditional release. (FN66)

In conversation later with the GNIB officer who detained this man, the researcher learned that the asylum appeal hearing was indeed not expected until September at the earliest. Despite this, the prosecution claimed in court that the appeal was expected imminently. The same GNIB officer claimed that the circumstances that warranted a detention under s.9(8) were different to those that warranted a person being charged under s.12 of the Immigration Act, 2004, yet one of the instances that he indicated might warrant detention was when a non-Irish national charged under the provisions of the Immigration Act was released on bail prior to their identity being established. However, observations do indicate that District Court judges will not sanction the continued detention of persons under these provisions when they consider the period of detention to be excessive and unreasonable.

Irregular Migration Status Viewed as an Active Choice

It was evident from various comments made by judges that they tended to view those charged with immigration offences as persons who had actively engaged in a process of dissembling to circumvent the laws of the state, rather than persons who may have had to resort to extraordinary measures to ensure their own safety. Almost every defendant charged with an immigration offence, and particularly those arrested at Dublin airport, was presented to the court as an asylum applicant. Judges therefore listened with a certain amount of jaded ennui to the information that the defendant before them had lodged an asylum application. The designation of defendants charged with immigration offences as asylum applicants was so commonplace it effectively lacked any currency in court. It was not unusual to detect a sort of disbelieving tone in the comments made by District Court judges who at times seemed to find it almost impossible to fathom that a person had arrived in Ireland without any ID. This scepticism was bolstered if the court was told that defendants had taken a circuitous route to get to Ireland, passing through a number of different countries before reaching Dublin, or when defendants simply refused to provide any details of their travel routes. Judge Cahill's comment, 'they arrive in on the last flight on a Saturday night, the ID is flushed down the lav, and they take an emory board to their finger tips' (FN67), encapsulates this view of irregular immigrants as actively trying to dodge the immigration laws of the state. Efforts to present clients as desperate, persecuted persons were generally responded to with trite comments regarding the person's ability to get him/herself half way around the world. Despite this view regarding the agency of defendants, as the field note extract set out below highlights, generally once the identity of the defendant was established to the satisfaction of the Gardaí, judges did not seek to impose any additional punishment on defendants charged under the provisions of s.12 of the Immigration Act, 2004.

> Yu Wong is before the court on immigration charges. This woman appears very young. She is extremely thin, which makes her appear especially vulnerable. A Garda from the GNIB gives evidence and notes that the defendant is claiming religious persecution. Hearing this, Judge Murray comments: 'That's a good story . . . but you don't get on a plane without a passport . . . and then you arrive here with no passport . . . the mystery is what happened to the passport in between.' The solicitor indicates that the defendant claims that she gave it to another traveller. The solicitor also tells the court that the defendant has lodged an asylum application. Judge Murray says: 'Nothing previous?' and the solicitor replies: 'No, Judge.' The charges are dismissed under the provisions of the Probation Act and the woman is released. (FN3)

The claim by this defendant that she had given her travel documents to another traveller echoes the claim of a solicitor in SDC who said that Chinese traffickers have people in the departure airports to collect passports/documentation from would-be immigrants who then arrive in Ireland and are unable to establish their identity (FN4).

Identity an Issue for Some Irish Defendants

It should be noted that questions may also arise at times regarding the identity of Irish defendants. Gardaí are currently only allowed to fingerprint persons arrested in relation to specific offences. This means that the majority of persons arrested and charged with minor offences are not subject to fingerprinting (Lally, 2010).

The lack of a means to verify a person's identity can lead to some defendants using one or a number of aliases. On several occasions the same person was included on the court list under a number of different names. Sometimes the names were very similar, suggesting no real attempt to deceive, but on other occasions the names listed were quite different. Doubt over the identity of a defendant can lead to a period in custody before bail will be granted. During one court sitting observed, a young woman with a history of bench warrants came before the court. This woman may have feared that because of her past failures to appear in court she may not have been granted bail. In any event, she gave Gardaí a false name and address, and then compounded this by signing the custody sheet with another name. Perhaps not surprisingly, the state initially objected to bail. During the bail application her solicitor told the court: 'I'm satisfied she is Anne Joyce, and I think she's now satisfied she is Anne Joyce!' (FN9). Another Irish defendant with a history of using aliases observed in RC was refused bail and remanded in custody because of doubts about his identity. The court was told that the man had applied for a passport to satisfy Gardaí regarding his identity.

Conclusion

Immigration policies seek to achieve a number of competing objectives and can be contentious. National borders are permeable and the immigration status of non-citizens can change over time from regular to irregular. The EU aims to create an area of freedom, security and justice for citizens of EU member states but it has been criticised for failing to meet its obligations to third-country nationals who seek asylum. Ireland's decision to criminalise irregular migrants is contrary to the recommendations of the Council of Europe Commissioner for Human Rights.

Observations indicate that those charged under the provisions of s.12 of the Immigration Act, 2004 were frequently subject to a period of pre-trial detention, which in some instances has been lengthy. Judges at times refused to allow persons charged under these provisions to enter guilty pleas until their identity had been verified. Persons convicted under these provisions were rarely sentenced to imprisonment or indeed to any penalty, leading to the conclusion that these provisions were used as a device to allow persons to be detained while the Gardaí verified their identity. Attention has been drawn in particular to the use of s.12 of the Immigration Act, 2004 as a means of controlling members of the Roma community and inappropriately harassing asylum applicants, and to concerns regarding the inappropriate policing of ethnic minorities which may stem from such legislation. The chapter notes that following the introduction of the Civil Law (Miscellaneous Provisions) Act, 2011 amendments to the Immigration Act, 2004 have been introduced which have narrowed the definition of 'non-nationals' to exclude EU citizens and also provide for persons to enter a defence against charges on the grounds of having reasonable cause for not producing a passport.

Foreign nationals may be detained in Irish prisons for breaches of immigration legislation but may not face criminal charges and indeed may not in some instances appear before a court. It is regrettable that the statistics published by the IPS do not distinguish between those subject to civil or administrative detention and those detained pursuant to criminal charges.

Chapter 5 considers the provision and quality of interpretation services in the District Court. The chapter also highlights reluctance on the part of courtroom actors to modulate the pace of proceedings to accommodate interpreters.

Chapter 5

LEP Defendants and Interpretation Services

Introduction

Foreign nationals now regularly appear before Irish courts charged with criminal offences, and many need the assistance of an interpreter to ensure that they fully understand the court proceedings. As the number of foreign defendants has increased, the presence of court interpreters in Irish courts has changed from being almost an exotic oddity to becoming quotidian and unremarkable. Most interpreters are themselves foreign nationals and in many courts they may be the only non-Irish persons, apart from the defendants, who play a role in the courtroom proceedings.

While the CS has put in place arrangements to ensure that when requested by a District Court judge interpreters are provided for criminal defendants, this does not ensure that court proceedings are organised in such a way as to ensure that they can be fully interpreted, or that an interpreter is provided for all defendants who have limited proficiency in English (LEP). There are also ongoing concerns that the service provided is not appropriately regulated, and that the standard of interpreting is not uniformly high.

This chapter points out that at least some court interpreters do not adequately interpret court proceedings, and do not always interact appropriately with defendants. The chapter also presents evidence which suggests that District Court proceedings are frequently not paced in such a manner as to allow interpreters to interpret proceedings fully and accurately. In addition, it appears some courtroom actors in the District Court view the provision of an interpreter for LEP defendants as being something that can be dispensed with if an interpreter is not readily available. This is particularly the case when court appearances effectively only constitute an application for an adjournment. Even when interpreters are provided, there seems to be no expectation that they should diligently endeavour to accurately translate all the court proceedings, and at times their presence constitutes little more than window dressing.

It seems therefore that while interpreters are now frequently present during District Court sittings, there is a reluctance to change the way in which proceedings are conducted to allow the interpreter to accurately and fully translate all courtroom exchanges. The evidence presented suggests that all District Court actors – judges, solicitors, barristers, court presenters, registrars, probation officers and Gardaí – need guidance regarding the work of the court interpreter and the rights of defendants with LEP. This chapter begins by outlining how and by whom interpretation services are provided in the District Court, and draws on courtroom observations to highlight concerns about the competency of some of those appointed as interpreters and the behaviour of both interpreters and other courtroom actors.

Provision of Interpreters

Until recent years, discussions around language and the issue of court interpretative services in Ireland centred around the rights of native Irish speakers (Waterhouse, 2009). However, the sustained and extensive inward migration experienced by Ireland between 1996 and 2008 (CSO, 2009) has resulted in the rapid transformation of Ireland's population, so that the proportion of foreign nationals resident in Ireland in 2008 was estimated as being higher than that in traditional immigrant destination countries such as Britain and France (Vasileva, 2009). In addition, cheaper and more extensive air transport has made Ireland more accessible, leading to greater diversity in short-term visitors to Ireland. Although the recent economic recession has resulted in greatly reduced migrant inflows, the evidence suggests that Ireland will remain a multi-cultural society (Trinity Immigration Initiative, 2010). A consequence of Ireland's more heterogeneous population and its greater accessibility is greater diversity among criminal defendants in Irish courts. This has meant that whereas in the past interpreters were rarely required for court proceedings, they are now commonly present, especially in the District Court, which deals with a far higher number of defendants than any other court.

Waterhouse notes the absence of a statutory right to an interpreter in Ireland and adds: 'There is effective reliance for the right on the court's interpretation of the due course of law and the principles of natural justice, and on the ECHR' (2009:60). The right to an interpreter is addressed under Article 6(3)(e) of the European Convention on Human Rights (ECHR), which stipulates that a person accused of a criminal offence must have the free assistance of an interpreter if he cannot understand or speak the language used in court. In its judgement in *Kamasinski v Austria*, the European Court of Human Rights also stipulates that authorities have a duty not just to provide an interpreter but to exercise control over the adequacy of the interpretation provided (Irish Translators' and Interpreters' Association (ITIA), 2008:3). In practice, the absence of an explicit statutory right to the assistance of an interpreter does not seem to impede the provision of interpretative services in the Irish District Court, and no instances were observed during the course of the fieldwork conducted when a request for the assistance of an interpreter was refused.[1]

The response of the DJELR to the Green Paper on procedural safeguards for suspects and defendants in criminal proceedings throughout the European Union indicates that defence lawyers for defendants awarded legal aid may also independently appoint an interpreter for the defendant (DJELR, undated). Based on courtroom observations, it does not seem to be normal practice for solicitors representing defendants in the District Court to appoint independent interpreters. On occasions, solicitors did indicate that an interpreter would be required for a consultation with their client and the court was requested to certify the interpreters required for these consultations. Judges certify for an interpreter either following the request of a defence lawyer, a Garda or the court presenter, or as a result of their own assessment of the needs of the defendant.

Some defendants erroneously think that requesting an interpreter may somehow derail the court proceedings or result in the court adopting a more lenient approach to the charges. Observations indicate that even when a defendant who has previously displayed good English requests an interpreter in court he will, despite any protests by the arresting Garda, be provided with an interpreter.

> Adam Mabiele was not in court when his name was called and a
> bench warrant was issued for his arrest. A French interpreter

came forward when his name was called and when he failed to appear, the interpreter immediately went to the court clerk with her attendance sheet and as soon as it was signed she left the courtroom. Adam Mabiele later appeared and the case was recalled. Judge Murray asked: 'Does the man speak English?' The arresting Garda replied: 'Yes, Judge, he has very good English.' Judge Murray then asked the defendant again: 'Mr Mabiele, do you speak English?' The defendant raised his hands as if to suggest that he was unclear what was being said. The Garda looked in disbelief at the defendant. Judge Murray asked the defendant: 'Do you understand the charge? It's a charge of drink-driving.' The defendant then said: 'Yes', but waved his hands as if to indicate he disagreed with it. Judge Murray put it back until a French interpreter was in court. (FN22)

The Garda believed that the defendant in this case was feigning an inability to understand the proceedings. In most other instances when a Garda and a defendant present different versions of the facts, the Garda will almost always be believed, but in this instance the court acceded to the defendant's request for an interpreter even though this request was considered unreasonable by a Garda. However, Phelan provides examples of the different approaches taken by Gardaí regarding the provision of interpreters and points out that if Gardaí decide that an interpreter is not required, this may result in no interpreter being provided by the court (Phelan, 2011).

The demand for court interpretation services has increased very markedly in recent years. In 2000, the cost of court interpretation services was €103,000. Costs increased dramatically between 2000 and 2005 when they reached €1,257,000 (CS, 2006:38). From mid-2006 the CS contracted out the provision of interpretation services, and costs are no longer disclosed but are estimated to be in the region of €3m annually (Reilly and McArdle, 2010). The rapid increase in costs suggests that court interpreters have quickly become part of the everyday fabric of Irish courts. The 2010 annual report for the Courts Service notes that interpretation services were provided in over 10,000 cases and in sixty-three languages (CS, 2011:26). A similar level of provision was noted in the 2008 annual report although the level of diversity was greater as interpretation services were provided in seventy-one languages (CS 2009:34). The 2010 CS annual report does not provide any information regarding the most common languages for court interpretation services but in 2008 interpretation services were most commonly provided in Polish, Romanian, Lithuanian, Russian, Mandarin Chinese, Latvian, Portuguese, French, Czech and Arabic (CS, 2009:34). Language cannot always be conflated with nationality or ethnicity. French is an official language of several European countries as well as a range of African countries. Similarly, Portuguese is spoken in a number of African and South American countries as well as in Portugal.

Observations indicate that sometimes when an interpreter in a defendant's first language is not immediately available, they may be offered an interpreter in a language other than their own in the hope that they might understand that language. Many, but not all, defendants from Eastern European countries understand Russian and may be willing to accept a Russian interpreter. On occasion it seemed as if courtroom actors did not quite believe that defendants needed interpreters for a specific language, and that for example Cantonese speakers could not understand Mandarin interpreters. There was also often an unreasonable expectation that because an interpreter was in court they would be able to assist any defendant with LEP. Gardaí were often surprised that the interpreters present could not assist defendants who spoke only Hungarian, or Czech, or Slovak.

The view consistently expressed to the researcher by a variety of court actors was that while the present structure within which interpretative services are provided is not entirely satisfactory, it nevertheless represents a very substantive improvement on the sort of *ad hoc* arrangements in place some years ago when the demand for interpretative services began to increase. Solicitor O'Brien described as 'very chaotic' the situation that pertained a number of years ago when interpreters began to be required regularly in court. She added:

> It was also somewhat unseemly where interpreters were kind of jostling for business . . . it's bad enough when solicitors are but when interpreters were somewhat involved in, you know, trying to promote themselves, and get work in the court . . . then my impression was that they were developing relationships with particular solicitors and sort of almost acting as go-betweens and bringing them the business. It was all *highly* [emphasis in transcript] undesirable.

Following a public tender process, the CS entered into a four-year contract in 2006 with a private company, Lionbridge Ireland, to provide court interpretative services. When Lionbridge are unable to provide an interpreter promptly, CS staff may use other, often locally based, companies to secure an interpreter. Interpreters are paid directly by Lionbridge and receive a modest hourly rate (Tighe, 2009). Interpreters who are hired for the day rather than by the hour receive a lower hourly rate of pay. The ITIA contend that the current rates of pay are 'so low that it is surprising that any qualified interpreters are still willing to work in the courts' (2011:6).

The 2010 CS Annual Report indicates that a procurement exercise commenced in late 2010 to replace the single national provider with regional providers (CS 2011:26). The only information provided regarding the outcome of this procurement exercise is a statement in the 2011 CS Annual Report that 'a review during the year resulted in additional value for the Service in respect of the quality and cost of the interpretation service being provided' (CS 2012:17)

In many courts interpreters will only be present if they are requested by CS staff. However, in courts with a high proportion of foreign defendants a small number of interpreters who interpret the most commonly requested languages may be present during all court sittings. Polish, Russian and Romanian interpreters were always present in CCC during the fieldwork period. For the initial period of the fieldwork a Chinese interpreter was also present in CCC but due to low numbers of Chinese defendants it was decided that a full-time Chinese interpreter was not required. Full-time interpreters were also present towards the end of the fieldwork period in SDC. In some courts, cases involving foreign defendants requiring interpretation services are scheduled for the same court session in an effort to reduce the cost of interpretation services (Reilly and McArdle, 2010).

Which Foreign Defendants Receive the Assistance of an Interpreter?

While the CS previously expressed a commitment to providing an interpreter for defendants for whom neither Irish nor English is their first language (CS, 2005), this commitment has not been restated in the most recent strategy document (CS, 2008b) and the policy of the CS regarding the provision of interpreters to foreign criminal defendants is now unclear (Waterhouse, 2009:60). Observations indicate that in practice interpreters are provided when requested by defence solicitors or court presenters or when a judge assesses the defendant's English to be too limited to allow him to fully comprehend the court proceedings. However, sometimes, as can be seen from the following field note extract, even though it may seem clear that a defendant's English is poor, no effort will be made to provide the defendant with an interpreter.

> When Lukasz Grozinski was called, a young man with a fair complexion came forward. When asked, 'Who is your solicitor?' he answered: 'My name is Lukasz Grozinski.' When Judge Murray was told by the court presenter that his solicitor was not in court, the matter was put back to a second calling. When the matter was later recalled, it proceeded without an interpreter even though it seemed that this man had little or no English. His solicitor indicated that the defendant wished to enter a plea of guilty to a charge of criminal damage. The court was told that the man has no previous convictions and wishes to return to Poland when this matter is concluded. The damage to the property was valued at €210. An amount of €100 had been paid but the solicitor indicated that his client had now lost his job and was not in a position to pay the balance. Judge Murray applied the Probation Act. (FN44)

Pragmatism seems to have greatly influenced both court procedures and the outcome in this case. Presumably the solicitor was aware that his client's English was poor, but his primary objective was to bring the case to a conclusion, and so he did not request an interpreter in case this resulted in an adjournment. Similarly, while Judge Murray would have preferred if the defendant had paid an amount equivalent to the damage caused, his decision to waive the amount unpaid seems almost certainly to have been influenced by the declaration that the defendant was returning to Poland.

Delays in providing an interpreter

When persons arrive in court on foot of a summons, there may be no advance notice that the defendant is not sufficiently proficient in English to understand the court proceedings without the assistance of an interpreter. Interpreters may also not be on hand if Gardaí have not indicated to the courts service that an interpreter is required. This can mean that the defendant is asked to remain in court while efforts are made to locate an interpreter or matters are adjourned. Both courses of action are subject to misinterpretation and misunderstanding on the part of the defendant. On other occasions observed, defendants with LEP were in custody and no efforts were made to ascertain what language they spoke until they were called in court. If the defendant is Polish or Romanian or Ukranian there may be an interpreter on hand but this will not be the case if the defendant is Iraqi or from Brazil. Delays in obtaining an interpreter can result in defendants being unnecessarily detained in custody.

Competency of Interpreters

Court interpreting is a highly skilled job. If court interpreters do not faithfully interpret court proceedings a defendant's right to a fair trial may be infringed. If those employed as court interpreters are not appropriately qualified, they are unlikely to discharge their duties adequately. Some disquiet was expressed by solicitors regarding the uneven quality of court interpretative services. In an interview, a solicitor, Mr Corrigan, commented:

> Interpreting live is probably, just from my own limited experience of different languages, it's probably one of the hardest things a linguist can do, and I don't feel that the standards are there, I'm not aware of standards actually being applied at the moment . . . it's very unsatisfactory and I think there really needs to be a system of regulation and accreditation for interpreters who work in formal court or quasi-judicial-type hearings.

It has been claimed that the qualification standards required for court interpreters are not sufficiently rigorous and that not all those employed as court interpreters under the current system are adequately or appropriately qualified (Bacik, 2007; O'Brien, 2010). Phelan (2011) provides several examples of incompetent interpreters who have been rejected by Irish judges.

Lionbridge indicated that it would be in a position to provide interpreters with the highest level of qualifications (Level 4)[2] stipulated by the CS for the most frequently used languages in court (Bacik, 2007:121). However, the most frequently used languages in court have changed over time, and it is not clear if in fact the qualifications of individual court interpreters are being monitored by the CS. The ITIA have claimed that even Level 4 interpreters may not be qualified to act as court interpreters as:

> . . . a person with a third-level qualification in translation and interpreting would probably not have studied legal terminology

and would not be aware of the ethical challenges that can arise in court. Untrained interpreters may be tempted to act as advocates, to give legal advice or to speak on behalf of a defendant or witness. (2008:6)

In a recent submission to the Courts Service the ITIA suggest that it would be best if the stratification of qualifications was expanded to include a Level 5 which would encompass persons with a qualification in court or community interpreting (ITIA, 2011:3–4).

Discussions with interpreters in court indicate that a very large proportion of those provided by Lionbridge do not have any qualification in translating or interpreting and therefore do not have Level 4 qualifications. It should also be noted that the present payment structures do not reward those with higher qualifications or incentivise inadequately qualified persons to upgrade their qualifications (ITIA, 2008). Nor do they encourage the service provider to recruit qualified interpreters. Lionbridge provides newly recruited interpreters with training in the form of a short induction course and a day spent observing court proceedings in the company of an experienced interpreter. The level of training provided has been criticised by the ITIA (ITIA, 2011).

The Irish Translators' and Interpreters' Association note that:

> Interpreters need advanced linguistic skills that include legal terms, Latin expressions, idioms and slang. They need to actually be able to interpret simultaneously and consecutively. To do this they need to have a good memory and to have note-taking skills. They may be asked to do sight translation of documents in court where they are given a document in a foreign language and asked to read it aloud in English. They also need to have the confidence and integrity to tell the court if they cannot hear what is being said or to ask for clarification if they have not grasped a particular concept. An understanding of court procedures is essential. (2008:6)

The extensive skill set identified by the ITIA as being essential for a court interpreter was often lacking in the court interpreters observed. On several occasions the researcher was asked by interpreters to explain basic legal terms such as 'bench warrant' or 'remand' or 'bail bond'. A number of interpreters were also unclear as to the role of the probation officer. Several did not seem to understand the court proceedings at all. Some left the court when a matter had been 'let stand' and therefore did not seem to understand that the matter would be recalled later in the court sitting. Others remained in court after an adjournment had been granted and the defendant had been remanded on continuing bail even though they were not required to give assistance to any other defendants. Many had excellent English but a small number observed did not appear to have fluent English.

Despite the concerns expressed regarding the competency of interpreters the recent tender for interpretation services issued by the Courts Service only specifies qualifications up to Level 3 and not, as previously, up to Level 4. This is criticised by the ITIA, which points out that the level of competency required from inter-preters is going down rather than up and the low standards set by the Courts Service are not in keeping with the EU Directive on the Right to Interpretation and Translation in Criminal Proceedings, based on planned publication date of October 2013 (see below) (ITIA, 2011).

Confidence to Interrupt Proceedings

District Courts can be noisy places and many witnesses, Gardaí and solicitors do not use the microphones provided. This can mean that only those positioned very adjacent to persons speaking will be able to fully hear what they say. When asked by the researcher if she ever had difficulty hearing testimony in court, one of the interpreters said this was a frequent problem and did a parody of someone mumbling incoherently (FN15). Despite proceedings often being inaudible, interpreters almost never told the court that they were unable to hear clearly enough to interpret properly. One or two interpreters were confident enough to put up their hand and ask that evidence be repeated, but most seemed reluctant to intervene in the flow of proceedings. Sometimes judges will intervene in proceedings when they realise that the interpreter may not be able to hear, or when the speed at which evidence is being given needs to be slower.

> When Yu Wang was called, a young Chinese man was produced from the custody cells and the Chinese interpreter stepped forward to assist him. The court was told that this man's identity had now been verified. The prosecuting Garda was sworn in and began to rattle off evidence regarding this man's arrest. Judge Healy looked at the interpreter and said to her: 'Can you hear?'

> He clearly realised that the interpreter could not accurately trans-
> late the Garda's evidence because of the speed and the volume at
> which it was being delivered. The interpreter said: 'Can you
> speak a little louder and a little slower please . . . thank you.'
> Judge Healy turned to the Garda and said: 'Louder and slower.'
> The Garda repeated the evidence he had already given, pausing
> at intervals. (FN55)

Silent Interpreters

Despite the general perception that the arrangements for the provision of interpreters have improved in recent years and that the
quality of interpretation services has also improved, observations
indicate that some of the interpretative services provided are still of
an unacceptable standard. During the court sittings observed, on
multiple occasions it was noted that interpreters quite simply made
no attempt to interpret court proceedings and just stood mutely
beside the defendant. Solicitors and court presenters generally stand
in front of the defendant and face the judge, and hence have their
back to the interpreter, and so may not be in a position to assess
whether the interpreter is endeavouring to translate the court proceedings. Judges, however, do have a good view of how interpreters
perform their duties, but despite this many did not intervene even
when interpreters were doing nothing except standing silently beside
the defendant. Judge Nolan did interject when he realised that a
Chinese interpreter was not translating the evidence of a Garda and
said: 'You're giving evidence and she's not translating' (FN43). On
another occasion he took a Polish interpreter to task when he felt he
wasn't interpreting the court proceedings and said: 'Are you translating all this?' The Polish interpreter told him that he had agreed
with the defendant to assist him when necessary (FN44).

While in many instances appearances by defendants before the
District Court will be very brief and the interpreter may be able to
easily explain the substantive content of any courtroom exchanges
to the defendant, in other instances when matters are contested, or
bail applications are opposed, matters can be before the court for
quite a considerable length of time. Even on such occasions several
interpreters were observed who simply made no attempt to interpret
the court proceedings to the defendant. A hearing observed in CCC
regarding immigration charges brought against two Roma women

lasted well over an hour (see Chapter 5) and involved complex legal arguments. As this brief field note extract highlights, the bulk of this hearing was not interpreted.

> While both defendants were assisted by a Romanian interpreter, it was very notable that for large tracts of time the Romanian interpreter simply sat on the bench beside the defendants and said nothing. He didn't attempt to translate the lengthy representations made to the court by both the prosecution and defence in relation to the legal substance of the charges. (FN34)

It should be noted, however, that the pace of the exchanges in this matter took no account of the fact that an interpreter was provided to assist the defendants. There could have been no reasonable expectation that the interpreter would have been able to fully translate everything that was said in court.

Another almost-silent interpreter was observed during a lengthy bail application made on behalf of a woman charged under the provisions of s.12 of the Immigration Act, 2004 who had been remanded in custody for four weeks and separated from her minor child while in custody. During the application, the interpreter spoke no more than a handful of words to the defendant. The outcome of this bail application was of the utmost importance to the defendant, and one would have thought that it was absolutely essential that if the process was to be fair, the procedures in place had to ensure that the defendant could understand everything that was said in court; but the procedures in place failed to ensure this.

The interpreter was not within the range of vision of the defence solicitor, and so he did not realise that the interpreter was not endeavouring to interpret the proceedings for the client. The bail application was not successful, but the matter was relisted just two days later. The same interpreter was in court for the second bail application but it seems that the defence solicitor had been told by other courtroom actors that she had done a very poor job, so as he approached her prior to the court session he said: 'I want you to interpret every word that is said in court . . . it is very important that you interpret everything that is said' (FN18). The solicitor later confirmed in a conversation with the researcher that he had been unaware of the interpreter's silence until after the first bail hearing had concluded, but he added: 'Mind you, she [the defendant] does speak English.'

Inappropriate Behaviour of Interpreters

On a number of occasions observed, the behaviour of interpreters appeared not to accord with generally accepted codes of behaviour for court interpreters (see Edwards, 1995). At times interpreters engaged in conversation with defendants and did not simply seek to interpret what was said in court. Rather than an interpreter primarily relaying court proceedings, from time to time it was clear that there was a two-way, and occasionally animated, conversation between the defendant and the interpreter, which sometimes began before the court proceedings commenced or extended after court proceedings were concluded. One instance was also observed where the interpreter inappropriately intervened in a case. The defendant was charged with using a false instrument. The case against the defendant centred on the authenticity of a Romanian driving licence. A Garda from the documents section was in court to support the state's claim that the licence was not authentic. The interpreter intervened by producing his own Romanian driving licence and passing it to the defence solicitor, who then passed it to the expert from the documents section suggesting that it could be used as a comparator. Judge Murray rebuked the interpreter sharply and said it was not his role to assist the defence (FN44).

Interpreters Aware of Poor Interpreting Standards

Many court interpreters are aware that some of those who are employed as interpreters in the District Court are not competent. On several occasions interpreters asked the researcher: 'Have you come across interpreters who don't speak English yet?' One said she was often appalled by the quality of court interpretative services. While observing proceedings in CCC, the researcher saw what appeared to be two Chinese defendants, a man and a woman, before the court, standing silently side by side. However, as details of the case were disclosed it became apparent that only the man was a defendant. The researcher turned to the Romanian interpreter who was sitting beside her and asked: 'Is the woman an interpreter?' The Romanian interpreter nodded and said: 'Yes, but not a very good one.'

Interpreters are also aware that proceedings in many District Court venues are not recorded and therefore the accuracy of their work cannot subsequently be reviewed. One interpreter told the researcher that he no longer took assignments in the Circuit Court because his work was subject to scrutiny via court transcripts and audio recordings. He told the researcher: 'I'm not paid enough for that – I can work here [District Court].'

Defence Counsel and Interpreters

Observations indicate that in practice the provision of interpreters is somewhat ad hoc, with the same defendant appearing on occasions with an interpreter and on other occasions without an interpreter. While solicitor O'Brien commented during interview that in her view, 'It's just unacceptable that people don't have an interpreter if English isn't their first language. There's too much at stake . . . too much can be missed if they're not following everything', observations of court proceedings indicate that other solicitors are not quite as concerned that their clients fully understand court proceedings. Solicitors seem willing on occasion to dispense with interpreters when they are not readily available. This attitude is clearly revealed in the following brief field note extract.

> A solicitor called out prior to the commencement of the court session: 'Is there a French interpreter in court?' Getting no response, he spoke to a plain-clothes Garda and said: 'Sure we can fire ahead without the interpreter if need be.' (FN7)

Whether or not a defendant is assisted by an interpreter may depend on who represents him in court. Tomas Varannai was observed in CCC without an interpreter (FN42), and then in RC some ten weeks later where he was assisted by a Russian interpreter (FN67). Lech Rutyna was assisted in court in CCC by a Polish interpreter (FN32), and then was observed in court some six weeks later without an interpreter (FN47). This man's seemingly shifting requirement for an interpreter was noted and commented on by Judge Power, who said simply: 'I think he has been here without an interpreter on other occasions' (FN32). During the court proceedings observed when this man was provided with an interpreter, his solicitor described him as a man who had studied literature at third level and who had 'an excellent grasp of the English language' (FN32). Perhaps the solicitor did not realise how incongruous this statement seemed given that his client was assisted by an interpreter in court.

Many instances were observed when solicitors representing foreign nationals who were not assisted by interpreters in court indicated that an interpreter would be required for future court appearances or for a hearing date. It seemed that among some solicitors at least, there is a belief that interpreters are only really necessary when a case comes to a conclusion. On other occasions, despite the court having previously certified for an interpreter, on finding that an interpreter was not immediately available, solicitors waived the provision of an interpreter claiming that their client's English was in fact adequate.

> When Robert Rukas was called, Judge Power asked if there was a Slovak interpreter in court. The judge, the registrar and the solicitor turned towards the interpreters' bench and were met by shaking heads. The defendant's solicitor told the court that he was satisfied to proceed without the interpreter and that his client's English was good. The judge was clearly irritated by this remark and said: 'What is the point of having an interpreter assigned when it doesn't appear to be necessary . . . I don't see why the state is paying for interpreters that are not required.' (FN32)[3]

Sometimes proceedings are 'let stand' to allow time for an interpreter to be procured but eventually go ahead without the interpreter (FN42), or commence when the interpreter is not present (FN45). There seems to be a very widespread view among District Court actors that the provision of an interpreter for defendants with LEP is something that can be dispensed with when the procurement of an interpreter results in an inconvenient delay. Interpreters are not viewed as being essential to ensure fair procedures are applied in respect of defendants with LEP.

Frequently interpreters are asked by defence lawyers to accompany them to explain matters to their clients after the matter has come before the court. Gardaí may also ask interpreters to assist them to communicate with defendants. The general view seems to be that pre- and post-court conversations with the aid of an interpreter can adequately explain to the defendant what is expected to happen in court or what has just happened in court and it is not critical that actual courtroom proceedings are fully interpreted.

Adjusting the Pace of Court Proceedings to Accommodate Interpretation

If interpreters are to fully interpret courtroom exchanges, the conduct and pace of courtroom proceedings must be adjusted. It is essential that as far as possible courtroom actors speak in turn and when speaking at length adopt a slower speech pattern, or pause at intervals to accommodate the interpreter. Observations indicate that very often there is no adjustment to the pace of courtroom proceedings when an interpreter is provided, and there almost seems to be an expectation that the interpreter will be able to explain matters to the defendant afterwards, and so not take up any additional court time. Much of what is said in court is routine and formulaic. Courtroom actors may not be conscious that they are speaking at a pace which hampers efforts to interpret. When defendants are assisted by an interpreter, courtroom actors must accept that it is necessary to adopt a slower pace of speaking as otherwise interpreters will not be able to fully interpret what is said.

When District Court judges are faced with very lengthy case lists, they may feel that the dictates of the court list preclude the allocation of the extra time needed to allow interpreters to do their job properly. A solicitor (Ms O'Brien) commented in interview on how District Court proceedings can be rushed, and noted:

> Sometimes you definitely get the impression that things are being missed and that the defendant hasn't quite followed the significance of the proceedings or got all the nuances of it . . . it's probably to do with the turnover in the District Court and the time allotted to each case . . .

On occasions, even though defendants are provided with an interpreter, they may answer questions in English. As solicitor O'Brien noted:

> It can get frustrating sometimes where a defendant has been assigned an interpreter but he or she has relatively good English and then they're inclined to answer in English, perhaps when a hearing is being run, and the defendant himself or herself is giving evidence, and then whilst the question is being translated into their own language for them they reply in English but not so well . . . and then you're in a position where you just say, 'Look would you just answer in your own language and then we're not missing anything', and then that can be interpreted . . . so sometimes that can happen.

When a defendant is being cross-examined by a Garda or a prosecutor, they can be reluctant to accommodate the interpreter. They may interrupt the defendant, speak rapidly and adopt a hectoring and even an intimidating stance. Some defendants may then feel pressured to answer questions in English. In one case observed the defendant was provided with a Russian interpreter. The charges against him were contested and the subject of a hearing. The defendant gave his evidence partially in English and partially in Russian. He was interrogated by the arresting Garda, who largely ignored the interpreter. The rapid-fire nature of the Garda's questioning made it impossible at times for the interpreter to interpret fully. The interpreter did not ask for the pace of the proceedings to be adjusted and the judge (Judge Williams) did not seek to choreograph the proceedings in a more orderly fashion so that the interpreter could do her job properly. Only the defending barrister seemed to feel that the proceedings were not being conducted in a fair manner and at one point he did speak sharply to the Garda (FN47).

It seems that there are no plans afoot to adjust the pace of court proceedings to accommodate full and complete interpretation of proceedings. The tender document recently issued by the CS indicates that the interpretation services that are required are 'consecutive interpretations only'.[4] This is described by the ITIA as 'alarming' as 'interpreters do not have to interpret what the judges, lawyers and witnesses are saying apart from when they address the defendant directly in the form of questions' (2011:4). The ITIA note the need to provide both consecutive and whispered simultaneous interpretation to defendants throughout the course of a court case. They claim that the defendant cannot understand the case without whispered simultaneous interpretations. The ITIA claim that the limited form of interpretation stipulated by the CS is contrary to the ECHR. The ITIA also points out that inadequate or incomplete interpreting may provide grounds for an appeal or for claims of a mistrial (ITIA, 2011).

The Interpretative Role of Defence Counsel

It should perhaps be remembered that the language used in legal settings and in the District Court may at times be impenetrable to many English-speaking defendants. The social milieu of many District Court defendants bears little resemblance to that of many legal professionals and, as can be seen from the following field note extract, this is evident from differences in the language used by both groups and can lead to misunderstandings and frustration on both sides.

> At one point during today's proceedings the background noise grew to an unacceptable volume. The courtroom was very crowded and quite a number of people were standing at the back of the court. Judge O'Higgins addressed one man and said: 'Have you any business in court?' He replied: 'Yeah.' Judge O'Higgins asked: 'What business?' and the reply was: 'I'm in court.' Judge O'Higgins looked exasperated and asked: 'As what?' The man who was being interrogated now looked puzzled and repeated: 'I'm in court.' Judge O'Higgins then asked: 'Are you a defendant?' and the man replied: 'Yeah', as if to say: 'That's what I already told you!' (FN82)

Courtroom discourse is framed in formal, measured phrases, some of which are commonly used only in legal settings, and in the District Court some of the phrases used are specific to the District Court. The argot of the court is quite frankly an alien language to most of those who appear as defendants, whether or not they are Irish nationals. Defendants are not expected to be proficient in the argot of the court, and generally are given very limited opportunities to speak in court. Unrepresented defendants have more opportunities to address the court than those who have legal counsel but are often encouraged to seek legal representation. The court may recommend that a defendant seeks legal representation primarily to ensure that the interests of the defendant are protected, but such recommendations may also be partially motivated by the recognition that the work of the court will generally proceed at a faster pace when matters are handled by legal professionals who effectively interpret courtroom exchanges for their clients. It is routine for defence lawyers to explain to defendants, either outside the court or within the body of the courtroom, the substantive outcome of their court appearance in a language which more closely approximates to their vernacular.

Conclusion

The rapid growth in demand for court interpretation services in Ireland has resulted in a compromise between the speedy delivery of interpretative services and the quality of the services provided. The view seems to have been taken that it is better to have any interpreter, however poorly qualified, than no interpreter at all. While there is evidence that the standard of court interpreting has improved, the continued absence of audio recordings of many

District Court sittings makes it impossible to adequately monitor or assess the quality of interpreting in the court.

The need for interpretative services has not been fully embraced by many courtroom actors, who continue to view it as something which can be dispensed with or used intermittently and sparingly. Indeed the CS seem reluctant to accept that defendants may not gain a full understanding of courtroom proceedings from the interpretation only of exchanges between the defendant and other courtroom actors. Properly accommodating defendants who require the assistance of court interpreters will mean reducing the current length of court lists and allowing more time for the court to deal with defendants with LEP. All courtroom regulars need to be educated regarding the role of the interpreter (Phelan, 2011), and there must be recognition that the interpreter is essential to ensuring that LEP defendants are treated fairly.

The European Commission (EC) passed a directive on 20 October 2010 regarding the right to interpretation and translation in criminal proceedings (EU, 303, 2010). The directive came into force in October 2013. Article 5 of the directive sets out the requirement to safeguard the quality of interpretation and translation provided to those facing criminal charges. EU member states[5] now have an obligation to ensure that interpreters used in criminal court settings are appropriately qualified. The implementation of this directive will require the establishment of a system which will provide for the accreditation and regulation of interpreters and the management of a register of qualified interpreters. The recommendations of the European Parliament Committee on Civil Liberties, Justice and Home Affairs (LIBE), which have been supported by the ITIA (2010), point to specific issues which need to be addressed to implement the directive. The recommendations are as follows:

- Training for judges, lawyers, the police and relevant court personnel so they have a better understanding of when it is appropriate to call an interpreter and of what exactly is involved in the interpreter's work.
- A right of appeal against a decision that there is no need for interpreting.
- A system of training, qualification and accreditation of translators and interpreters for legal work.
- A national register of independent professional translators and interpreters.
- Sufficient time to produce translations and to provide interpreting.

If these recommendations were embraced and implemented, the District Court could claim that fair procedures are applied to LEP defendants there. At present no such claim can be made.

Chapter 6

Conclusion

Introduction

This book focuses on the lowest tier of the Irish criminal court system, the Irish District Court, and in doing so provides not only a detailed account of the work of the court but valuable insights regarding the wider Irish criminal justice system. The book draws on courtroom-based research for which the primary research subjects were non-Irish/non-UK District Court defendants who are referred to as foreign defendants. The research set out to consider whether fair procedures are applied to all defendants before the court; to determine whether there are structural biases within the Irish criminal justice system which contribute to the criminalisation of foreign nationals; to assess the scale of the presence of foreign nationals in the Irish District Court; and to assess the sentencing decisions of the Irish District Court. Conclusions regarding each of these issues are presented later in this chapter. As the research progressed some activities of other arms of the Irish criminal justice system also came under scrutiny.

The overwhelming majority of committals to Irish prisons arise from decisions made by the District Court, therefore it provides the ideal location to study the processes which culminate in committals to Irish prisons. A series of decisions by various criminal justice actors can result in accused persons being remanded in custody and in the imprisonment of offenders. The sentences of Irish District Court judges are undoubtedly shaped by the personal orientations and philosophies of individual judges, but judges also take account of the actions and attitudes of other criminal justice actors in deciding whether or not to impose a sentence of imprisonment. So, certain offences may be policed more diligently than others and certain charges may be prosecuted with vigour rather than with a kind of benign disapproval; similarly, assessments by probation officers may be subtly disapproving rather than optimistic in tone; judges are sensitive to these differences and will be slow to disregard the views of other criminal justice actors. The observation of courtroom processes provides insights into the decisions and actions of all the various actors which culminate in imprisonment.

The Irish criminal justice system and the criminal justice systems of all developed countries now process defendants whose origins can be traced across the globe. This presents challenges to criminal justice systems which are based on local and national traditions and practices. This book recognises those challenges by focusing largely on foreign rather than Irish defendants. This conclusion begins by considering the perceptions of and evidence for an immigration–crime nexus, and the link between immigration and recent penal expansionism.

Immigration, Crime and Penal Expansionism

Despite the somewhat contradictory empirical evidence (see, *inter alia*, Sun and Reed, 2007; Ousey and Kubrin, 2009), perceptions of an immigration–crime nexus are long-standing (Abbott, 1931), and can be linked to historical rituals and practices of expulsion (see Bremner, 1983; Stern, 1991; Vazsonyi and Killias, 2001), and especially the practice of transportation. The British found that the transportation of criminals conveniently removed many who were considered maladjusted or malevolent from the British mainland while also providing a much-needed source of labour to the colonial settlers (Abbot, 1931). American independence finally halted the westward journeys of British convict ships. The use of off-shore prison ships known as 'Hulks' provoked great contention, so Britain turned to the 'desperate experiment' of founding a colony in the distant lands discovered by Captain Cook to exclusively house criminals (Lewandowski, 1993:8). Australia and Tasmania became the new destinations for Britain's unwanted convicts, and Britain's Eastern colonies continued to receive convict ships until transportation finally halted in 1868.

Other European countries followed the example of the British and instituted their own versions of transportation. Penal colonies were established by the Dutch in the East Indies, by the Portuguese in Angola, and by the French in Algeria, New Caledonia, and French

Guiana, and it was 1952 before the last penal colony finally closed (see Bender, 1992; Toth, 2006). So, well into the twentieth century the practice of transporting convicted criminals to distant foreign lands continued, a practice which can only have served to support already existing suspicions and fears of foreigners and strangers.

In recent years, research suggests that the perceived immigration–crime nexus has strengthened both internationally (Simon and Sikich, 2007) and in Ireland (Watson et al., 2007). The perception that immigration is linked to crime has been used by right-wing politicians to stoke up support and inflame anti-immigrant sentiments (Collins, 2003). Modern insecurities about national (De Koster et al., 2008:722) and individual identity also contribute to negative views of immigration which help to perpetuate the perception of the immigration–crime nexus. In addition, increased rates of transnational and international crime (Berdal and Serrano, 2002) fuel the belief that foreigners are dangerous and crime-prone. Widespread fear of crime (Garland, 2001) has made crime and criminal justice processes more politicised than in the past, and linking crime to foreigners can be a convenient way of displacing state responsibility for crime. Increased suspicion and surveillance of immigrants in Europe may therefore be a product of these processes and not simply stem from their economic marginalisation.

Until recently, social theorists have provided us with a selection of heuristic frameworks which explain why immigration is a force that will increase crime, either through the actions of immigrants themselves or due to the disproportionate targeting and harsher treatment of immigrants by criminal justice processes. Immigration has also been linked to increasing levels of social disorder and instability which undermine the informal social controls that discourage criminal behaviour.

However, newly emerged theoretical perspectives on the relationship between immigration and crime suggest that immigration may not contribute to increases in crime, and indeed may be associated with a reduction in crime in certain contexts (Hagan and Palloni, 1999; Martinez and Lee, 2000; Sampson, 2006, 2008; Hagan et al., 2008; Lee and Martinez, 2009). The crime-reducing impact of immigration has been explained by reference to factors such as selective migration, higher levels of traditional family structures and economic revitalisation of poor areas.

Theoretical understandings of immigration as a criminogenic force are not supported by the bulk of the limited available empirical research. Recent North American research suggests that immigration does not increase crime and may even be a crime-reducing force (Lee et al. 2001; Reid et al., 2005; Sampson 2008; Ousey and Kubrin, 2009). However, this picture is not replicated in Europe.

It should be noted that our knowledge about how and why foreign nationals come into contact with European criminal justice systems, and how they are treated by such systems, is remarkably limited, especially when one considers the growth in the proportion of foreign nationals in European prison populations (Van Kalmthout et al., 2007). Claims of hyper-incarceration and hyper-criminalisation of immigrants (Wacquant, 1999; De Giorgi, 2010) lack authority because of the absence of supporting empirical evidence. Research efforts are constrained by limitations in statistical databases. While details of nationality appear to be routinely collected by European prison authorities, there is no standard practice regarding the collection and publication of the nationality and residency status of individuals who come into contact with other arms of European criminal justice systems such as the police, the courts and the probation services. The limited research that has been carried out in Europe suggests that recent immigrants, or at least some groups of immigrants, have a greater involvement in criminal activity than the native population (Vazsonyi and Killias, 2001; Martens, 2007; Sun and Reed, 2007; Killias, 2009).

It seems clear that the relationship between crime and immigration is not predetermined; diversity in the profiles of recent immigrants, host country characteristics, and local area features all influence the relationship between crime and immigration. Before considering the relationship between immigration and crime in Ireland, let us consider one of the most influential perspectives presented with regard to immigration and crime.

Immigration and the Political Economy of Punishment

The critical materialist theoretical perspective, known as the political economy of punishment, stems from the work of Rusche and Kirchheimer (1939) and contends that the penal apparatus of capitalist societies is used to ensure a flexible, compliant supply of labour. The penal arm of the state is therefore understood as being integral to the working of capitalist economies because of the role it plays in controlling the labour force. Workers are induced to provide their labour and avoid criminal sanctions by ensuring that the conditions of penal confinement are more unattractive than the living conditions of even the lowest-paid worker (De Giorgi, 2010).

However, penal confinement is not used at the same rate in all capitalist societies, and the conditions of confinement also vary greatly. Analysts who put forward a 'soft' version of the political economy of punishment recognise that the high levels of penal punitiveness that are associated with the relatively unfettered capitalism found in liberal regimes are not found in all capitalist societies (Cavadino and Dignan, 2006; Lacey, 2008).

The individualistic ethos of liberal welfare regimes marginalises and excludes those who do not add value in the economic arena, and is consistent with the exclusion and punishment of those who break the law. In contrast, social democratic welfare states (Esping-Andersen, 1990) are characterised by a commitment to social equality which is evidenced by generous and universal state social welfare provision. The social institutions of such societies are therefore more inclusive, and primarily seek to re-socialise rather than exclude those who engage in crime. This form of capitalism is consistent with low levels of penal punitiveness and humane conditions of confinement (Cavadino and Dignan, 2006). Conservative corporatist welfare states (Esping-Andersen, 1990) adopt centrist and consensual rather than majoritarian democratic processes, and support traditional family structures. Such regimes provide conditional rather than universal social rights and moderate levels of welfare support, and are less inclusive than social democratic welfare regimes. Moderate levels of penal punitiveness are associated with conservative corporatist regimes (Cavadino and Dignan, 2006).

Lacey (2008) also distinguishes between levels of punitiveness in liberal and coordinated market economies. Firms in Liberal Market Economies (LMEs) are highly sensitive to short-term market mechanisms and inter-firm relationships are competitive. Firms demand flexible workforces which are adjusted in accordance with shifts in demand (Hall and Soskice, 2001). This results in widespread job insecurity. She points out that LMEs produce large pools of unskilled labour, and many unskilled workers are at risk of coming under the control of the penal arm of the state.

In contrast, the institutional structures of Coordinated Market Economies (CMEs) produce workers with high levels of vocational skills which are required to produce the high-quality goods that are typical of CMEs. Job security and income support are high in CMEs and relationships between firms are co-operative (Hall and Soskice, 2001). The institutional structures in CMEs therefore promote a stable and inclusive environment which offers workers greater protection against economic marginalisation than they are afforded in LMEs. This results in lower levels of penal punitiveness than those found in LMEs (Lacey, 2008). However, 'outsiders', who may not have the necessary vocational skills required to fit into CMEs, may have difficulty integrating into such regimes, and if present in sufficient numbers may undermine support for inclusionary policies.

Kilcommins et al. (2004) illustrate how a country's political economy may be structured so that punitiveness is subtly disguised, and imprisonment may be engineered through the use of institutions outside the criminal justice system. They establish that Ireland's low crime rates in the early decades after independence were largely a product of its stagnant economy, which prompted many to emigrate, and the reliance on a whole collection of coercive institutions such as mother and baby homes, Magdalene laundries, industrial and reform schools and county homes to 'manage' those that were surplus to the needs of the Irish economy. They provide a detailed account of the extent of repressive control exercised in Ireland over groups such as unmarried mothers, orphans, the mentally ill and the destitute of all ages who were 'sentenced' to confinement, often for very long periods, in an array of institutions and asylums, not for criminal behaviour but simply by virtue of their marginal position on the fringes of Irish social and economic life.

Proponents of the political economy of punishment have explained recent penal expansionism by pointing to economic restructuring in developed capitalist societies (see Wacquant, 2001, 2009). Economic restructuring has resulted in the loss of many manufacturing jobs as low-cost manufacturing bases in less-developed countries have replaced many higher-cost manufacturing facilities in developed countries. Competition from manufacturers in cheaper, less-developed countries has also eroded the pay and reduced the security attaching to the jobs that remain. Technological advances have also resulted in lower labour inputs in many manufacturing and agricultural processes. This means that in developed capitalist economies many of those with low levels of education, and especially young men, are surplus to the requirements of the labour market, or can only access employment which yields minimum wage rates. Economic restructuring has therefore resulted in a bigger proportion of the workforce of developed capitalist societies being at risk of economic and social marginalisation.

It is contended that the economically marginalised are increasingly controlled by the state through a combination of 'workfare' and 'prisonfare' (Wacquant, 2009). Policy shifts which result in restrictive and contingent welfare and an expansion of the penal arm of the state are presented as devices to control those who are decoupled from, or who have only a tenuous attachment to, the labour force (Wacquant, 2009, 2010). These shifts have resulted in the 'double regulation of poverty by the joint action of punitive welfare-turned-workfare and an aggressive penal bureaucracy' (Wacquant, 2010:202).

In America, penal expansionism has disproportionately affected the African-American community (Pettit and Western, 2004; Western, 2006; Lynch, 2007), and in particular young African-American men who face rates of incarceration eight times those of white men (Western and Pettit, 2006:16). In Europe, analysts have claimed that penal expansionism is largely fuelled by foreigners and immigrants who as a group are especially at risk of economic marginalisation (Wacquant, 1999; De Giorgi, 2006, 2010). The higher risk of economic marginalisation of migrants stems from lower job security and their limited access to, or exclusion from, the formal labour market and the income supports offered to the native population. The economic marginalisation of migrants is also linked to regulations which seek to privilege native workers by restricting access to labour markets. Migrants who are excluded from the formal economy are especially vulnerable. When breaches of immigration legislation are criminalised, immigrants also have more opportunity to breach the criminal code and may be subject to greater surveillance by law enforcement officers.

Drawing on evidence of the experience of Irish migrants, this book presents a more nuanced view of the link between immigration and penal expansionism than that which has been suggested previously by proponents of the political economy of punishment (see Wacquant, 1999; De Giorgi, 2006, 2010).

Understanding the Immigration–Crime Nexus in Ireland

The relationship between immigration and crime in Ireland is complex. There are a number of reasons why migrants might be expected to have higher offending rates than Irish nationals (gender/age profile) but also reasons which point to lower offending rates (higher levels of education/higher rates of employment), and the risk of offending differs significantly between national groups (see Chapter 2). Statistical limitations mean that in the Irish context rates of offending among non-Irish nationals are not known and can only be inferred from their presence among the Irish prison population.

The rapid growth in the committal of foreign nationals to Irish prisons has been documented and analysed in this book. Such growth during a period of economic boom and substantial inward migration was not unexpected, although the scale and speed of the increase was perhaps surprising. The changes in the pattern of committals to Irish prisons since the end of the economic boom are particularly interesting.

Ireland has been in a period of economic recession since 2008. Migrants in Ireland are more at risk of economic marginalisation, which is linked to a higher risk of offending, than the native population. Although most national groups of migrants had very high rates of employment and low rates of unemployment in 2006 (CSO, 2008), the contraction in employment that has accompanied the current economic recession has disproportionately affected foreign nationals so that the unemployment rate of foreign nationals in Ireland is now higher than the unemployment rate of Irish nationals (OECD, 2010). Discrimination may also contribute to the unemployment rate of foreign nationals (McGinnity et al., 2009). Foreign nationals are also more likely than natives to have difficulty satisfying the habitual residency condition which is necessary to receive state income supports.

As Irish legislation provides that certain breaches of immigration legislation are criminal offences, this means that foreign nationals face a higher risk of criminalisation than the native population. The criminalisation of immigration breaches may result in foreign nationals being subject to greater police surveillance than the native population.

One might therefore expect that a significant contraction in the labour market, such as that recently experienced, would result in a higher proportion of the more economically vulnerable foreign nationals being committed to Irish prisons. However, the proportion of foreign nationals committed to Irish prisons fell in 2008, and again in 2009 (see Prologue), when the number of jobs in the Irish labour market fell sharply. This fall coincided with a very substantial reduction in the number of PPS numbers allocated to foreign nationals joining the Irish labour market in 2008 and 2009 (OECD, 2010), and a return to net outward migration (CSO, 2009). Therefore, since 2008 fewer new migrants have arrived in Ireland and some existing migrants have left. This suggests that migrants' response to changed economic conditions and economic marginalisation may be as important as structural conditions in determining the risk of criminalisation.

As migrants may be more likely than the native population to respond to unemployment by moving to a location where employment opportunities are more plentiful (see Schundeln, 2007), the impact of greater levels of economic marginalisation may be different for both groups. While greater levels of economic marginalisation may contribute to higher rates of offending in the native population, offending rates in the migrant population may not increase, or increase to a lesser degree, as migrants' response to economic marginalisation may be to return to their country of origin or to move to another host country, or they may simply choose not to come. Migrants with higher levels of education are more likely to match the skill profiles sought by other host countries,[1] and are also more likely to have the financial resources to relocate. As, on average, migrants to Ireland in recent years have had very high levels of education, many may be able to relocate easily if they so choose.

Ireland's migrant population also includes the highest proportion of EU citizens of any EU member state with the exception of Luxembourg (Vasileva, 2009). As EU citizens can move freely within the EU, and as many EU member states have intra-EU-oriented labour policies, EU migrants are likely to have higher levels of mobility than non-EU migrants.

In comparison to most OECD countries, family-based migration to Ireland is small (see Crosscare Migrant Project, 2008; Lowell, 2009). This reflects Ireland's very short history as a destination country for migrants. Most Irish migrants in recent years were pulled to Ireland by the strength of its economic performance and the prospect of employment. While Ireland's economy continues to shed jobs it is unlikely to remain an attractive location for unemployed migrants who are motivated largely by economic considerations. Thus, economic migrants without work who view Ireland as a temporary destination may well choose to return home or move elsewhere. Migrants who were pushed into migration because of conflict or religious or political persecution are unlikely to respond in the same way to changes in the labour market.

The experience in Ireland suggests that the extent to which immigrants drive penal expansionism will be greatly influenced by the characteristics of the immigrant population. Penal expansionism is less likely to be fuelled by foreign nationals in European countries that attract mainly economic migrants, especially economic migrants who are well educated and therefore likely to be more mobile. Within Europe, EU citizens are especially mobile.

Thus, penal expansionism is more likely to be driven by foreign nationals in countries that attract a large proportion of migrants who are relatively immobile. The mobility of irregular, and low-skilled, migrants is likely to be especially limited and hence the presence of a large cohort of such migrants may be linked to penal expansionism.

As discussed in Chapter 2, unexpectedly low numbers of several of the largest national groups of foreign nationals were observed among the defendants before the District Court. Despite the greater mobility of EU citizens and the ease with which EU citizens can access the Irish labour market, EU citizenship or the absence thereof was not found to be consistent with low or high levels of offending.

Therefore, while acknowledging the structural disadvantages faced by immigrants, and their higher risk of criminalisation, it is argued that we should expect local and national economic, legislative and procedural differences, along with variations in migration patterns, to produce a disparate rather than a consistent pattern of immigrant criminalisation and incarceration. Claims of hyper-incarceration and hyper-criminalisation rely on statistics that do not distinguish between permanent and temporary foreign nationals or indeed foreign nationals who may have been arrested and charged prior to entering a country (O'Nolan, 2011); they are simply not adequately supported by empirical evidence.

Immigrants' contribution to penal expansionism will be greatly dependent on key characteristics of the immigrant population, and in particular their level of education and socio-economic status. EU citizenship was not found to be a crucial determinant of criminalisation in Ireland and consequently the evidence presented in this book does not support claims regarding the hyper-criminalisation of non-EU immigrants (De Giorgi, 2010).

Socio-economic class rather than nationality was found to be the most crucial factor which influenced the risk of criminalisation. Higher socio-economic class protects citizens and non-citizens alike from the structural bias within law enforcement processes, discussed below, which results in resources being targeted at particular types of offences and offenders.

Blanket claims of hyper-criminalisation of immigrants ignore national and local variations in policies and practices and indeed in patterns of migration. Macro-level analysis of criminal justice statistics may also cloak important variations in patterns of offending.

Fair Procedures

The research conducted revealed a certain tension in the District Court between ensuring procedural fairness and achieving procedural efficiency. It can seem at times that the court is unduly orientated towards getting to the end of its lengthy caseload rather than dispensing justice; this can result in impatience with cases/procedures which are considered to take up too much of the court's time.

The main issue of concern in relation to the procedures applied to foreign nationals arose in relation to court interpreters. The research revealed a number of concerns regarding the provision of interpreters in the District Court. Not all interpreters appeared to have the skills necessary to competently interpret court proceedings. There was also an observed reluctance to adjust the pace of court proceedings to accommodate interpreters and at times a willingness to proceed despite the absence of a requested interpreter. The interpretation services sought by the Courts Service only provide for interpretation of direct exchanges with defendants rather than the interpretation of all courtroom exchanges (ITIA, 2011). It is argued that this level of court interpretation is not sufficient to ensure fair procedures are in place for defendants with limited proficiency in English. It also reflects the very passive and minor role that is generally afforded to District Court defendants.

Structural Bias in the Irish Criminal Justice System and Foreign Nationals

The research conducted in the Irish District Court which forms the basis for this book set out to establish whether structural provisions within the Irish criminal justice system contribute to the criminalisation and imprisonment of foreign nationals. The research shows that structural bias against foreign nationals does exist in the Irish criminal justice system through the criminalisation of immigration offences. Although the European Commissioner on Human Rights has strongly argued that irregular migrants should not be criminalised (COECHR, 2010), Ireland has not followed the recommendations of the commissioner in this regard. The criminalisation of immigration offences and in particular the provisions of section 12 of the Immigration Act, 2004, prior to amendment (see below), and the potential discriminatory use of this legislation are discussed in some detail in Chapter 4.

In March 2011 the High Court found that certain provisions of the Immigration Act, 2004 were unconstitutional. This decision resulted in an amendment of this legislation (see Civil Law (Miscellaneous Provisions) Act, 2011, s.34). The amended legislation now effectively excludes EU nationals from the definition of 'non-national' and allows persons to present a defence of 'reasonable cause' against any charges brought. These changes are welcomed but it is still the case that certain non-Irish persons may be criminalised due to their irregular immigration status.

The High Court's decision was reported in the press (see, *inter alia*, Carolan, 2011; *The Irish Times*, 16 May 2011) but the reporting did not generate widespread controversy or debate. There seems to be little public interest or concern in Irish society that immigration legislation may sanction the differential policing of non-Irish persons in Ireland, regardless of their residency status. Immigration legislation does not address how non-Irish nationals are to be identified by Gardaí, but the research conducted has shown that people of non-European appearance and people with limited English are most likely to be stopped by Gardaí under the provisions of this legislation. This is consistent with previous research which has highlighted that sub-Saharan Africans, and to a lesser extent Eastern Europeans, are subject to a high rate of Garda stops (European Union Agency for Fundamental Rights, 2009; Amnesty International, 2001, cited in Ionann, 2004). The evidence presented in this book also suggests that immigration legislation may sanction inappropriate racial and ethnic profiling by the police.

Why has more controversy not been generated by legislation which has allowed certain sections of the population to be policed differently from others? It is only very recently that Ireland's minority ethnic population has constituted more than a very tiny component of the total population. Recent inward migration has greatly increased the size of the resident minority ethnic population and the majority of people in the minority ethnic communities in Ireland are recent arrivals. Perhaps Irish people still think of these people primarily as immigrants who are not embedded in society rather than as neighbours, friends, co-workers and sometimes fellow citizens.

The relatively small numbers of Irish citizens in the Irish ethnic minority community may weaken the voice, and the power, of these communities and their ability to draw on the support of the wider Irish community. This may mean that laws which excite controversy in countries with more sizeable and established ethnic minority communities do not generate the public debate in Ireland, and in similar countries, that they warrant. Although some members of the minority ethnic population are Irish citizens, the expensive and lengthy naturalisation process and the high refusal rate of applications are likely to dissuade many from applying for naturalisation (Immigrant Council of Ireland (ICI), 2009).

Presence of Foreign Nationals in the Irish District Court

The foreign nationals observed in the District Court are described in detail in Chapter 2. The mobility of life in the twenty-first century is evident when we look at Irish District Court defendants. Irish District Court defendants now include people of truly catholic origins who are citizens in countries across the globe or in some cases persons who are stateless. Foreign nationals who appear as District Court defendants may be living in Ireland but District Court defendants also include foreign nationals holidaying in Ireland, doing business in Ireland, studying in Ireland as well as persons not previously resident in Ireland arrested while seeking to enter the state.

The research conducted revealed that foreign defendants accounted for a larger proportion of defendants than the proportion of foreign nationals in the Irish population, although local population features partially explained the disproportionate presence of foreign defendants. However, the proportion of foreign defendants who appear before the court should be understood as a by-product of mobility and not simply as an indication of levels of offending among the resident foreign national population. In addition, as already noted, the criminalisation of irregular migrants contributes to the numbers of foreign national defendants who appear before the court.

Sentencing Decisions of the Irish District Court

The research conducted did not suggest that sentencing decisions were influenced by the nationality/ethnicity of the defendant. However, the sentencing practices of the District Court raised a number of general concerns which collectively serve to undermine the court's important role in the Irish criminal justice system. The issues identified are summarised below and addressed in greater detail in Chapter 3.

A number of issues of concern stem directly from the inconsistent sentencing that is evident in the Irish District Court. One of the side-effects of this inconsistency is a tendency by courtroom regulars to dismiss proceedings as unimportant and inconsequential. District Court outcomes are unduly dependent on which judge passes sentence, and consequently applications and representations made by defence advocates are at times little more than rituals invested with symbolic rather than instrumental value. The description of courtroom proceedings by one defence solicitor as a 'game' (FN3) encapsulates a widely held view among defence solicitors that outcomes are uncertain and affected by chance rather than being primarily determined by the facts of the case. It is contended that sentencing inconsistency devalues the work of the court to such a degree that even courtroom regulars question the legitimacy of court outcomes, and the value of the work of the court.

Many of the offences dealt with by the court are offences defined by law in an unequivocal manner, even though the moral character of the actions which constitute those offences may be subject to a variety of interpretations. The law overrides any individual moral uncertainty by creating a boundary between what is legal and what is illegal. The court's role is to reinforce the moral boundaries as defined by the law, and to reduce the ambiguity of the law (Cohen, 1966). However, the sentencing inconsistency that is a feature of District Court decisions does little to dispel ambiguity and can even call into question the law itself when convictions are not returned, or are returned in respect of lesser charges, despite evidence of a breach of the law.[2]

Inconsistency in the sentencing decisions of Irish District Court judges is an inevitable product of the absence of sentencing guidelines and information on sentencing practices. As judges are not directed to adopt specific sentencing rationales, and are not in a position to assess sentencing norms for specific offences, there can be no expectation of sentencing consistency. We cannot expect consistency in sentencing to emerge in an organic fashion.

Greater consistency in sentencing would increase public confidence in the work of the District Court. Addressing the lack of court transcripts would also improve the accountability of the court and so boost public confidence in the justice system. A pilot introduction of digital audio recording (DAR) in the District Court commenced in December 2009 (CS, 2010:23) and since then DAR has been introduced in some District Court venues. However, the 2010 CS annual report indicated that facilities for DAR were still outstanding in seventy-five District Court venues (CS, 2011:26). The absence of court transcripts may also constrain the introduction of the long-awaited judicial council.[3]

Appeals of District Court verdicts result in a full rehearing in the Circuit Court while appeals against sentences result in a partial rehearing of the case (Rottman and Tormey, 1985). The court therefore produces decisions which, when challenged, are routinely put aside. This system inherently devalues the decisions of the court.

District Court judges frequently decide that it is appropriate to impose a custodial sentence. In 2008, the outcome for approximately one in eight of all cases not dismissed by the court was a period of incarceration (DJELR, 2010). Incarceration has been described as a punishment of last resort (Whitaker, 1984), yet in the Irish District Court the use of imprisonment is an everyday and commonplace occurrence. This seems to inure many regular court actors to its imposition. The pace at which court proceedings are conducted does not lend itself to reflection on, or the analysis of, decisions in specific cases. The role played by the probation services in the District Court is very peripheral. The proportion of referrals to the probation services is very low, and when probation reports are presented to the court they are often read hurriedly by judges in the courtroom. In most instances, no significant amount of time is spent in assessing or considering the contents.

It is argued that this system has encouraged judges to rely largely on a limited range of criminal sanctions. Recent legislation may prompt a change in sentencing in the District Court and in particular in the use of short-term prison sentences. The Criminal Justice (Community Service Amendment) Act, 2011 requires judges to consider the imposition of a Community Service Order as an alternative to the imposition of a custodial sentence for a period of twelve months or less. This is a welcome initiative particularly as additional capacity has been identified in existing community service schemes (DJELR, 2009), and the probation service has sought to increase the number of CSOs (DJELR, 2010); this is therefore an opportune time for a reduction in the use of short-term prison sentences.

Power of An Garda Síochána in the District Court

The picture of the District Court presented in this book is of a court in which the presumption of innocence can often seem to be tentative rather than robust. Most prosecutions in the District Court are conducted by a Garda officer and in many instances the chief prosecution witness is a member of An Garda Síochána, whose evidence is often afforded a great deal more credibility by the court than the evidence given by the defendant. The weight routinely given to the evidence of Gardaí means that when the chief, and indeed often only, prosecution witness is a member of An Garda Síochána, defendants who plead 'not guilty' may effectively have to prove their innocence. This situation places a great deal, and perhaps an inordinate, amount of power in the hands of An Garda Síochána. It could be argued that this power is especially inappropriate as many of the offences prosecuted in the District Court are 'regulatory' offences (see Whitman, 2003; Lacey, 2008) i.e. where the underlying behaviour is forbidden, rather than inherently wrong. Regulatory offences could, as in many other jurisdictions, be dealt with as administrative breaches rather than as criminal offences.

Lower-Tier Courts and the Definition of 'Crime' and 'Criminals'

In many ways lower-tier courts play a greater role in defining moral boundaries than do higher criminal courts which deal with more serious offences whose moral character is rarely in question. The offences and offenders that appear before lower-tier courts tell us a great deal about how 'crime' is defined in a society and who is designated as 'criminal'.

In the Irish context, the caseload of the Irish District Court tells us that a great deal of priority is given to regulating and policing behaviour in public spheres. Those who tend to be unruly in public spheres are young men, and in particular young men from lower economic backgrounds. Policing efforts are also concentrated on those who engage in unsophisticated thefts of tangible property. Such crimes are readily detectable, and situational anti-theft devices such as alarms and cameras may even identify the perpetrator. These crimes are also likely to be largely committed by those in the lower socio-economic classes. Contrast these crimes with more sophisticated cyber-crime and fraud which may not be detected for some time after they are committed and which are likely to require significant levels of education both to carry out and to solve. The resources needed to tackle crimes of this nature are considerable and it seems likely that many perpetrators never appear before our courts.

The research presented in this book suggests that for the most part, 'crime' and 'criminals' are narrowly defined in Ireland; this means that the minor crimes committed by those in lower socio-economic classes are more likely to be detected and prosecuted than the crimes committed by those in higher socio-economic classes. It should be remembered that this reflects policing priorities and practices and the legislative framework, and not necessarily the attitudes of District Court judges.

The Continuing Importance of Social Class and Local Cultures and Practices in a Globalised World

This book set out to present a detailed ethnographic account of the work of the Irish District Court and to record and explain the presence of foreign nationals among District Court defendants. It includes numerous field note extracts which not only allow us to hear the voice of the court but also probe and scrutinise court decisions and outcomes. Collectively the extracts presented, and the related analysis, provide an in-depth understanding of what the court does and the roles played by various courtroom actors. The account presented in this book ensures that the work of the District Court can now be more readily understood than before.

The picture of the District Court that emerges is of a court in which the vast majority of defendants, regardless of their nationality or ethnicity, are from the lower socio-economic classes. A superficial reading of this disparity might suggest that minor criminal offences are disproportionately committed by the less well-off in Irish society. However, in the main the Irish District Court is only called upon to deal with a limited range of offences committed largely by a small section of our society. The court is rarely called upon to deal with 'white collar' crimes, which are more likely to be committed by those in the middle and higher socio-economic classes. It seems very likely that the vast bulk of 'white collar' crimes are never detected and the perpetrators are never prosecuted (see Whitaker, 1984; Kilcommins et al., 2004; Coulter, 2010); this creates an erroneous impression that those who commit crime are predominantly from the ranks of the poor and less educated.

The socio-economic composition of District Court defendants is a product of how crime is defined and policed in Irish society rather than a reflection of the distribution of crime in Irish society. All criminal offences are not policed and prosecuted with equal vigour and the criminalisation of certain behaviour disproportionately impacts the less well-off in Irish society. In practice, the tag of 'criminal' in Irish society is largely reserved for those who are economically and socially vulnerable and therefore, for the most part, the Irish District Court punishes and regulates the poor.

It is argued that the institution of punishment in Irish society is very largely used to regulate and control those who have no attachment or only a tenuous attachment to the labour market and who therefore do not contribute to the production of wealth as measured in capitalist economies.

In Ireland, migrants face a higher risk of economic marginalisation and of criminalisation than the native population. Some migrants may also be subject to undue police surveillance due to racial/ethnic profiling. However, these risks do not necessarily translate into higher rates of criminalisation for all migrants because, as outlined above, police resources and efforts are primarily targeted at offences committed by the less well-off in society. Hence, migrants of high socio-economic status are largely insulated from the risk of criminalisation, whereas migrants of low socio-economic status are especially at risk of criminalisation. Overall, therefore, although the origins of Irish District Court defendants are now extraordinarily varied, defendants are still overwhelmingly from the lower social classes in society.

Irish District Court defendants now have global origins but the organisation, practices and decisions of the court are embedded in local cultures and context. This book highlights that, despite global influences, local cultures are enduring and must continue to be taken into account. It also demonstrates that situated, local, micro-level research can provide insights and knowledge which can inform and guide macro-level theories and analysis.

Appendix

Research Methodology

Introduction

Methodology choices for social researchers are often shaped and limited by constraints. The researcher may well have to decide 'what can I do?' rather than 'what would I like to do?' Research methodologies employed therefore reflect practical accommodations necessary to get the work done. Research constraints may take many forms, such as limited resources, restricted access, lack of willing informants, inadequate statistical databases, and ethical considerations. Ethical considerations act as an over-arching constraint on the methodology adopted for social research projects, and given the requirement within most academic institutions that ethical approval must be obtained prior to embarking on research, they can be a very important determinant of what research takes place and how it is conducted. The choice of methodology for this research was mainly constrained by the limited information recorded pertaining to District Court defendants, which ruled out the possibility of quantitative research and essentially dictated that a qualitative research methodology be adopted for this.

This appendix sets out the research methodology adopted in conducting qualitative research of proceedings in the Irish District Court. The appendix describes how a preliminary perspective of District Court proceedings was gleaned from interviews conducted with one sitting District Court judge and one retired District Court judge. The quasi-ethnographic approach adopted is located in relation to traditional ethnographic research, with the differences between traditional or 'pure' ethnography and quasi-ethnography highlighted and discussed.

The appendix outlines and discusses the factors that determined the choice of research locations and provides a detailed description of the various locations where research was conducted, and sets out the length of time spent at each site. The process of negotiating access to the 'field' is noted and discussed and the method adopted to write and code field notes and organise field note extracts thematically is described. The discussions held on an informal basis with various courtroom regulars during the course of the research are outlined, as is the process of seeking and conducting interviews with criminal law solicitors. Measures taken to protect research participants are outlined and departures from normal ethical practice are also discussed.

Preliminary Interviews

Prior to deciding on the research approach to be adopted, interviews were conducted with a retired District Court judge and a sitting District Court judge. Interviews were not recorded in accordance with the wishes of both judges. The objective of these interviews was to get an insider's perspective of the day-to-day work of the court and an assessment of the impact of foreign defendants on the work of the court, and to use this information to devise a research strategy that was both appropriate and implementable.

The interviews highlighted that procedural efficiency was a key concern of District Court judges and CS staff. Given the heavy caseload faced daily in most District Courts, it was essential that the research did not impinge on the work of the court or make undue demands on the time of CS staff. Judge Doyle expressed the view that most judges would not be keen to engage directly by way of interview with the research. After careful consideration it was decided that the most suitable methodology for this research project was quasi-ethnographic courtroom-based observation supplemented with informal discussions with various courtroom 'insiders' (Rock 1993), and more formal interviews with a number of selected solicitors. The term quasi-ethnographic and its application to other socio-legal research are explored below.

Quasi-Ethnographic Research

Ethnographic research methods have been used extensively in the study of deviance and hard-to-reach subcultures (see, *inter alia*, Shaw et al., 1938/2006; Shaw and McKay, 1942/2006; Agar, 1971; Inciardi et al., 1993; Whyte, 1993) and in the research of criminal justice processes (Cicourel, 1968; Punch, 1979; Travers, 1992; Norris, 1993; Rowe, 2007; Travers, 2007). In looking at research focused on the work of criminal courts, it is helpful to distinguish between studies which use the tools of ethnography but do not adopt an ethnographic stance; those that present an 'ethnographic perspective'; and true ethnographic studies.

Hogarth (1971), Crow and Simon (1987) and Ashworth et al. (1984) used a range of research methods which included courtroom observations and interviews with judges/magistrates. However, although these studies used methods commonly used by ethnographers, they are not ethnographic in character.

Travers (2007) presents an 'ethnographic perspective' of an examination of sentencing in a children's court. Travers employs ethnographic methods and an interpretative stance in exploring the work of the court but his research is not comprehensive enough to be described as ethnography and the term 'ethnographic perspective' is therefore appropriate. Similarly Mileski (1971), who observed proceedings in a lower criminal court on two days a week for three months, describes her research as an 'observational study' rather than as ethnography.

Blumberg's account (1967) of the practice of criminal law, in which he describes defence lawyers as 'double-agents' and 'con-men', is based on his extensive experience working as a lawyer in criminal courts. His account presents a fascinating 'insider's' perspective of court bureaucratic processes, the shared goals of judges, prosecutors and defence lawyers, and their collegial rather than adversarial relationships. But his essay employs generalisations and a broad, sweeping approach, and lacks the detailed references to specific events which are usual in ethnographic studies.

Bogira (2005) spent a year observing proceedings in the busiest felony courthouse in Chicago and enjoyed access to all areas of the courthouse including the lock-up, the jury room and the judges' chambers. Bogira also interviewed a range of court actors and defendants. His research methods were ethnographic in character, and his account is nuanced and complex. However, Bogira's main aim is to tell a compelling story rather than to present the findings of the social research he has conducted. His account is journalistic in tone, and is not sufficiently supported by references to other academic studies or commentaries, which results at times in an overly subjective picture of courtroom processes and participants.[1]

Although much of the research based in criminal courts and the observation of court processes has not resulted in true ethnographic studies, we can point to several ethnographies of criminal courts. Emerson (1969) and Cicourel (1968) focused on juvenile courts, and combined observation of courtroom processes with other research methods such as observation of informal encounters in courtroom corridors (Emerson, 1969), and analysis of background information in probation files and discussions with police and probation officers (Cicourel, 1968), to arrive at a multi-layered and 'thick' description of how courts deal with juvenile offenders. Bennett and Feldman (1981) spent more than a year conducting their courtroom-based ethnography of criminal trials. They combined courtroom observations with informal interviews with various participants and the analysis of videotapes of trial proceedings. Rock's (1993) fieldwork was also lengthy and was conducted over a ten-month period during which time he observed proceedings in the Crown Court and interviewed a range of court 'insiders'.

This research, following Owen (1998), adopts the designation 'quasi-ethnography'. This designation recognises that while the research has key ethnographic features (such as naturalism, and a commitment to a detailed exposition of the work of the court), the research methods adopted depart in some ways from the methodology of traditional ethnographers.

The first such departure concerns the total immersion of the researcher. Criminal courts only sit for limited periods of time; all courtroom actors therefore have lives outside the court, and to that extent none are completely immersed in the life and culture of the court. The researcher was able to carry on with most elements of her 'normal' life while conducting this research and can only therefore legitimately claim a partial immersion in the 'culture' of the District Court. The second departure from traditional ethnographies relates to the time spent conducting this research. Although the period of time spent observing District Court proceedings was lengthy, it does not equate to the extensive periods spent by those conducting ethnographies in the anthropological tradition. Thirdly, the research was conducted at a number of different locations, whereas traditionally ethnography is associated with a single research site. Finally, the researcher was not a participant in the court. She did not assume the role of the advocate, prosecutor, judge, probation officer, interpreter, witness or defendant. She was always an 'outsider', and undoubtedly this will have resulted in some interactions with courtroom 'insiders' being marked by suspicion and caution.

Using these criteria, Brickey and Miller's study of a traffic court could more accurately be described as a 'quasi-ethnographic' study than an ethnographic study (1975). Similarly, Wandall's study of decisions by a Danish District Court to impose sentences of immediate incarceration could also be described as 'quasi-ethnographic' (2008).

Gaining Access

As most courtrooms are designated by law as public places, researchers do not usually have to negotiate access and gain permission for their research. Hence, Brickey and Miller, who observed proceedings in a traffic court over a period of five months, note that:

> . . . entry into the court was quite easy. There were no posted restrictions for observers and there was no pressure to account for our presence. Consistent with state law, traffic court was a public proceeding. However, since the number of defendants rarely exceeded twenty-five and the room was quite small, we thought it best to introduce ourselves to the judge as students of the court (1975:689).

Brickey and Miller seem to have considered that in light of the public nature of the proceedings they were observing, the disclosure of their status as researchers was warranted by concerns around social etiquette rather than because they needed permission to conduct their research. Researchers may also make their presence known as a gesture of respect to the court and in recognition of the fact that good relationships with court administrators and the judiciary will facilitate requests for additional information and future research.

In the context of this research project, and the plan to spend extensive periods of time in specific court locations, it was evident that the co-operation of the CS and the judiciary would facilitate this research. Failure to secure this co-operation could also have adversely impacted the evaluation of this project by the Research

Ethics Committee (REC), and without ethical approval from the REC the research could not have been undertaken. The researcher therefore sought to secure the CS's co-operation with the planned research. The chief executive officer (CEO) of the CS was informed of the planned research and provided with details of courtroom-based research conducted in Ireland and in other jurisdictions. The response of the CEO of the CS indicated that he considered it was more appropriate to seek judicial sanction for the research. A written submission was then made to the president of the District Court. The president replied indicating that the researcher should contact a named member of the CS staff (S1). When contact was made with S1 she asked a number of questions which were designed to assess how obtrusive the researcher's presence would be in court. The answers she received were presumably satisfactory as she then indicated that there was no objection to the research being conducted.

Prior to conducting research at each location, the researcher contacted S1, who gave the researcher the name of a staff member to contact in the relevant office. Normally when the researcher contacted the staff member, S1 had already informed her of the planned research. In one of the locations chosen, S1 indicated that the sitting judge might raise objections to the presence of a researcher in court. Initial feedback from staff at the court office indicated that the judge was not happy to have the researcher in court. The researcher offered to meet the judge and discuss the research with him. It was then indicated that the judge would agree to the researcher's presence in court provided that she did not make any notes of matters said. It was not possible to agree to this condition so with the assistance of CS staff the researcher made an appointment to meet the judge. On the morning of the scheduled appointment the judge indicated to CS staff that he no longer had any objections and did not wish to meet the researcher. This was the only instance when an individual judge expressed reservations about the researcher's presence in court.

Courtroom Locations

The selection of locations where courtroom proceedings were to be observed was guided by the dual aims of selecting locations where foreign nationals were likely to be well represented, and locations which were representative of the work of the court as a whole. It was impossible to find both of these qualities in equal measure in any given courtroom location, but locating the research in a number of different sites ensured that an appropriate balance of these qualities could be achieved. Overall, however, it is likely that the presence of foreign nationals in the District Court as a whole is somewhat less than the level observed during the course of the fieldwork. A brief description of each court where research was conducted is set out below.

Dublin Suburban Court

Dublin Suburban Court (DSC) is located in a suburban area (DSA) to the north-west of Dublin city. DSA is located in close proximity to the Dublin motorway ring and is only a short distance from Dublin city centre and from Dublin airport. It is served by a number of different bus routes and a limited rail transport system. It boasts a wide range of amenities which include a hospital, an Institute of Technology (IT), a theatre, a major retail centre, local government offices and business and industrial parks.

Current population is estimated to be close to 100,000, with a planned capacity of 150,000. In the decade between 1996 and 2006 the population grew by approximately 65% making it one of the fastest-growing areas in Ireland. The population of non-Irish nationals in DSA is over 20%, more than double the national average. Non-Irish nationals are clustered in certain areas within DSA so that in some parts the population of non-Irish nationals is greatly in excess of 20%. The three biggest groups of non-Irish nationals in DSA are citizens of Nigeria, Poland and the UK. The area offers a large stock of affordable rental accommodation and has succeeded in attracting a number of large high-tech and service companies. These features may have contributed to the concentration of migrant workers in the area. The area also houses a large cluster of non-Irish nationals who are asylum seekers.

The socio-economic status of the population is varied. A number of areas within DSA are classified as 'disadvantaged' or 'marginally below average' and receive funding under the RAPID[2] programme which is aimed at improving the quality of life and the opportunities available to residents of the most disadvantaged communities in Irish cities and towns. DSA also includes areas that are classified as 'affluent' and 'very affluent'.

City Centre Court

City Centre Court (CCC) is located on the north side of Dublin city (NDC), just a short walk or a brief tram ride away from many busy shopping thoroughfares. The nineteenth-century building which houses CCC and another court has been used as a District Court since the foundation of the state. NDC contains a number of prestigious department stores and buildings of historic importance such as the GPO, the Four Courts complex, and the Custom House, but is noticeably less affluent than the area south of the River Liffey. The area has long been associated with high levels of unemployment and deprivation but has undergone a process of partial gentrification in recent years. Old local authority flat complexes have been joined by newer privately owned apartment developments. This juxtaposition of affluence and deprivation means that aggregate figures for Dublin's inner city do not accurately reflect levels of spatial deprivation experienced in many inner-city areas. Many of Dublin's homeless services are located within a short radius of the CCC and both homelessness and drug use is very much a feature, which is apparent in the vicinity of the court and in the defendants who appear before CCC.

However, many defendants in CCC are not residents of NDC. A large transitory population is a feature of any large city and CCC deals with a higher proportion of people who do not live adjacent to the court than would courts located outside the capital city.

North East Court

North East Court (NEC) is located in a town (NET) on the eastern seaboard approximately 70km north of Dublin and close to the border with Northern Ireland. Its proximity to the border results in high levels of cross-border traffic, which is evident from the number of Northern Ireland-registered vehicles on the streets of the town. An army barracks is also located in the town. NET has excellent road links to both Dublin and Belfast and is also served by the Dublin to Belfast rail corridor and by regular rail services to Dublin. Both Dublin and Belfast airports are within easy reach. The excellent road linkage between NET and both Dublin and Belfast, coupled with easy access to seaports and airports, has helped it to attract a wide range of international industrial and service companies as well as assisting the development of indigenous companies.

NET also has an IT offering both undergraduate and postgraduate courses. Retail outlets in the town have struggled in recent times, as many shoppers have opted to cross the border to take advantage of lower prices.

The population of the town and its environs grew by almost 8% between 2002 and 2006, when it amounted to over 35,000. The non-Irish national population of NET was just over 11% in 2006, which was only marginally above the national average of 10.2%. The three biggest groups of non-Irish nationals in NET are citizens of Nigeria, the UK and Lithuania.

Remand Court

Remand Court (RC) is located in the grounds of a male remand prison situated west of Dublin city. Adjoining the remand prison is a closed medium-security committal prison. RC is located in a modern purpose-built building adjacent to the visitors' centre for the prison. The court is linked to the prison by an underground passageway. Sports grounds and a pitch-and-putt course are sited on the road opposite the court. There is very little pedestrian traffic on the road leading to RC and most of it consists of people heading towards the court or the prison.

The vast majority of defendants appearing before this court are in custody; just a small number of defendants are on bail. This greatly reduces the body of people in the courtroom as most defendants are only in court very briefly and are contained in an area of the court which is directly linked to the prison. RC can be accessed by bus, although the nearest bus routes are a ten to fifteen minute walk away. The court's limited accessibility to public transport may also reduce the volume of people in the court.

In the 'Field'

Duration of Research

Observation of court proceedings took place over a fifteen month period.[3] At each court location proceedings were observed for approximately a two-month period. DSC, CCC and RC dealt almost entirely with criminal matters and during the observation period in each of these courts the researcher spent two to three days per week in court. In NEC, however, only one day a week was reserved for criminal matters. Criminal matters were dealt with by the court as necessary on an intermittent basis on other days. Observations were conducted in NEC on the one day reserved for criminal matters.

In DSC, CCC and RC the normal remand period was two weeks, and it was often possible to chart the progress of individual cases and to observe defendants on several occasions. In NEC, however, the remand period was typically two months. This meant that the progress of cases could not be tracked in the same manner as was possible in the other courts.

Conducting Observations

UK Nationals

Census 2006 indicated that the single biggest group of immigrants in Ireland are UK nationals who accounted for more than a quarter of the recorded non-Irish resident population (see http://cso.ie/statistic-snationalityagegroup.htm). In 2011 the number of Polish nationals outstripped the number of UK nationals who accounted for just over one fifth of the recorded non-Irish resident population (see http://www.cso.ie/en/census/census2011reports/census2011profile6mig rationanddiversity-aprofileofdiversityinireland/). The presence in Ireland of UK nationals is long-standing and largely problematic. The proportion of non-Irish persons committed to Irish prisons grew rapidly from 16.4% in 2001 to 33.1% in 2007 (see IPS Annual Reports, 2001–7). Since 2008 the proportion of non-Irish persons among those committed to prison has declined (2008: 29.4%; 2009: 24.1%; 2010: 22.2% – see IPS, 2009, 2010, 2011). In 2001, UK nationals accounted for 2.4% of persons committed to Irish prisons. This proportion remained stable but with a slight downward trend during the period from 2001 to 2010.[4] We can see therefore that the growth in the flow of non-Irish persons committed to prison was accounted for by a growth in the numbers of 'new' migrants within the Irish prison system. Given this and the difficulty of distinguishing UK nationals from Irish nationals, observations of non-Irish nationals concentrated on non-Irish, non-UK nationals, who are referred to as foreign nationals.

Identifying Foreign Nationals

Foreign nationals were identified based on features such as the defendant's name, proficiency in English, appearance, accent, comments by court officials, and the nature of the charge. In many cases the defendant could be categorically identified as being foreign. This was the case when the charges faced were immigration charges; the defendant was provided with an interpreter; or specific reference was made in court to the defendant's nationality or period of residence in the country. It is thought that the method used to identify foreign defendants is likely to have understated rather than overstated the presence of foreign nationals in the court.

In the Courtroom

While conducting courtroom observations, the researcher tried to sit in a location which provided her with a good view of the court, and a reasonable chance of hearing the proceedings. In two of the courts observed, RC and NEC, the level of background noise was relatively low and on most occasions it was possible to hear exchanges in court without any difficulty. In RC there were very few defendants in the body of the court and usually there were also few family members and other members of the public in court. In addition, there were far fewer Gardaí in this court than in other courts, which helped to reduce the level of background noise. The background noise in NEC was somewhat louder than in RC but not unduly intrusive. However, at times it was very difficult to hear proceedings in DSC and CCC. In both these courts there was a constant hum of background noise, a good part of which emanated from conversations between Gardaí, and between solicitors and their clients. Not surprisingly, defendants and members of the public in these courts seemed to think that they too could carry on conversations and, on occasion, discreet, and sometimes not so discreet, phone calls.

Pronouncements by judges were generally clearly audible but it was frequently very difficult to hear the testimony of witnesses, the bulk of whom were Gardaí, as they simply did not seem to appreciate that they should use the microphones provided. Even judges sometimes had difficulty hearing the evidence of Gardaí. On one occasion observed, Judge Nolan said to a Garda who was giving evidence in an inaudible voice: 'Is there any chance you could use that microphone, and you have my permission to shout, by the way' (FN44).

In all locations where proceedings were observed, court proceedings routinely took on the form of a conversation between the judge and the arresting Garda, who was usually the main prosecution witness, or between the judge and the defence counsel or prosecutor. Little acknowledgement was made of the wider audience in the court.

As far as possible, the researcher observed interactions between solicitors/barristers and their clients after cases were dealt with by the court. Such interactions were normally very brief and took place in the body of the court.

Field Notes

Field notes were recorded in abbreviated form during court proceedings and were re-written in greater detail as soon as possible after the conclusion of court proceedings. Letters and symbols were used to denote features such as the gender and ethnicity of the defendant, whether or not he/she was in custody prior to his/her court appearance, the presence or absence of an interpreter, and legal representation by a solicitor or barrister. When possible, a brief description of the defendant was also recorded, including details of his/her clothes, and distinguishing marks such as tattoos or facial scars, which were remarkably common among young male defendants of all nationalities. The defendant's demeanour was also noted, especially if he/she appeared aggressive, agitated or upset, or appeared to be drunk or under the influence of drugs. Recording this information allowed the researcher to re-assemble an image of the defendant as he/she appeared in court.

The researcher then sought to record the substance of the court hearing as faithfully as possible. In many instances, cases are dealt with in a matter of seconds when the defence simply seeks and is granted an adjournment, but if matters are contested and go to a full hearing they can take up a substantial amount of court time. Consequently, the account of court hearings varied with the length of court time they received. It was possible to record many routine processes such as bail applications or applications for adjournment using a type of shorthand.

Informal Discussions and Interviews

At times, opportunities arose for the researcher to engage in informal discussions with courtroom insiders. Opportunities presented themselves in a variety of circumstances, such as conversations that were struck up while walking to or from court or while waiting for court proceedings to begin or while the court was in recess. The discussions that ensued were spontaneous rather than scheduled, and usually determined by factors outside the control of the researcher, such as the workload of individual court actors, the timing of court recesses and the interest/curiosity of court actors.

Courtroom observations were supplemented by a number of semi-structured interviews with solicitors. Interviews were only requested from solicitors practising in criminal law or with a special interest in immigration. Such interviews were requested in writing and solicitors who wished to contribute to the research responded by contacting the researcher. Those who were interviewed therefore clearly consented to the interview and were informed as to the nature of the research. Given the expert knowledge of the solicitors and their professional training, they were very much in control of the interview process, and of the information they chose to disclose. Interviews were taped with the permission of solicitors.

Maintaining Objectivity

Maintaining the objective, dispassionate stance of a researcher was often difficult. Many of those who appeared before the court were clearly very vulnerable and it often seemed that they were more deserving of assistance than of punishment. This was particularly the case when defendants had psychiatric difficulties or had a drug or alcohol addiction. It was not uncommon to see defendants with a history of mental illness who exhibited signs of mental distress in court. Some Irish offenders with a history of mental illness were accompanied to court by elderly parents; somehow this made their court appearances especially poignant for this researcher. For LEP defendants with mental illness, the court process, and remands in custody, can be especially difficult.

While at times the researcher found the histories and the vulnerability of defendants distressing, those that worked in the court seemed unaffected by what they saw and heard. For those who spend their working lives in the District Court, it must often seem as if they listen to countless versions of essentially the same story. It seems that rather than exciting sympathy, the repetition of troubled backgrounds and addiction problems were considered by many to be simply excuses, and not very good excuses at that. The belief that structural disadvantages can be surmounted by individual agency allows courtroom regulars to distance themselves from the upsetting details of defendants' lives that are routinely recounted in court.

While acknowledging and recognising the vulnerability of many defendants, the researcher was also aware that the work of the court placed a heavy and burdensome responsibility on judges, defence lawyers and court presenters. She was also keenly aware of the demanding and challenging situations that Gardaí and prison officers often faced, particularly in their interactions with violent and unruly defendants. The danger of the work carried out by Gardaí and prison officers was often visibly attested to by bruises and marks on their person. Although relationships between some Gardaí and defendants were marred by animosity, which at times seemed personal rather than professional, many Gardaí were a helpful point of contact for defendants in court, and could often be seen explaining the court process and sentences to defendants and their families. It was not at all unusual for defendants to seek out Gardaí after matters were concluded, to shake their hands.

Overall, the researcher often found the experience of observing court proceedings to be dispiriting and depressing. There were very few success stories to offset the accounts of personal failures, setbacks and disasters. One could see that over time it would be very easy for those working in the court to distance themselves emotionally from the dysfunction and chaos that often characterised the lives of offenders.

Measures Adopted to Protect Research Participants

A key concern in designing the research methodology for this project was the protection of research participants. Normally researchers seek to prevent harm to participants by protecting the confidentiality of information collected and in some instances assuring research participants of anonymity. Research participants will also normally be required to indicate in writing that they consent to be involved in the research. However, the particular features of this research meant that some departures from normal practice were unavoidable, but as is detailed below, every effort was made to ensure that the research process did not result in harm to any research participant.

The research conducted relied primarily on information collected from observations carried out in Irish courtrooms, which are public places. The public nature of Irish courtrooms is determined by

Article 34 of the Irish Constitution, which requires that, except in exceptional circumstances, court proceedings are open to the public.[5] The constitutional provisions make it clear that there can be no expectation of privacy in Irish courts. The public nature of court proceedings is intended to provide an important counterbalance to the power of the Irish judiciary, which derives from the very broad sentencing discretion afforded to Irish judges and the security and privileges which attach to judicial appointments.

The public nature of criminal court proceedings also recognises that criminal proceedings allege an offence against the state rather than an individual. Part of the price paid by people convicted of criminal offences is the public ignominy that attaches to criminal convictions. Similarly, the innocence of those accused but found 'not guilty' of criminal offences is a matter of public record.

One of the situations in which the usual requirement for informed consent is negated is when research is conducted in a public place. Although it was not necessary, and neither would it have been possible, to obtain informed consent from courtroom participants, a number of methodological devices were employed to protect the identity of research participants; these are detailed below.

The field note extracts that are interspersed throughout this book have been selected to highlight aspects of behaviour of key court actors, or features of court processes, or to provide illumination on factors that influence sentencing decisions, rather than because of any particular interest in any individual defendant. All defendants are referred to by pseudonyms, and on occasion other personal details have been altered to ensure the anonymity of defendants is protected. In addition, field notes are referred to by number rather than date, which further protects the identity of individual defendants.

Each of the court locations where research was conducted has been assigned a pseudonym. Given the limited number of courtroom locations in Ireland it is not possible to guarantee that the research locations will not be identifiable. This is not considered problematic. At each court location, proceedings were observed on multiple occasions over a two-month period, and in each location more than one judge presided during the period of research. Even if a court location could be identified, it would not be possible to identify an individual defendant from the observations reported because of the high volume of cases dealt with in every court location and the fact that references to field notes are undated and simply referred to by number (e.g. FN1).

Judges observed are referred to by pseudonyms. The researcher endeavoured to make individual judges aware of the research process and to offer them an opportunity to discuss the research with her if they so wished. Courts Service staff were requested to advise presiding judges of the researcher's presence in court and the nature of the research, and to inform them that the researcher was available to provide further information regarding the research on request. Solicitors are not identified by name in transcripts of interviews, and are referred to in the text by pseudonyms.

From Non-Participant Observer to Participant Observer

The researcher's task in court was to observe court proceedings. No interactions with defendants were planned but at times unplanned interactions with defendants occurred. In NEC and DSC, quite often the researcher found that the person sitting beside her was a defendant in court. In RC and CCC, the physical organisation of the court almost always ensured that the researcher was not sitting beside a defendant.[6] The researcher always had a court list and this prompted a variety of people, including defendants, to approach her simply so that they could have access to the list. In one instance, outlined below, the researcher initiated contact with a defendant in an effort to assist her. In this instance the researcher momentarily became a participant observer rather than simply an observer.

> Adeola B was seated at the very back of the court on a bench which is behind the rows of seats and right at the rear wall of the court. When her name was called out by the registrar, she stood up but did not come forward. No-one else in the courtroom appeared to realise that the defendant was in court. The court presenter indicated to the judge that the defendant was not in court and the judge issued a bench warrant at 10.37am. I was unsure as to what I could or should do. I turned to a Garda seated behind me and told him that the woman was actually in court and pointed her out to him. The Garda simply shrugged his shoulders and made no move to intervene. It was clear that he had no interest in the woman's case. Meanwhile, the court session proceeded, but I frequently turned around to check if the woman was still in court. She seemed to have no understanding that her presence had not been noted or indeed that a bench

warrant had been issued, but it appeared that she wasn't sure whether she was required to stay in court or not. At one point the woman moved from her seat on the bench when she recognised a man in the court who it later transpired was also a defendant. The two chatted quietly together at the back of the court until the man's case was called. Towards the end of the morning's session I realised that the woman had moved again and was now sitting behind me. I decided that it was best to let her know that a bench warrant had been issued. I explained as best I could that her presence in the court had not been recorded and that a warrant had been issued as a result and advised her to make herself known to the court presenter (who I pointed out to her) when there was a break in the proceedings. Ms B did this and the court presenter spoke to her briefly. It was some time later before her name was re-called, and in the interim she waited anxiously. The court presenter intimated to the judge that the woman had now turned up in court (whereas in fact she had been in court all along), and asked the judge for permission to rescind the bench warrant. The judge agreed, and after noting that the woman had no solicitor he asked her would she like the court to assist her in appointing a solicitor. A solicitor present in the court was then assigned her case, the judge issued a 'Gary Doyle' order and she was remanded on continuing bail for a further two weeks (FN3).

Research involving human subjects can result in unexpected revelations or unanticipated situations. Planned research methodology may have to be adjusted to take account of unforeseen situations. Researchers may have to decide 'on the spot' on the ethically appropriate course of action and must be able to weigh up the relative harms and benefits of different courses of action. It had not been anticipated that during the course of the fieldwork the researcher might initiate contact with a defendant. The intervention that was made was 'natural' in that it was unplanned; it was triggered by the specific circumstances that arose when the researcher found that she was in a position to clear up a misunderstanding which would have had adverse consequences for the woman in question, and it was nothing more or less than what most observers in court would have done.[7] By initiating this contact, the researcher was preventing harm to the defendant, and although the intervention altered the 'field', it was ethically justifiable.

Bibliography

Abbott, E. 'Crime and the Foreign Born: Public Opinion', US National Commission on Law Observance and Enforcement (Wickersham Commission), Report no. 10, 1931.

Agar, M. *Ripping and Running: A Formal Ethnography of Urban Heroin Addicts* (New York: Seminar Press, 1971)

Alscher, S. 'Knocking at the Doors of "Fortress Europe": Migration and Border Control in Southern Spain and Eastern Poland', Working Paper 126, November 2005, The Centre for Comparative Immigration Studies, University of California, San Diego, http://www.ccis-ucsd.org/PUBLICATIONS/wrkg126.pdf [accessed 22 April 2010]

Archibold, R.C. 'Arizona Enacts Stringent Law on Immigration', *New York Times*, 23 April 2010

Ashworth, A. 'Criminal History in England: The Search for the Snark', *Federal Sentencing Reporter*, vol. 17, no. 3, 2005, pp. 207–8

Ashworth, A., Genders, E., Mansfield, G., Peay, J. and Player, E. 'Sentencing in the Crown Court', Occasional Paper 10, Oxford Centre for Criminological Research, 1984

Bacik, I. 'The Practice of Sentencing in the Irish Courts', in P. O'Mahoney (ed.), *Criminal Justice in Ireland* (Dublin: Institute of Public Administration, 2002)

Bacik, I. 'Breaking the Language Barrier: Access to Justice in the New Ireland', *Judicial Studies Institute Journal*, 2, 2007, pp. 109–23

Bacik, I., Kelly, A., O'Connell, M. and Sinclair, H. 'Crime and Poverty in Dublin: An Analysis of the Association Between Community Deprivation, District Court Appearance and Sentence Severity', in I. Bacik and M. O'Connell (eds), *Crime and Poverty in Ireland* (Dublin: Round Hall Sweet & Maxwell, 1998)

Bacik, I., Costello, C. and Drew, E. *Gender Injustice: Feminising the Legal Professions* (Dublin: Trinity College Law School, 2003)

Bagaric, M. 'Double Punishment and Punishing Character: The Unfairness of Prior Convictions', *Criminal Justice Ethics*, vol. 19, no. 1, 2000, pp. 10–28

Becker, H. 'Offences and Penalties in the Immigration Residence and Protection Bill 2008: Do the Punishments Fit the Crime?', paper presented at ACJRD 11th Annual Conference, Dublin, 9 October 2008, http://www.immigrantcouncil.ie/images/8470_091008_ACJRDpaper.pdf [accessed 22 April 2010]

Bender, G.J. *Angola Under the Portuguese: The Myth and the Reality* (Berkeley, CA: University of California Press, 1992)

Bennett, W.L. and Feldman, M.S. *Reconstructing Reality in the Courtroom* (London: Tavistock Publications, 1981)

Berdal, M. and Serrano, M. *Transnational Organised Crime and International Security: Business as Usual?* (Boulder, CO: Lynne Rienner Publishers, 2002)

Blumberg, A.S. 'The Practice of Law as a Confidence Game: Organisational Cooperation of a Profession', *Law and Society Review*, vol. 1, no. 2, 1967, pp. 15–39

Bogira, S. *Courtroom 302* (New York: Alfred A. Knopf, 2005)

Boswell, C. 'The "External Dimension" of EU Immigration and Asylum Policy', *International Affairs*, vol. 79, no. 3, 2003, pp. 619–38

Boyle, K. 'Appendix II: The Galway District Court Study', in *The Criminal Justice System: Policy and Performance* (Dublin: National Economic and Social Council (NESC), 1984)

Bremmer, J. 'Scapegoat Rituals in Ancient Greece', *Harvard Studies in Classical Philology*, 87, 1983, pp. 299–320

Brewer, J.D., Lockhart, B. and Rodgers, P. *Crime in Ireland, 1945–1995: Here Be Dragons* (Oxford: Clarendon Press, 1997)

Brickey, S.L. and Miller, D.E. 'Bureaucratic Due Process: An Ethnography of a Traffic Court', *Social Problems*, vol. 22, no. 5, 1975, pp. 688–97

Brown, I. and Hullin, R. 'A Study of Sentencing in the Leeds Magistrates' Courts: The Treatment of Ethnic Minority and White Offenders', *British Journal of Criminology*, vol. 32, no. 1, 1992, pp. 41–53

Cahill, A. 'Asylum Seekers to Ireland Double the EU Average', *Irish Examiner*, 9 May 2009

Carbery, G. 'Judge Apologises for Saying Social Welfare a Polish Charity', *The Irish Times*, 2 August 2012

Carolan, M. 'Identity Papers Challenge Upheld', *The Irish Times*, 25 March 2011

Carroll J. 'You Be the Judge – Part II: The Politics and Processes of Judicial Appointments in Ireland', *Bar Review*, vol. 10, no. 6, 2005, pp. 182–8

Cavadino, M. and Dignan, J. 'Penal Policy and Political Economy', *Criminology and Criminal Justice*, vol. 6, no. 4, 2006, pp. 435–56

Central Statistics Office (CSO), *Census 2002, Volume 8: Irish Traveller Community* (Dublin: The Stationery Office, 2004)

Central Statistics Office (CSO), *Census 2006, Volume 5: Ethnic or Cultural Background (including the Irish Traveller Community)* (Dublin: The Stationery Office, 2007)

Central Statistics Office (CSO), *Census 2006: Non-Irish Nationals Living in Ireland* (Dublin: The Stationery Office, 2008)

Central Statistics Office (CSO), *Population and Migration Estimates: April 2009*, http://www.cso.ie/en/media/csoie/releasespublications/documents/population/2009/popmig_2009.pdf [accessed 24 April 2010]

Central Statistics Office (CSO), *Population and Migration Estimates: April 2010* (Dublin: The Stationery Office, 2010)

Chiricos, T.G. and Crawford, C. 'Race and Imprisonment: A Contextual Assessment of the Evidence', in D.F. Hawkins (ed.), *Ethnicity, Race and Crime: Perspectives Across Time and Place* (Albany, NY: State University of New York Press, 1995)

Chiricos, T.G. and Waldo, G.P. 'Socioeconomic Status and Criminal Sentencing: An Empirical Assessment of a Conflict Proposition', *American Sociological Review*, vol. 40, no. 6, 1975, pp. 753–72

Cicourel, A.V. *The Social Organisation of Juvenile Justice* (New York: Wiley & Sons, 1968)

Clarke, S.H. and Koch, G.G. 'The Influence of Income and Other Factors on Whether Criminal Defendants go to Prison', *Law and Society Review*, 11, 1976, pp. 57–92

Codd, H. *In the Shadow of Prison: Families, Imprisonment and Criminal Justice* (Cullompton, Devon: Willan Publishing, 2008)

Cohen, A. *Deviance and Control* (Englewood Cliffs, NJ: Prentice Hall, 1966)

Collins, J. 'Immigrant Crime in Europe and Australia: Rational or Racialised Responses?', National Europe Centre Paper No. 80, pp. 1–35. Paper presented at the 'Challenges of Immigration and Integration in the European Union and Australia' conference, University of Sydney, 18–20 February 2003

Comptroller and Auditor General, 'Chapter 6: Courts Service' (2002), from the 2001 annual report, http://audgen.irlgov.ie/documents/annualreports/2001/Chap6pdf [accessed 20 March 2010]

Connolly, J. *Drugs and Crime in Ireland*, Overview 3 (Dublin: Health Research Board, 2006)

Conroy, B. and Gunning, P.G. 'The Irish Sentencing Information System (ISIS): A Practical Guide to a Practical Tool', *Judicial Studies Institute Journal*, vol. 9, no. 1, 2009, pp. 37–53

Coulter, C. 'Wall Around Site of Planned Prison "Poor Use of Money"', *The Irish Times*, 24 September 2010

Council of Europe, *Consistency in Sentencing: Recommendation No. R (92) 17* (Strasbourg: Council of Europe, 1993)

Council of Europe Commissioner for Human Rights (COECHR), *Criminalisation of Migration in Europe: Human Rights Implications*, Issue Paper, 4 February 2010 (Strasbourg: Council of Europe Commissioner for Human Rights, 2010)

Courts Service (CS), *Courts Service Strategic Plan 2005–2008* (2005), http://www.courts.ie/Courts.ie/library3.nsf/%28WebFiles%29/61E4912A

714C602680257123005C112F/$FILE/Strategic%20Plan%202005%20-%202008.pdf [accessed 25 June 2010]

Courts Service (CS), *Courts Service Annual Report 2005* (2006), http://www.courts.ie/Courts.ie/library3.nsf/%28WebFiles%29/86639819A92CC0F3802571AF00391DE2/$FILE/CS%20Annual%20Report%202005%20-%20pt%201.pdf [accessed 20 June 2010]

Courts Service (CS), *Courts Service Annual Report 2006* (2007), http://www.courts.ie/Courts.ie/library3.nsf/%28WebFiles%29/58AC1A582768C2F58025731E003E60DD/$FILE/AR%202006%20-%20EN%201.pdf [accessed 20 June 2010]

Courts Service (CS), *Courts Service Annual Report 2007* (2008a), http://www.courts.ie/Courts.ie/library3.nsf/%28WebFiles%29/B67ECF620606DCEE8025748900571B56/$FILE/Courts%20Service%20Annual%20Report%202007%20-%20Pt%201%20.pdf [accessed 20 June 2010]

Courts Service (CS), *Courts Service Strategic Plan 2008-2011* (2008b), http://www.courts.ie/Courts.ie/library3.nsf/%28WebFiles%29/EF10878F58250E908025756800579524/$FILE/Strategic%20plan%202008%20-%202011%20LR.pdf [accessed 25 June 2010]

Courts Service (CS), *Courts Service Annual Report 2008* (2009), http://www.courts.ie/Courts.ie/Library3.nsf/%28WebFiles%29/AC5D8C4F7765B6C080257766005D1B58/$FILE/Courts%20Service%20Annual%20Report%202009.pdf [accessed 20 June 2010]

Courts Service (CS), *Courts Service Annual Report 2009* (2010), http://www.courts.ie/Courts.ie/Library3.nsf/%28WebFiles%29/AC5D8C4F7765B6C080257766005D1B58/$FILE/Courts%20Service%20Annual%20Report%202009.pdf [accessed 20 June 2010]

Courts Service (CS), *Courts Service Annual Report 2010* (2011), http://www.courts.ie/Courts.ie/library3.nsf/%28WebFiles%29/4523C03355124B90802578CC0033B0AF/$FILE/Courts%20Service%20Annual%20Report%202010.pdf [accessed 7 January 2012]

Courts Service (CS), *Courts Service Annual Report 2011* (2012), http://www.courtsservice.ie [Retrieved online on 1 July 2013]

Crosscare Migrant Project, 'Family Reunification Legislation and Migrant Integration', Crosscare Migrant Project, January 2008, http://www.migrantproject.ie/images/Family%20reunification.pdf [accessed 23 September 2010]

Crow, I. and Simon, F. *Unemployment and Magistrates' Courts* (London: National Association for the Care and Resettlement of Offenders, 1987)

De Giorgi, A. *Re-thinking the Political Economy of Punishment: Perspectives on Post-Fordism and Penal Politics* (Aldershot: Ashgate, 2006)

De Giorgi, A. 'Immigration Control, Post-Fordism, and Less Eligibility: A Materialist Critique of the Criminalization of Immigration Across Europe', *Punishment and Society*, vol. 12, no. 2, 2010, pp. 147–67

De Koster, W., van der Waal, J., Achterberg, P. and Houtman, D. 'The Rise of the Penal State: Neo-Liberalization or New Political Culture?' *British Journal of Criminology*, vol. 48, no. 6, 2008, pp. 720–34

Delsol, R. and Shiner, M. 'Regulating Stop and Search: A Challenge for Police and Community Relations in England and Wales', *Critical Criminology*, vol. 14, no. 3, 2006, pp. 241–63

Department of Justice, Equality and Law Reform (DJELR), 'Value for Money and Policy Review of the Community Service Scheme' (2009), http://www.probation.ie/pws/websitepublishing.nsf/Content/Value+for+Money+and+Policy+Review+of+the+Community+Service+Scheme,+October+2009+News+Item [accessed 22 July 2010]

Department of Justice, Equality and Law Reform (DJELR), *White Paper on Crime, No. 2, February 2010: Criminal Sanctions Discussion Document* (Dublin: DJELR, 2010)

Department of Justice, Equality and Law Reform (DJELR), 'Green Paper on Procedural Safeguards for Suspects and Defendants in Criminal Proceedings Throughout the European Union: Response of the Minister for Justice, Equality and Law Reform, Ireland' (undated), http://ec.europa.eu/justice_home/fsj/criminal/procedural/responses/28pdf [accessed 20 June 2010]

Devins, M.C. 'Selectivity in Prosecution in the District Court', *Judicial Studies Institute Journal*, vol. 9, no. 2, 2009, pp. 26–41

Dickey, W.J. 'Sentencing, Parole and Community Supervision', in L.E. Ohlin and F.R. Remington (eds), *Discretion in Criminal Justice: The Tension Between Individualization and Uniformity* (Albany, NY: State University of New York Press, 1993)

Dowds, L. and Hedderman, C. 'The Sentencing of Men and Women', in C. Hedderman and L. Gelsthorpe (eds), *Understanding the Sentencing of Women* (London: Home Office, 1997)

Drummond, A. 'Cultural Denigration: Media Representation of Irish Travellers as Criminal', in M. Hayes and T. Acton (eds), *Counter-Hegemony and the Postcolonial 'Other'* (Cambridge: Cambridge Scholars Press, 2006)

Drummond, A. 'Irish Travellers and the Criminal Justice Systems Across the Island of Ireland', unpublished PhD thesis, University of Ulster, 2007

Edwards, A.B. *The Practice of Court Interpreting* (Amsterdam and Philadelphia: John Benjamins, 1995)

Eisenstein, J. and Jacob, H. *Felony Justice: An Organisational Analysis of Criminal Courts* (Boston and Toronto: Little, Brown & Company, 1977)

Eley, S., McIvor, G., Malloch, M. and Munro, B. *A Comparative Review of Alternatives to Custody: Lessons from Finland, Sweden and Western Australia*. Final report commissioned by the Scottish Parliament Information Centre for the Justice 1 Committee (Edinburgh: Scottish Parliamentary Corporate Body, 2005)

Emerson, R.M. *Judging Delinquents: Context and Process in Juvenile Court* (Chicago: Aldine Publishing, 1969)

Equality and Human Rights Commission (EHRC), 'Stop and Think' (2010), http://www.equalityhumanrights.com/fairer-britain/race-in-britain/stop-and-think [accessed 19 April 2010]

Esping-Andersen, G. *The Three Worlds of Welfare Capitalism* (Cambridge: Polity Press, 1990)

European Commission, 'The European Union Policy Towards a Common European Asylum System' (2006), http://www.ec.europa.eu/justice_home/fsj/asylum/fsj_aslum_intro_en.htm [accessed 20 April 2010]

European Migration Network (EMN), 'Ad-Hoc Query on Criminal Penalties against Illegally Entering or Staying Third-Country Nationals' (2009), http://www.emn.fi/files/96/COMM_145_EMN_Ad-Hoc_Query_Criminal_penalties_against_illegally_entering_or_staying_third_country_nationals [accessed 20 April 2010]

European Parliament Committee on Civil Liberties, Justice and Home Affairs (LIBE), 'Draft Report on the Directive of the European Parliament and of the Council on the Right to Interpretation and Translation in Criminal Proceedings' (00001/2010-C7-005-/2010/0801(COD)) (2010), http://www.europal.europa.eu/meetdocs/2009-2014/documents/libe/pr/807/807292/8 [accessed 24 June 2010]

European Union Agency for Fundamental Rights (FRA), *European Union Minorities and Discrimination Survey: Main Results Report* (2009), http://fra.europa.eu/fraWebsite/attachments/eumidis_mainreport_conference-edition_en_.pdf [accessed 23 June 2010]

Eurostat, 'Asylum in the EU in 2008', Eurostat news release, 8 May 2009, http://europa.eu/rapid/press-release_STAT-09-66_en.htm [accessed 23 June 2010]

Eurostat, 'Population and Social Conditions: Asylum Applications' (2012), http://epp.eurostat.ec.europa.eu/cache/ITY_OFFPUB/KS-QA-12-012/EN/KS-QA-12-012-EN.PDF [accessed 15 May 2013]

Fallon, J. 'Two Jailed Men Refuse to Reveal Identities', *The Irish Times*, 11 February 2008

Farrington, D.P. and Painter, K.A. *Gender Differences in Offending: Implications for Risk-Focused Prevention.* Home Office Research Findings No. 196, September 2004, www.homeoffice.gov.uk/rds/pdfs06/r196pdf [accessed 16 June 2010]

Farrington, D.P. and Morris, A.M. 'Sex, Sentencing and Reconviction', *British Journal of Criminology*, vol. 23, no. 3, 1983, pp. 229–48

Feeley, M.M. *The Process is the Punishment: Handling Cases in a Lower Criminal Court* (New York: Russell Sage Foundation, 1979)

Franko-Aas, K. *Sentencing in the Age of Information: From Faust to Mackintosh* (London: GlassHouse Press, 2005)

Free Legal Aid Centre (FLAC), *One Size Doesn't Fit All: A Legal Analysis of Direct*

Provision Ten Years On (2010), http://www.flac.ie/publications/one-size-doesn't-fit-all [accessed 5 July 2010]

Garland, D. *The Culture of Control: Crime and Social Order in Contemporary Society* (Oxford: Oxford University Press, 2001)

Garner, S. 'Babies, Bodies and Entitlement: Gendered Aspects of Access to Citizenship in the Republic of Ireland', *Parliamentary Affairs*, 60, 2007, pp. 437–51

Greenwood, P., Model, K., Rydell, C. and Chiesa, J. (1996) 'Diverting Children from a Life of Crime: What Are the Costs and Benefits?', http://www.rand.org/pubs/researh_briefs/RB4010/index1html [accessed 11 November 2011]

Hagan, J. 'Extra-Legal Attributes and Criminal Sentencing: An Assessment of a Sociological Viewpoint', *Law and Society Review*, vol. 8, no. 3, 1974, pp. 357–84

Hagan, J. and Bumiller, K. 'Making Sense of Sentencing: A Review and Critique of Sentencing Research', in A. Blumstein, J. Cohen, S.E. Martin and M. Tonry (eds), *Research on Sentencing: The Search for Reform, Volume II* (Washington: National Academy Press, 1983)

Hagan, J., Levi, R. and Dinovitzer, R. 'The Symbolic Violence of the Crime-Immigration Nexus: Migrant Mythologies in the Americas', *Criminology and Public Policy*, vol. 7, no. 1, 2008, pp. 95–112

Hagan, J. and Palloni, A. 'Sociological Criminology and the Mythology of Hispanic Immigration and Crime', *Social Problems*, vol. 46, no. 4, 1999, pp. 617–32

Hall, P.A. and Soskice, D. 'An Introduction to the Varieties of Capitalism', in P. Hall and D. Soskice (eds), *Varieties of Capitalism* (Oxford: Oxford University Press, 2001)

Hamilton, C. 'Sentencing in the District Court: "Here Be Dragons"', *Irish Criminal Law Journal*, vol. 15, no. 3, 2005, p. 9

Hammerberg, T. 'It is Wrong to Criminalise Migration' (2008), http://www.coe.int/t/commissioner/Viewpoints/080929_en.asp [accessed 3 March 2010]

Hatton, T.J. 'European Asylum Policy', Discussion Paper No. 1721, August 2005, http://www.iza.org/en/webcontent/publications/papers/viewAbstract?dp_id=1721 [accessed 20 April 2010]

Healy, D. and O'Donnell, I. 'Crime, Consequences and Court Reports', *Irish Criminal Law Journal*, vol. 20, no. 1, 2010, p. 2

Hedderman, C. and Gelsthorpe, L. (eds), *Understanding the Sentencing of Women* (London: Home Office, 1997)

Hogarth, J. *Sentencing as a Human Process* (Toronto: University of Toronto Press, 1971)

Hood, R. and Cordovil, G. *Race and Sentencing: A Study in the Crown Court. A Report for the Commission for Racial Equality* (Oxford: Clarendon Press, 1992)

Hudson, B. 'Discrimination and Disparity: The Influence of Race on Sentencing', *New Community*, 16, 1989, pp. 23–34

Immigrant Council of Ireland (ICI), 'Citizenship Processes in Need of Overhaul'. Press release, 7 July 2009, http://www.immigrantcouncil.ie/press_detail.php?id=91 [accessed 21 July 2010]

Inciardi, J.A., Lockwood, D. and Pottiger, A.E. *Women and Crack Cocaine* (New York: Macmillan, 1993)

Ionann Management Consultants, 'An Garda Síochána Human Rights Audit'. Report prepared for the Human Rights Working Group of An Garda Síochána, June 2004, http://www.minelres.lv/reports/ireland/PDF_Ireland)Comhlamh_GardaHreport.pdf [accessed 27 June 2010]

Irish Criminal Law Journal, 'Cases and Comment: District Judge Brady and DPP (respondents) v David Joyce (applicant) [HC 2006/92 JR], Feeney J., April 24, 2007', *Irish Criminal Law Journal*, vol. 17, no. 2, 2007(a), p. 29.

Irish Criminal Law Journal, 'Cases and Comment: District Judge Brady and ANOR (respondents) v Martin Moore (applicant) [HC 2005 1336/JR] [2006] IEHC 434, Feeney J., November 16, 2006', *Irish Criminal Law Journal*, vol. 17, no. 2, 2007(b), p. 29

Irish Penal Reform Trust (IPRT), 'IPRT Position Paper 2: Spent Convictions Bill, 2007' (2008), http://www.iprt.ie/files/IPRT_Position_Paper_2__Spent_Convictions.pdf [accessed 10 March 2010]

Irish Penal Reform Trust (IPRT), 'IPRT Position Paper 3: Mandatory Sentencing' (2009), http://www.iprt.ie/files/IPRT_Position_Paper_3__Mandatory_Sentencing.pdf [accessed 30 May 2012]

Irish Prison Service (IPS) *Irish Prison Service Annual Report 2001* (Dublin: The Stationery Office, 2003a)

Irish Prison Service (IPS), *Irish Prison Service Annual Report 2002* (Dublin: The Stationery Office, 2003b)

Irish Prison Service (IPS), *Irish Prison Service Annual Report 2003* (Dublin: The Stationery Office, 2004)

Irish Prison Service (IPS), *Irish Prison Service Annual Report 2004* (Dublin: The Stationery Office, 2005)

Irish Prison Service (IPS), *Irish Prison Service Annual Report 2005* (Dublin: The Stationery Office, 2006)

Irish Prison Service (IPS), *Irish Prison Service Annual Report 2006* (Dublin: The Stationery Office, 2007)

Irish Prison Service (IPS), *Irish Prison Service Annual Report 2007* (Dublin: The Stationery Office, 2008)

Irish Prison Service (IPS), *Irish Prison Service Annual Report 2008* (Dublin: The Stationery Office, 2009)

Irish Prison Service (IPS), *Irish Prison Service Annual Report 2009* (Dublin: The Stationery Office, 2010)

Irish Prison Service (IPS), *Irish Prison Service Annual Report 2010* (published 2011), http://www.justice.ie/en/JELR/Irish_Prison_Service_2010_Annual_Report.pdf/Files/Irish_Prison_Service_2010_Annual_Report.pdf [accessed 2 February 2012]

Irish Translators' and Interpreters' Association, 'Submission of the Irish Translators' and Interpreters' Association on the Courts Service Statement of Strategy, 2008–2011' (2008), http://translatorsassociation.ie/component/option,com_docman/task,cat_view/gid,28/Itemid,16 [accessed 24 March 2010]

Irish Translators' and Interpreters' Association (ITIA) 'Submission of the Irish Translators' and Interpreters' Association to the Joint Committee on Justice, Equality, Defence and Women's Rights Concerning the Proposed EU Directive on the Right to Interpretation and to Translation in Criminal Proceedings' (2010), http://www.translatorsassociation.ie [accessed 24 June 2011]

Irish Translator' and Interpreters' Association (ITIA), 'Submission of the Irish Translators' and Interpreters' Association to the Courts Service on the New Tender for Interpreting and Related Issues' (2011), http://www.translatorsassociation.ie [accessed 18 November 2011]

Johnson, L.M. 'Steve Bogira, Courtroom 302', *Critical Criminology*, vol. 15, no. 4, 2007, pp. 365–8

Joint Committee on European Affairs, 'Eleventh Report: The Position of Minority Groups in Europe: An Examination of Roma Policies in the European Union'. Rapporteur: Senator Terry Leyden, Houses of the Oireachtas, December 2009

Joyce, C. *European Migration Network Annual Policy Report on Migration and Asylum 2008: Ireland.* Economic and Social Research Institute (ESRI) Survey and Statistical Report Series 015 (Dublin: ESRI, 2009)

Joyce, C. and Quinn, E. *Policies on Unaccompanied Minors in Ireland.* Report by European Migration Network (Dublin: ESRI, 2009)

Juchno, P. 'Asylum Applications in the EU' (2007), Eurostat, Statistics in Focus, Population and Social Conditions, 110/2007, http://www.epp.eurostat.ec.europa.eu [accessed 24 June 2010]

Judicial Appointments Advisory Board (JAAB), *Judicial Appointments Advisory Board Annual Report 2008* (published 2009), http://www.courts.ie/Courts.ie/library3.nsf/%28WebFiles%29/A0F32FE287A3F5DD802575E5005720E0/$FILE/JAAB%20Annual%20Report%202008.pdf [accessed 30 May 2012]

Judicial Appointments Advisory Board (JAAB), *Judicial Appointments Advisory Board Annual Report 2009* (published 2010), http://www.courts.ie/courts.ie/library3.nsf/%28WebFiles%29/6394D92252CA383F80257749004C012E/$file/JAAB%20Annual%20Report%202009.pdf [accessed 30 May 2012]

Judicial Appointments Advisory Board (JAAB), *Judicial Appointments Advisory Board Annual Report 2010* (published 2011), http://www.courts.ie/Courts.ie/library3.nsf/%28WebFiles%29/CBCCECD7D8C85348802578 C7002F98BC/$FILE/JAAB%20Annual%20Report%202010.pdf [accessed 30 May 2012]

Kapardis, A. and Farrington, D.P. 'An Experimental Study of Sentencing by Magistrates', *Law and Human Behavior*, vol. 5, nos 2 & 3, 1981, pp. 107–21

Kilcommins, S., O'Donnell, I., O'Sullivan, E. and Vaughan, B. *Crime, Punishment and the Search for Order in Ireland* (Dublin: Institute of Public Administration, 2004)

Killias, M. 'Paradise Lost? New Trends in Crime and Migration in Switzerland', in W.F. McDonald (ed.), *Immigration, Crime and Justice* (Bingley, Yorkshire: Emerald Group Publishing, 2009)

Kleck, G. 'Racial Discrimination in Criminal Sentencing: A Critical Evaluation of the Evidence, with Additional Evidence on the Death Penalty', *American Sociological Review*, vol. 46, no. 6, 1981, pp. 783–805

Kopp, I. (2008) 'Review of Resource Needs in the Forensic Science Laboratory and the Wider Scientific Context in Ireland' (2008), http://www.justice.ie/en/JELR/Pages/Kopp_Review [accessed 25 June 2010]

Koser, K. 'Irregular Migration, State Security and Human Security'. A paper prepared for the Policy Analysis and Research Programme of the Global Commission on International Migration, www.gcim.org/attachments/TPF.pdf [accessed 25 May 2010]

Kuhn, A. (1997) 'Prison Populations in Western Europe', in M. Tonry and K. Hatlestad (eds), *Sentencing Reform in Overcrowded Times: A Comparative Perspective* (Oxford: Oxford University Press, 1997)

Lacey, N. *The Prisoners' Dilemma: Political Economy and Punishment in Contemporary Democracies* (Cambridge: Cambridge University Press, 2008)

Lally, C. 'Greens Seek Anti-Racism Training for Judiciary', *The Irish Times*, 21 February 2003

Lally, C. 'Gardaí Seek New Fingerprint Laws', *The Irish Times*, 14 April 2010

Lavenex, S. *Safe Third Countries: Extending the EU Asylum and Immigration Policies to Central and Eastern Europe* (Budapest: Central European University Press, 1999)

Law Reform Commission (LRC), *Report on Sentencing* (Dublin: Law Reform Commission, 1996)

Law Reform Commission (LRC), *Consultation Paper on Penalties for Minor Offences* (LRC CP18-2002) (Dublin: Law Reform Commission, 2002)

Law Reform Commission (LRC), *Report on Penalties for Minor Offences* (LRC 69-2003) (Dublin: Law Reform Commission, 2003)

Law Reform Commission (LRC), *Consultation Paper on Prosecution Appeals from Unduly Lenient Sentences in the District Court* (LRC CP33-2004) (Dublin: Law Reform Commission, 2004)

Law Reform Commission (LRC) (2005) *Report on Court Poor Box: Probation of Offenders* (LRC 75-2005), Dublin: Law Reform Commission.

Law Society of Ireland, 'Solicitors' Advertising Regulations: Summary' (undated), http://www.lawsociety.ie/Documents/membersadv_regs_summary.pdf [accessed 24 June 2010]

Law Society of Ireland, Spent Convictions Group, *The Disclosure of Criminal Convictions: Proposals on a Rehabilitation of Offenders Bill* (2009), http://www.lawsociety.ie/documents/committees/hr/spentconvictionreport09.pdf [accessed 10 March 2010]

Lee, M.T. and Martinez, R. 'Immigration Reduces Crime: An Emerging Scholarly Consensus', in W.F. McDonald (ed.), *Immigration, Crime and Justice* (Bingley, Yorkshire: Emerald Group Publishing, 2009)

Lee, M.T., Martinez, R. and Rosenfeld, R. 'Does Immigration Increase Homicide? Negative Evidence from Three Border Cities', *Sociological Quarterly*, vol. 42, no. 4, 2001, pp. 559–80

Lewandoski, K. 'A New Transportation for the Penitentiary Era: Some "Household Words" on Free Emigration', *Victorian Periodicals Review*, vol. 26, no. 1, 1993, pp. 8–18

Linehan, S., Duffy, D., O'Neill, H., O'Neill, C. and Kennedy, H.G. 'Irish Travellers and Forensic Mental Health', *Irish Journal of Psychological Medicine*, vol. 19, no. 3, 2002, pp. 76–9, http://www.ijpm.org/content/pdf/116/travellers.pdf [accessed 24 June 2010]

Lowell B.L. 'Immigration "Pull" Factors in OECD Countries over the Long Term', in Organisation for Economic Co-operation and Development (OECD), *The Future of International Migration to OECD Countries* (Paris: OECD, 2009)

Lyons, A. and Hunt, P. 'The Effects of Gender on Sentencing: A Case Study of the Dublin Metropolitan Area District Court', in M. Tomlinson, T. Varley and C. McCullagh (eds), *Whose Law and Order: Aspects of Crime and Social Control in Irish Society* (Belfast: Sociological Association of Ireland, 1988)

Lynch, M.J. *Big Prisons, Big Dreams: Crime and the Failure of America's Penal System* (New Jersey: Rutgers University Press, 2007)

Lysaght, C. 'The Court Poor Box', *Bar Review*, July 2004, pp. 124–5

Mac Cormaic, R. 'Ireland of the Unwelcomes?', *The Irish Times*, 26 September 2008

MacPherson, W. *The Stephen Lawrence Inquiry*. Presented to parliament by the Secretary of State for the Home Department by command of Her Majesty, February 1999 (London: The Stationery Office, 1999)

Maguire, N. 'Sentencing in Ireland: An Exploration of the Views, Rationales, and Sentencing Practices of District and Circuit Court Judges', unpublished PhD thesis, Trinity College Dublin, 2008

Martens, P.L. 'Immigrants as Victims of Crime', in J.D. Freilich and G.R.

Newman (eds), *Crime and Immigration* (Aldershot: Ashgate, 2000)

Martinez, R. and Lee, M.T. 'On Immigration and Crime', *Criminal Justice 2000: The National Institute of Justice*, 1, 2000, pp. 485–523

McCafferty, N. *In the Eyes of the Law* (Dublin: Ward River Press, 1981)

McCarthy, C. 'Minister is Complacent on the Realities of Racism', *Irish Examiner*, 18 January 2010

McConville, M. and Baldwin, J. 'The Influence of Race on Sentencing in England', *Criminal Law Review*, 1982, pp. 652–8

McCullagh, C. 'Unemployment and Imprisonment: Examining and Interpreting the Relationship in the Republic of Ireland', *Irish Journal of Sociology*, 2, 1992, pp. 1–19

McCullagh, C. *Crime in Ireland: A Sociological Introduction* (Cork: Cork University Press, 1996)

McEvoy, P. 'Research for the Department of Justice on the Criteria Applied by the Courts in Sentencing under s.15A of the Misuse of Drugs Act, 1977 (as amended)' (2005), http://www.jjustice.ie/en/JELR/Research.pdf/files/Research.pdf [accessed 12 April 2010]

McGinnity, F., Nelson, J., Lunn, P. and Quinn, E. *Discrimination in Recruitment: Evidence from a Field Experiment* (Dublin: Equality Authority/ESRI, 2009)

Menz, G. *The Political Economy of Managed Migration: Nonstate Actors, Europeanization, and the Politics of Designing Migration Policies* (Oxford: Oxford University Press, 2009)

Migrant Rights Centre Ireland (MRCI), *An Exploration of Irregular Migration in Ireland* (Dublin: MRCI, 2007)

Mileski, M. 'Courtroom Encounters: An Observation Study of a Lower Criminal Court', *Law and Society Review*, vol. 5, no. 4, 1971, pp. 473–538

Murray, J. 'The Effects of Imprisonment on Families and Children of Prisoners', in A. Liebling and S. Maruna (eds), *The Effects of Imprisonment* (Cullompton, Devon: Willan Publishing, 2006)

National Consultative Committee on Racism and Interculturalism (NCCRI)/Equality Authority, *Case Study: The Task Force on the Travelling Community*, study compiled for the European Monitoring Centre on Racism and Xenophobia, April 2003 (Dublin: NCCRI, 2003)

National Consultative Committee on Racism and Interculturalism (NCCRI), 'The Traveller Education Strategy – as Part of an Intercultural Education Strategy in Ireland' (2004), http://www.nccri.ie/submissions/04JanTrav Education.pdf [accessed 12 May 2010]

Needham, M. 'The District Court: An Empirical Study of Criminal Jurisdiction', unpublished thesis, University College Galway, 1983

Norris, C. 'Some Ethical Considerations on Field-Work with the Police', in D. Hobbs and T. May (eds), *Interpreting the Field: Accounts of Ethnography* (Oxford: Clarendon Press, 1993)

O'Brien, C. 'Hundreds of Court, Garda Interpreters Have No Qualification', *The Irish Times*, 7 June 2010

O'Donnell, I. 'Prison Matters', *Irish Jurist* (NS), 36, 2001, pp. 153–73

O'Donnell, I. and Milner, C. *Child Pornography: Crime, Computers and Society* (Cullompton, Devon: Willan, 2007)

O'Donnell, I., Teljeur, C., Hughes, H., Baumer, E. and Kelly, A. 'Punishment, Social Deprivation and the Geography of Reintegration', *Irish Criminal Law Journal*, vol. 17, no. 4, 2007, pp. 3–9

O'Donnell, I., Baumer, E.P. and Hughes, N. 'Recidivism in the Republic of Ireland', *Criminology and Criminal Justice*, vol. 8, no. 2, 2008, pp. 123–46

Office of the Director of Public Prosecutions (ODPP), *Office of the Director of Public Prosecutions Annual Report 2008* (published 2009), http://www.dppireland.ie/filestore/documents/Annual_Report_2008_ENG.pdf [accessed 24 June 2010]

O'Halloran, M. 'Amended Immigration Bill Expected Before Autumn', *The Irish Times*, 1 June 2010

O'Mahony, P. 'An Investigation of the Operation of the Bail System', unpublished report for the Minister for Justice, 1996

O'Malley, T. *Sentencing Law and Practice* (Dublin: Round Hall Sweet & Maxwell, 2000)

O'Malley, T. *Sentencing Law and Practice*, 2nd edn (Dublin: Thompson Round Hall, 2006)

O'Malley, T. 'Sentencing Recidivist Sex Offenders: A Challenge for Proportionality', in I. Bacik and L. Heffernan (eds), *Criminal Law and Procedure: Current Issues and Emerging Trends* (Dublin: FirstLaw, 2009)

O'Malley, T. 'Time Served: The Impact of Sentencing and Parole Decisions on the Prison Population', paper delivered to Irish Penal Reform Trust, Morrison Hotel Dublin, 28 June 2010, http://www.iprt.ie/files/Tom_OMalley_Presentation_IPRT_Open_Forum_28062010.pdf [accessed 15 May 2013]

O'Nolan, C. 'Penal Populations in a World in Motion: The Case of the Republic of Ireland (ROI)', *Howard Journal of Criminal Justice*, vol. 50, no. 4, 2011, pp. 371–92

Organisation for Economic Co-operation and Development (OECD), *International Migration Outlook: SOPEMI 2010* (Paris: OECD, 2010)

Ousey, G.C. and Kubrin, C.E. 'Exploring the Connection between Immigration and Violent Crime Rates in US Cities, 1980–2000', *Social Problems*, vol. 56, no. 3, 2009, pp. 447–73

Owen, B.A. *In the Mix: Struggle and Survival in a Women's Prison* (New York: State University of New York Press, 1998)

Pavee Point, 'A Review of Travellers' Health using Primary Care as a Model of Good Practice' (2005), http://paveepoint.ie/pdf/PrimaryHealth Care05.pdf [accessed 12 May 2010]

Pavee Point, *Assimilation Policies and Outcomes: Travellers' Experience* (Dublin: Pavee Point, 2006)

Pettit, B. and Western, B. 'Mass Imprisonment and the Life Course: Race and Class Inequality in US Incarceration', *American Sociological Review*, 69, 2004, pp. 151–69

Phelan, M. 'Legal Interpreters in the News in Ireland', *The International Journal for Translation and Interpreting Research*, vol. 3, no. 1, 2011, pp. 76–105

Pope, C. 'Judge Issues Apology for Improper Comments', *The Irish Times*, 20 February 2003

Punch, M. *Policing the Inner City* (London: Macmillan, 1979)

Redmond, D. *Imprisonment for Fine Default and Civil Debt* (Dublin: Nexus Research, 2002)

Reid, L., Weiss, W.H.E., Adelman, R.M. and Jaret, C. 'The Immigration–Crime Relationship: Evidence Across US Metropolitan Areas', *Social Science Research*, vol. 34, no. 4, 2005, pp. 757–80

Reilly, M. *The Irish Prison Population: An Examination of Duties and Obligations Owed to Prisoners*, report presented by Inspector of Prisons on 29 July 2010 to the Minister for Justice and Law Reform pursuant to Part 5 of the Prisons Act, 2007, http://www.iprt.ie/contents/1862 [accessed 30 May 2012]

Reilly, J. and McArdle, P. 'Pilot Scheme Aims to Slash €3m Court Translation Bill', *Sunday Independent*, 20 June 2010

Remington, F.J. 'The Decision to Charge, the Decision to Convict on a Plea of Guilty and the Impact of Sentence Structure on Prosecution Practices', in L.E. Ohlin and F.R. Remington (eds), *Discretion in Criminal Justice: The Tension Between Individualization and Uniformity* (Albany, NY: State University of New York Press, 1993)

Ring, E. 'Asylum Seekers Discouraged by Changes to System', *Irish Examiner*, 12 November 2008

Riordan, D. 'Diversion To Treatment: A Study of Drug-Related Cases in the Dublin Metropolitan District Court', thesis submitted to Trinity College Dublin in part fulfilment of the requirement for the MSc Drug and Alcohol Policy (2000), www.drugsandalcohol.ie/4343/1/1289-1055pdf [accessed 10 October 2012]

Riordan, D. 'Immigrants in the Criminal Courts', *Judicial Studies Institute Journal*, 2, 2007, pp. 95–108

Roberts, J.V. 'Impact of Previous Convictions on Sentencing: Recent Developments in England and Wales', *Federal Sentencing Reporter*, vol. 17, no. 3, 2005, pp. 171–4

Roberts, J.V. *Punishing Persistent Offenders: Exploring Community and Offender Perspectives* (Oxford: Oxford University Press, 2008)

Rock, P. *The Social World of an English Crown Court: Witness and Professionals in the Crown Court Centre at Wood Green* (Oxford: Clarendon Press, 1993)

Rottman, D.B. *The Criminal Justice System: Policy and Performance* (Dublin: National Economic and Social Council, 1984)

Rottman, D.B. and Tormey, P.F. 'Criminal Justice System: An Overview', in *Report of the Committee of Inquiry into the Penal System* (chairman T.K. Whitaker) (Dublin: The Stationery Office, 1985)

Rowe, M. 'Tripping Over Molehills: Ethics and the Ethnography of Police Work', *International Journal of Social Research Methodology*, vol. 10, no. 1, 2007, pp. 37–48

Ruhs, M. and Quinn, E. 'Ireland: From Rapid Immigration to Recession' (2009), Migration Policy Institute, http://www.migrationinformation.org/Feature/display.cfm?ID=740 [accessed 20 July 2010]

Rusche, G. and Kirchheimer, O. *Punishment and Social Structure* (New York: Columbia University Press, 1939)

Russell, M. 'The Irish Delinquent in England', *Studies*, 53, Spring 1964

Sampson, R.J. 'Open Doors Don't Invite Criminals: Is Increased Immigration Behind the Drop in Crime?' *New York Times*, 11 March 2006

Sampson, R.J. 'Rethinking Crime and Immigration', *Contexts*, vol. 7, no. 1, 2008, pp. 28–33, http://contexts.org/articles/winter-2008/sampson [accessed 3 April 2010]

Schündeln, M. 'Are Immigrants More Mobile Than Natives? Evidence from Germany', IZA Discussion Paper 3226, December 2007 (Bonn: Institute for the Study of Labour, 2007)

Schweppe, J. 'Definition of a "Sentence" in the Law Reform Commission's Consultation Paper on Prosecution Appeals from Unduly Lenient Sentences in the District Court', *Irish Criminal Law Journal*, vol. 15, no. 3, 2005, p. 24

Seymour, M. *Alternatives to Custody* (Dublin: Business in the Community in Ireland and Irish Penal Reform Trust, 2006)

Shaw, C. R., McKay, H.D. and McDonald, J.F. 'Brothers in Crime', in P. Beirne (ed.), *The Chicago School of Criminology, 1914–1945, Volume V* (London and New York: Routledge, 2006 [1938])

Shaw, C.R. and McKay, H.D. 'Juvenile Delinquency and Urban Areas: A Study of Rates of Delinquents in Relation to Differential Characteristics of Local Communities in American Cities', in P. Beirne (ed.), *The Chicago School of Criminology, 1914–1945, Volume V* (London and New York: Routledge, 2006 [1942])

Simon, R.J. and Sikich, K.W. 'Public Attitudes Toward Immigrants and Immigration Policies across Seven Nations', *International Migration Review*, vol. 41, no. 4, 2007, pp. 956–62

Smith, M.D., Devine, J.A. and Sheley, J.F. 'Crime and Unemployment: Effects across Age and Race', *Sociological Perspectives*, vol. 35, no. 4, 1992, pp. 551–72

Socio-Legal Studies Association, 'Statement of Principles of Ethical Research Practice' (2009), http://www.kent.ac.uk/nslsa/images/slsadownloads/-

ethicalstatements/slsa20%ehtics20%statement20%_final_%5B1%5D.pdf [accessed 7 January 2010]

Spohn, C. and Holleran, D. 'The Imprisonment Penalty Paid by Young, Unemployed Black and Hispanic Male Offenders', *Criminology*, vol. 38, no. 1, 2000, pp. 281–306

Stern, J. 'Scapegoat Narratives in Herodotus', *Hermes*, vol. 119, no. 3, 1991, pp. 304–11

Sun, H.-E. and Reed, J. 'Migration and Crime in Europe', in D. Freilich and G.R. Newman (eds), *Crime and Immigration* (Aldershot: Ashgate, 2007)

Task Force on the Travelling Community, *Report of the Task Force on the Travelling Community: Executive Summary* (1995), http://www.lenus.ie/hse/handle/10147/45449 [accessed 30 May 2012]

Tighe, M. 'Interpreters in Court Pay Row', *Sunday Times*, 29 March 2009, http://www.timesonline.co.uk/tol/news/world/ireland/article5993267ece [accessed 24 June 2010]

Tonry, M. 'Real Offense Sentencing: The Model Sentencing and Corrections Act', *Journal of Criminal Law & Criminology*, vol. 72, no. 4, 1981, pp. 1550–96

Tonry, M. 'More Sentencing Reform in America', *Criminal Law Review*, 1982, pp. 157–67

Tonry, M. *Sentencing Matters* (New York and Oxford: Oxford University Press, 1996)

Toth, S.A. *Beyond Papillon: The French Overseas Penal Colonies, 1854–1952* (Lincoln, NE and London: University of Nebraska Press, 2006)

Travers, M. 'Persuading the Client to Plead Guilty: An Ethnographic Examination of a Routine Morning's Work in the Magistrates' Court', *Manchester Sociology Occasional Papers*, 33, 1992, pp. 1–43

Travers, M. 'Sentencing in the Children's Court: An Ethnographic Perspective', *Youth Justice*, vol. 7, no. 1, 2007, pp. 21–35

Trinity Immigration Initiative, *Addressing the Current and Future Reality of Ireland's Multi-Cultural Status* (Dublin: Trinity Immigration Initiative, 2010)

Ugba, A. 'Ireland', in A. Triandafyllidou and R. Gropas (eds), *European Immigration: A Sourcebook* (Aldershot: Ashgate, 2007)

Van Kalmthout, A., van der Meulen, F.B. and Dunkel, F. (eds), *Foreigners in European Prisons* (Nijmegen: Wolf Legal Publishers, 2007)

Vasileva, K. 'Citizens of European Countries Account for the Majority of the Foreign Population in EU-27 in 2008', Eurostat Statistics in Focus, 16 December 2009, http://epp.eurostat.ec.europa.eu/cache/ITY_OFFPUB/KS-SF-09-094-EN-PDF [accessed 9 January 2010]

Vaughan, B. *Towards a Model Penal System* (Dublin: Irish Penal Reform Trust, 2001)

Vazsonyi, A.T. and Killias, M. 'Immigration and Crime among Youth in Switzerland', *Criminal Justice and Behavior*, vol. 28, no. 3, 2001, pp. 329–66

Von Hirsch, A. *Censure and Sanctions* (Oxford: Clarendon Press, 1993)

Von Hirsch, A. 'Proportionate Sentencing: A Desert Perspective', in A. Von Hirsch, A. Ashworth and J. Roberts (eds), *Principled Sentencing Readings on Theory and Policy*, 3rd edn (Oxford: Hart Publishing, 2009)

Von Hirsch, A. and Ashworth, A. *Proportionate Sentencing: Exploring the Principles* (Oxford: Oxford University Press, 2005)

Wacquant, L. '"Suitable Enemies": Foreigners and Immigrants in the Prisons of Europe', *Punishment and Society*, vol. 1, no. 2, 1999, pp. 215–22

Wacquant, L. 'Deadly Symbiosis: When Ghetto and Prison Meet and Mesh', *Punishment and Society*, 3, 2001, pp. 95–133

Wacquant, L. *Punishing the Poor: The Neoliberal Government of Social Insecurity* (Durham, NC: Duke University Press, 2009)

Wacquant, L. 'Crafting the Neoliberal State: Workfare, Prisonfare, and Social Insecurity', *Sociological Forum*, vol. 25, no. 2, 2010, pp. 197–220

Walsh, D. and Sexton, P. *An Empirical Study of Community Service Orders in Ireland* (Dublin: The Stationery Office, 1999)

Wandall, R.H. *Decisions to Imprison: Court Decision-Making Inside and Outside the Law* (Aldershot and Burlington, VT: Ashgate, 2008)

Ward, T. *Justice Matters: Independence, Accountability and the Irish Judiciary* (Dublin: Irish Council for Civil Liberties, 2007)

Waterhouse, K. 'Interpreting Criminal Justice: A Preliminary Look at Language, Law and Crime in Ireland', *Judicial Studies Institute Journal*, vol. 9, no. 2, 2009, pp. 42–75

Watson, I., Nic Ghiolla Phádraig, M., Kennedy, P.F. and Rock-Huspatel, B. 'National Identity and Anti-Immigrant Attitudes', in B. Hilliard and M. Nic Ghiolla Phádraig (eds), *Changing Ireland in International Comparison* (Dublin: Liffey Press, 2007)

Western, B. *Punishment and Inequality in America* (New York: Russell Sage Foundation, 2006)

Western, B. and Pettit, B. 'Mass Imprisonment', in B. Western, *Punishment and Inequality in America* (New York: Russell Sage Foundation, 2006)

Whitaker, K. (chairman), *Report of the Committee of Inquiry into the Penal System* (Dublin: The Stationery Office, 1984)

Whitman, J.Q. *Harsh Justice: Criminal Punishment and the Widening Divide between America and Europe* (New York: Oxford University Press, 2003)

Whyte, W.F. *Street Corner Society: The Social Structure of an Italian Slum*, 4th edn (Chicago: University of Chicago Press, 1993)

Working Group on a Courts Commission, *First Report: Management and Finance* (Dublin: The Stationery Office, 1996)

Working Group on the Jurisdiction of the Courts, *The Criminal Jurisdiction of the Courts* (Dublin: The Stationery Office, 2003)

Zatz, M.S. 'The Changing Forms of Racial/Ethnic Biases in Sentencing', *Journal of Research in Crime and Delinquency*, 24, 1987, pp. 69–92

Notes and References

PROLOGUE

1 This and all names used in respect of defendants, judges, solicitors, barristers, probation officers and Gardaí are pseudonyms.
2 A court presenter is a Garda of the rank of sergeant or higher who presents the case for the prosecution for the majority of offences adjudicated upon in the District Court.
3 Dóchas Prison is a women's prison in north Dublin City.
4 References to field notes are indicated throughout the text by the designation FN.
5 The 2001 annual report of the IPS was the first annual report to include information regarding the nationality of persons committed to Irish prisons.
6 The number of committals is higher than the number of persons committed to prison as some people are committed to prison more than once in a year. In 2008, for example, total committals to prison were 13,557 but only 10,928 people were committed to prison. Similarly, in 2009 total committals to prison were 15,425 but only 12,339 people were committed to prison.

1. ANATOMY OF A WORKHORSE

1 The maximum term of imprisonment that can be imposed by the District Court for a single offence is twelve months. The court can impose a term of imprisonment of up to twenty-four months in respect of two or more offences.
2 The unit of analysis used by the Courts Service is the court office.
3 Information is not provided which would make it possible to compare the severity of penalties imposed.
4 In the database offenders are designated as 'Irish' or 'foreign nationals'.
5 Recommended in both the consultation paper (LRC, 2002) and the ultimate report (LRC, 2003).
6 Vaughan sent a questionnaire to District Court judges and achieved a response rate of 33%. Some 50% of those who responded indicated support for a prohibition on short-term sentences (under three months), except in exceptional circumstances.
7 There has also been debate recently regarding the use of short-term prison sentences in England and Wales. See the report published by the National

Association of Probation Officers in June 2010 (Short-term Jail Sentences: An Effective Alternative, available online at http://www.napo.org.uk/publications/Briefings.cfm).

8 One could also point more recently to the very significant increase in the numbers committed to prison for the non-payment of fines; an 88% increase in committals for non-payment of court-imposed fines is revealed in the 2008 annual report of the Irish Prison Service (IPS, 2009:22) and in 2009 a further 91% increase on the 2008 level was reported (IPS, 2010:6).

9 In 2008, for example, €2,039,000 was collected for the Poor Box through District Court offices while only €262 was collected in Circuit Court offices and no Poor Box donations were collected in the High Court (CS, 2008:97).

10 A total of twenty-three judges participated in the research. Of these, eight were Circuit Court judges and fifteen were District Court judges.

11 'Sentence' is defined by the LRC in the consultation paper on Prosecution Appeals from Unduly Lenient Sentence in the District Court (LRC, 2004). Schweppe highlights that a sentence as defined by the LRC includes sentences made upon conviction and what the Commission terms 'conditional acquittals', which are sentences imposed following a finding of guilt without the making of a conviction (2005).

12 Fewer Gardaí are present in RC than in other courts as evidence of arrest charge and caution has normally already been given in another court.

13 However, during courtroom sittings observed, the probation officer in NEC sat with or beside the solicitors/barristers and had a much more collegial relationship with other courtroom regulars than was the case in other courts.

14 A request by the defence to be supplied with prosecution witness statements is known as a Gary Doyle order. The scope of the duty of disclosure in summary prosecutions has been defined by the Supreme Court in Director of Public Prosecutions v. Gary Doyle [1994] 2 IR 286. There is no general duty on the prosecution to provide the defence with statements of intended witnesses in advance of trial. The test to be applied by a court on an application by the defence to be furnished pre-trial with the statements on which the prosecution case will proceed is whether 'in the interests of justice on the facts of the particular case' this should be done (Gary Doyle's case, at p. 301). See Office of Director of Public Prosecutions, 'Disclosure' available from http://www.odpp.ie

15 References to the Probation Act are to the Probation of Offenders Act, 1907. The application of the Probation Act is explained in Chapter 4.

16 When judges apply the Probation Act they may also require the defendant to make a contribution to the 'Poor Box' or a designated charity. Defence counsel frequently suggest this course of action to the court by indicating that their client has available a sum of money which he is prepared to donate to charity.

17 Emphasis added.

18 He was referring to offences under s.4 and s.6 of the Criminal Justice (Public Order) Act, 1994. It is very common for a defendant to be charged with offences under the provisions of both of these sections.

19 An Irish judge may only be removed from office for 'stated misbehaviour or incapacity' (see Art. 35.4.1 of the Constitution and s.20 of the Courts of Justice (District Court) Act, 1946), and only if a joint resolution is adopted by both houses of the Oireachtas. To date no Irish judge has ever been removed from office. See Ward (2007:67–70) for a discussion on judicial accountability.

20 See Twenty-Ninth Amendment of the Constitution (Judges' Remuneration) Act, 2011.

21 In NEC, during all court proceedings observed a Garda inspector assumed the role of the court presenter. In RC, CCC and SDC, the role of the court presenter was carried out by a Garda sergeant.

22 See Devins (2009) for an explanation of 'hybrid' and 'either-way' offences. Devins also points to 'disquiet' regarding the level of nolle prosequi decisions made after a defendant has exercised his right to trial by indictment or where cases are sent forward to the Circuit Court after a District Court judge has refused jurisdiction.

23 This decision will be made by the Directing Division of the DPP.

24 He was referring to Judge Murray.

25 In one case observed, the defence did seek to play the tape in court but the quality was such that the images were not decipherable and the charges were dismissed. CCC did not have facilities to display CCTV footage and consequently many cases were referred to other courts.

26 The standard practice of relying on these certificates was unsuccessfully challenged in the case of DPP v. Omotoya Bakara (High Court, unreported, 20 October 2008). The applicant appealed his conviction in the District Court for possession of a controlled substance contrary to section 3 of the Misuse of Drugs Act, 1977 (as amended) to the Circuit Court, and claimed he should have been allowed the opportunity to cross-examine the forensic scientist who prepared the certificate. The appeal failed and the applicant then initiated a judicial review seeking an order of the High Court directing the prosecution to make the forensic scientist available. The High Court refused the relief sought, ruling that 'a certificate is of such a scientific nature that it has to be amenable to prima facie proof by certification' (see ODPP, 2009:18).

27 The analysis is carried out by the Irish Forensic Laboratory Service (FLS), which was unable to report on 33% of drug samples received between 2000 and 2006 (Kopp, 2008).

28 The prosecution also present a version of the 'facts'. See Devins (2009).

29 Stamp 4 indicates that the person is entitled to work without a work permit. It is issued to people on work visas/work authorisations, and also to, for example, spouses of Irish and EU citizens, refugees, people with Irish Born Child residency, and other people with long-term residency status.

30 Observations indicate that persons who appear before the District Court charged with immigration offences are almost always charged under the provisions of s.12(1) of the Immigration Act, 2004.

31 S.2(1).

32 The deaths occurred of two sitting District Court judges during the course of the fieldwork.

33 'Inappropriate locations' are defined in s.4(10) of the Solicitors' (Amendment) Act, 2002 as: 'a hospital, clinic, doctor's surgery, funeral home, crematorium, or other location of a similar character'.

34 Presumably because the prosecution are expected to have details of the accused person's criminal history ready to present to the court and failure to indicate a guilty plea in advance might therefore result in a delay and the matter being put back to a 'second calling'.

35 When Mr Buckley says, 'it's worse in prison', he seems to be suggesting that it's harder to stay drug-free in prison.

36 'Benzos' refers to benzodiazepines.

2. Ordinary Crimes and Ordinary Criminals

1 Travellers are an indigenous minority group who have a culture and lifestyle which is distinct from mainstream Irish society. Formerly nomadic, Travellers now mainly adopt a settled or semi-nomadic lifestyle. It is generally accepted that there is widespread discrimination against Travellers in Irish society (see Task Force on the Travelling Community, 1995; NCCRI/Equality Authority, 2003; Pavee Point, 2006).

2 The Luas is a light rail system that operates in Dublin.

3 The reference to 'Mountjoy' is to Mountjoy prison, which is located a short distance north of Dublin's city centre. Both Wheatfield and Mountjoy prisons are closed medium-security prisons for males. Judge O'Toole did not make it clear why he felt that Mountjoy would be unsuitable for this offender, but it seems clear from his comments that he considers this offender to be vulnerable and therefore perhaps more likely to have difficulty with the more serious inmate population housed in Mountjoy.

4 If one adjusted for children in both populations one would expect even fewer adult Travellers to appear before the District Court.

5 Foreign nationals are non-Irish and non-UK nationals.

6 These national groups were from China, Germany, Latvia, Lithuania, Nigeria, Poland, UK and USA.

7 This group comprised two men and two women who appeared to range in age from thirty to forty-five.

8 When bail is granted on the defendant's bond, no cash sum is required to be lodged but if the defendant later fails to appear in court the court will make an estreatment order as required by the Bail Act, 1997 and the Courts Service will seek to collect the amount of the bond (Comptroller and Auditor General, 2002).

9 He was charged under the provisions of section 26 of the Criminal Justice (Theft and Fraud) Act, 2001.

10 EU-12 countries are those that joined the EU in 2004 and 2007, namely Bulgaria, Cyprus, the Czech Republic, Estonia, Hungary, Latvia, Lithuania, Malta, Poland, Romania, Slovakia and Slovenia.

11 EU-13 countries refer to countries other than Ireland and the UK that were EU member states prior to 1 May 2004.

3. THE PUNISHMENT OF MINOR OFFENCES

1 Section 258 of the Children Act, 2001 stipulates that offences committed by those under eighteen years of age can be expunged from the record provided certain conditions are met. Efforts to draft legislation in this area are on-going (see The Criminal Justice (Spent Convictions) Bill, 2012).

2 In England and Wales, the purposes of sentencing are set out in the Criminal Justice Act, 2003. The purposes listed include punishment, reduction of crime, rehabilitation, protection of the public and reparation (Roberts, 2005).

3 In the database, offenders are designated as Irish or 'foreign national'.

4 The Road Traffic (No. 2) Act, 2011 now provides for certain limited situations when drink-driving does not result in a mandatory disqualification from driving.

5 The treatment of previous convictions for minor offences in determining sentence varies from jurisdiction to jurisdiction. The Criminal Justice Act, 2003 introduced in England and Wales requires courts to treat 'recent and relevant' convictions as aggravating factors. This provision has been criticised by Ashworth, who has linked this requirement to the possible imposition of disproportionately harsh punishments for minor offenders (Ashworth, 2005). Ashworth claims that the provisions inappropriately prioritise repetition above seriousness, fail to take account of the role of substance misuse and other social disadvantages, and do not take account of the limited efficacy of harsher sentences as a form of crime control. The Council of Europe's Committee of Ministers on Consistency in Sentencing recommended (and adopted on 19 October 1992) that the effect of previous criminal history should depend on the characteristics of the offender's prior criminal convictions, and that when the present offence is minor, or previous offences were minor, the effect of previous criminality should be reduced or nullified (1993:33). This would suggest that very little, if any, recognition should be given by lower-tier courts such as the Irish District Court to previous criminal convictions.

6 Just one of the judges observed routinely retired before pronouncing sentence. On occasions, other judges observed took a short recess before passing sentence or indicated that they would consider matters during the lunch recess.

7 Only a very small number of defendants charged under the provisions of s.12(1) of the Immigration Act, 2004 were observed in NEC.

8 The charge of endangerment is liable to a maximum term of imprisonment on conviction on indictment of seven years. On summary conviction, the maximum term of imprisonment is twelve months and/or a fine of €1,500.

9 A fictitious name has been substituted for this location.

10 The study of recidivism carried out by O'Donnell et al. (2008) examined recidivism rates of persons released from prison and used a prior prison sentence as a proxy for previous criminal history.

11 One Irish offender observed had 180 previous convictions.

12 The details of the location have been changed.

13 S.13 charges are charges arising out of a defendant's failure to appear in court.

14 A fictitious name has been substituted for this location.

15 Private Residential Tenancies Board.

16 This intervention was unusual in that the prosecution was handled by the court presenter but it seems likely that directions had been sought from the DPP.

17 For a discussion on gender differences in offending, see Farrington and Painter, 2004.

18 These were the decisions in *People (DPP) v. W.B.* (CCA, 21/12/1994, O'Flaherty, Keane and Carney JJ), and *People (DPP) v. A.C.* (CCA, 17/11/1997, Barron, Laffoy and O'Donovan JJ (see McEvoy, 2005:5).

19 Minor offences are offences which attract not more than one year's imprisonment and/or a fine of €3,000. However, the LRC (2003) exhorted District Court judges to reconceptualise the maximum penalty for minor offences. They considered that a more appropriate maximum penalty for minor offences is six months' imprisonment. Article 38.2 of the Irish Constitution states: 'Minor offences may be tried by courts of summary jurisdiction.'

4. IMMIGRATION OFFENCES

1 The term 'irregular' is used in preference to 'illegal' in relation to migrants who are in breach of immigration legislation. The use of terminology relating to the status of migrants is discussed in Koser (2005:4–6).

2 The exclusion of EU citizens may only be justified on the basis of public policy, public security or public health.

3 All EU countries with the exception of Ireland and the UK are parties to the Schengen Agreement (see Menz, 2009:40–1). Norway, Switzerland and Iceland are also Schengen countries. Third-country nationals can obtain a Schengen visa, which allows them to travel within the Schengen area. Passports or national ID cards may still be required for air travel and for hotels.

4 As set out in the Treaty of Amsterdam, 1997.

5 The EU Commission defines a third country as any non-EU country (see http:// www.europa.eu/abc/eurojargon/index_en.htm). A third-country national is a non-EU citizen.

6 In 2001, asylum applications to EU-27 countries totalled 424,180. In 2006, the total had fallen to 197,410. In 2007, total asylum applications were 222,635 and the indications are that this figure increased in 2008. The vast majority of applications are made to EU-15 countries (Juchno, 2007).

7 Non-EEA nationals are citizens of countries outside the European Economic Area (EEA). The EEA currently includes thirty countries: Iceland, Lichtenstein, Norway, and the twenty-seven EU member states.

8 EU-10 nationals are citizens of the ten accession countries which joined the EU on 1 May 2004. The ten countries are: Cyprus, Czech Republic, Estonia, Hungary, Latvia, Lithuania, Malta, Poland, Slovakia and Slovenia.

9 Usually in immigration matters a solicitor has been provided prior to the case coming to court.

10 Although there are no legislative provisions which prevent the deportation of unaccompanied minors or separated children, the practice is not to deport such children (Joyce and Quinn, 2009:46).

11 Persons charged in relation to a false instrument are generally charged under the provisions of section 26 or section 29 of the Criminal Justice (Theft and Fraud) Offences Act, 2001. Section 26 refers to the use of a false instrument while section 29 refers to the control of a false instrument.

12 There is some variation in the reported over-representation of minorities in stop and search exercises but it seems that black people are around six times more likely than, and Asians about twice as likely as, whites to be subject to stop and search by the police in England and Wales.

13 Directive 2004/38/EC.

14 However, since the interview with Ms Keane the Criminal Justice (Public Order) Act, 2011 (No. 5/2011) has put in place provisions which criminalise certain types of begging.

15 All of the Roma observed in court were described as Romanian nationals.

16 The case followed Judge Power.

17 The hearing lasted over an hour, which in the context of the District Court is lengthy.

18 It is not possible to provide these statistics for 2009 or 2008 as the charts included in the 2009 and 2008 annual reports of the IPS do not indicate numbers in each category. However, in both years the charts indicate that a very significant proportion of those detained for breaches of immigration legislation were held for less than eight days. In 2010, no information is provided in the annual report of the IPS regarding the period of detention of persons held regarding breaches of immigration legislation.

19 An applicant is a person who seeks asylum and leave to remain in the state (see s.8 Refugee Act, 1996).

20 Temporary release.

5. LEP Defendants and Interpretation Services

1 However, it was reported in *The Sunday Times* on 3 October 2010 that a judge queried the use of a court interpreter for two Polish men who had lived in Ireland for seven years (p. 17). The ITIA submission on the Courts Service Statement of Strategy 2008–2011 also highlights an instance reported in the *Galway Advertiser* in January 2007 when a judge refused to certify an interpreter because she thought it was ridiculous that a defendant who had been living in Ireland for five years could not speak English (ITIA, 2008:11). Phelan's analysis of court reports in national and provincial newspapers (2003–10) also establishes that the provision of interpreters to LEP defendants is not automatic and can be resisted by the court (2011).

2 Four levels of qualification are specified. For a person to be considered a Level 4 interpreter, they must be a native speaker of the language concerned, with a third-level qualification and qualifications specific to translating or interpreting (Bacik, 2007:121).

3 It appears from this comment that Judge Power does not realise that interpreters are paid only on foot of certified attendance in court.

4 Consecutive interpreting is when the speaker pauses after a few phrases, which are then interpreted by the interpreter. Whispered simultaneous interpreting is provided when pauses are not incorporated into speech to allow for interpretation.

5 With the exception of Denmark, which is not adopting this directive.

6. CONCLUSION

1 High-skill migration schemes exist in the Czech Republic, Austria, UK, Ireland, Latvia, Estonia and Sweden. Schemes are also under consideration in France and Germany (Menz, 2009:2).

2 On occasions, convictions were waived in respect of minor public order offences and RTOs on foot of a contribution to the court Poor Box. Convictions for driving without insurance were also waived on occasion by certain judges, with defendants in such incidences normally being convicted on the lesser charge of failing to produce documents.

3 A report on the implementation of the Public Service Agreement by the Courts Service (*The Justice Sector: Public Service Agreement 2010–2014. Action Plan: The Courts Service, March 2011,* http//:www.courts.ie) notes that 'the full implementation of DAR in all courts is a requirement for the operation of the proposed Judicial Council' (2011:3). The target date for full implementation of DAR set out in the report is the end of 2011.

APPENDIX

1 However, Johnson describes Bogira's work as 'participatory journalism' and claims that 'in many ways, Bogira's inquiry is comparable to good ethnography' (2007:367).

2 RAPID stands for Revitalising Areas by Planning, Investment and Development.

3 Observations were conducted between October 2008 and December 2009.

4 Details of the numbers of UK nationals committed to Irish prisons in 2003 and 2004 were not published by the IPS but UK nationals accounted for 2.2% of total committals in 2002 and 2005, which suggests that there was little change in these years.

5 At present, hearings of the Special Criminal Court, the Children's Court, and the Family Law Court are held in camera.

6 Very occasionally, a defendant who appeared before RC on bail sat in the area reserved for interpreters while his case was being dealt with. In CCC, on especially busy days defendants sometimes stood or sat beside the researcher.

7 The reluctance of the Garda to intervene has been noted. It seems that some observers may view proceedings with a somewhat jaded or cynical eye and therefore it cannot be claimed that all observers would seek to assist defendants in similar circumstances.

Index